LOOP HIKES
Washington

LOOP HIKES
Washington

Edited and Compiled by Dan A. Nelson
Photos by Alan Bauer

THE MOUNTAINEERS BOOKS

Published by
The Mountaineers Books
1001 SW Klickitat Way, Suite 201
Seattle, WA 98134

Published simultaneously in Great Britain by Cordee, 3a DeMontfort Street,
Leicester, England, LE1 7HD

Manufactured in Canada

Project Editor: Laura Drury
Editor: Joeth Whitney
Cover and Book Design: The Mountaineers Books
Layout: Mayumi Thompson
Mapmaker: Moore Creative Design
"Greentrails" is a trademark of Green Trails, Inc., P.O. Box 77734, Seattle,
WA 98177, (206) 762-MAPS.
Photographer: Alan Bauer unless otherwise noted.

Cover photograph: *Lupines at Sand Lake, Hike 85.*
Frontispiece: *Koppen Ridge, Hike 60* (Photo by Jim Cavin)

Library of Congress Cataloging-in-Publication Data

Best loop hikes, Washington / edited and compiled by Dan A. Nelson ;
photos by Alan Bauer.— 1st ed.
     p. cm.
Includes index.
  ISBN 0-89886-866-1 (pbk.)
  1. Hiking—Washington (State)—Guidebooks. 2. Hiking—Cascade
Range—Guidebooks. 3. Hiking—Washington (State)—Olympic
Mountains—Guidebooks. 4. Washington (State)—Guidebooks. 5. Cascade
Range—Guidebooks. 6. Washington (State)—Olympic
Mountains—Guidebooks. I. Nelson, Dan A.
  GV199.42.W2 B47 2003
  796.51'09797—dc21
                                            2002154384

CONTENTS

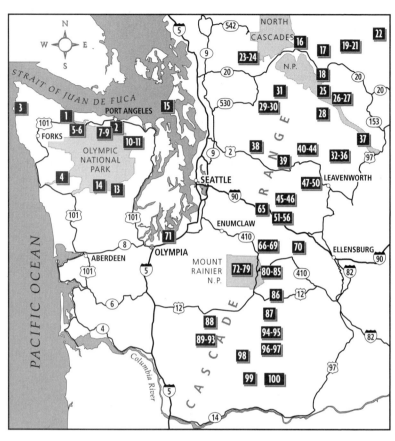

Paved Road

Unpaved Road

Featured Trail

Connecting Trail

State Boundary

River/Creek/Waterfall

Lake

Pass/Saddle

Peak

90 Interstate

101 U.S. Highway

410 State Route

9712 Forest Road

][Bridge

T Trailhead

P Parking

A Good Camping

Ranger Station

PREFACE

This book was created by scores of volunteers from Washington Trails Association and The Mountaineers Books who donated their time and sweat to research the routes included within. The work was sometimes grueling, as there were far more candidate routes than could fit in the book, and some of the trails our volunteer researchers hiked proved to be either unfit for consideration or simply unhikeable. Many times, researchers were prevented from completing what appeared to be a loop route on the map, only to find the trail had disappeared on the ground. Sometimes floods washed them out and sometimes nature just reclaimed its own. For a trail left unmaintained for too long will soon be covered with brush and debris, making it difficult to find, and nearly impossible to travel.

That's where the Washington Trails Association's volunteer trail teams come in. These teams of volunteers help maintain and rebuild the trails in Washington, keeping them safe and hikeable for all of us. To help keep the volunteer program going, portions of the proceeds from this book will be used to support the WTA volunteer trail maintenance program.

For that, and for the great work in researching the routes here, I'd like to thank all of those who contributed: Bree Barton, Alan Bauer, Jim Cavin, Helen Cherullo, Laura Drury, David Emblidge, Stephen Fox , John Howell, Tom Iurino, Rick Jakious, Kathy Kelleher, Elizabeth Lunney, Donna Meshke, Jim L. Nelson, Lisa Olson, Ellie Ottey, Linda Pearson, Adam Rynd, Jannel Rynd, Susan Saul, Abigail Selzer, Eric Strandberg, Hally Swift, Betty Swift, Julie Van Pelt, and Allison Woods.

Dan A. Nelson, Editor

INTRODUCTION

The idea of going in circles in day-to-day life—especially in the business world—makes most people cringe. There's something wrong, so the thinking goes, when you aren't making straight-ahead, linear progress.

Not so on trails. Nothing pleases hikers more than finding a great wilderness trail that allows them to wander in circles, never touching the same bit of trail twice. Hiking, after all, is hard work and it's nice when every step takes you into new country, with new scenery. Out-and-back hikes are okay, but a great loop hike? That's the holy grail of the trail world.

Historically, most trails were built to a specific destination—a lake, a mountaintop fire lookout, or a distant valley—and loops were built only when they served a functional purpose. As trails shifted from utility to recreation, the idea of visiting multiple destinations during a single hiking trip grew. Land managers started connecting the linear trails with secondary trails, making loops out of them.

Here in Washington, scores of great loop routes exist, ranging from short day hikes suitable for those looking for a quiet few hours in the woods, to the granddaddy of all loop trails, the 95-mile Wonderland Trail encircling Mount Rainier. Volunteers from Washington Trails Association and The Mountaineers Books endeavored to find the best loops in the Cascade and Olympic Mountains, and the results of their labor (of love) are presented here. Enjoy.

PERMITS AND REGULATIONS

You can't set off out your door these days without first making sure you're not breaking the rules. In an effort to keep our wilderness areas wild and our trails safe and well maintained, the land managers—especially the National Park Service and the U.S. Forest Service—have implemented a sometimes complex set of rules and regulations governing the use of public lands.

Virtually all trails in national forests in Washington (and Oregon) fall under the USFS Region 6 Forest Pass Program. Simply stated, in order to park legally at any national forest trailhead in USFS Region 6 (Washington and Oregon), you must display a Northwest Forest Pass decal in your windshield. These sell for $5 per day or $30 for an annual pass good throughout Region 6. The NW Forest Pass is also required at most trailheads within North Cascades National Park.

In addition to the parking pass, when hikers enter wilderness areas they must pick up and fill out a wilderness permit at the trailhead registration box (sometimes located at the wilderness boundary if the trail doesn't immediately enter a designated wilderness). These are free and unlimited (though that may change).

In Mount Rainier National Park, backcountry campers are required to register. There are a limited number of official backcountry campsites, but hikers can reserve sites up to two months in advance of their trip for a $20 fee. The permits are free for hikers who opt to chance it and get their backcountry permits the day of their hike.

Olympic National Park, on the other hand, charges hikers a trail free, and a camping fee on many trails, and has restrictive permits in select areas. Call the park's Wilderness Information Center (see Appendix) for specifics.

GENERAL TRAIL ETIQUETTE

Anyone who enjoys backcountry trails should recognize their responsibility to those trails and to other trail users. We each must work to preserve the tranquility of the wildlands, not only by being sensitive to the environment but to other trail users as well.

The trails in this book are open to an array of trail users. Some trails are open to hikers only, but others allow hikers, horseback riders, mountain bikers, dog hikers, and—on occasion—motorcycles. When you encounter other trail users, whether they are hikers, climbers, trail runners, bicyclists, or horseback riders, the only hard-and-fast rule is that common sense and simple courtesy must be observed. It's hard to overstate just how vital these two things—common sense and courtesy—are to maintaining an enjoyable, safe, and friendly situation on our trails when different types of trail users meet.

With that "Golden Rule of Trail Etiquette" firmly in mind as you encounter other users, there are things you can do to make your trip, and that of others on the trail, most enjoyable:

■ When hikers meet other hikers, the group heading uphill has the right-of-way. There are two general reasons for this. First, on steep ascents, hikers may be watching the trail before them and not notice the approach of descending hikers until they are face-to-face. More importantly, it is easier for descending hikers to break their stride and step off the trail than it is for those who have fallen into a good, climbing plod. If, however, the uphill hiker is in need of a rest, they may step off the trail and yield the right-of-way to the downhill hikers, but this is the decision of the climbers alone.

■ When hikers meet other user groups, the hikers should move off the trail. This is because hikers are generally the most mobile and flexible users, so it is easier for hikers to step off the trail than for bicyclists to lift their bikes off or for horseback riders to get their animals off the trail.

■ When hikers meet horseback riders, the hikers should step off the downhill side of the trail unless the terrain makes this difficult or dangerous. In that case, move to the uphill side of the trail, but crouch down a bit so you do not tower over the horses' heads. Also, do not stand behind trees or brush if you can avoid it as this could make you invisible to the animals until they get close, and then your sudden appearance could startle them. Rather, stay in clear view and talk in a normal tone of voice to the riders. This calms the horses.

■ Stay on trails and practice minimum impact. Don't cut switchbacks, take shortcuts, or make new trails. If your destination is off-trail, leave the trail in as direct a manner as possible. That is, move away from the trail in a line perpendicular to the trail. Once well clear of the trail, adjust your route to your destination.

■ Obey the rules specific to the trail you are visiting. Many trails are closed to certain types of use, including hiking with dogs or riding horses.

■ Hikers who take their dogs on the trails should have the dog on a leash—or under strict voice-command—at all times.

■ Avoid disturbing wildlife, especially in winter and in calving areas. Observe from a distance—even if you cannot get the picture you want, resist the urge to move closer to wildlife. This not only keeps you safer, but it prevents the animal from having to exert itself unnecessarily in fleeing from you.

■ Leave all natural things and features as you found them for others to enjoy.

■ Never roll rocks off trails or cliffs—you never know who or what is below you.

These are just a few of the things hikers can do to maintain a safe and harmonious trail environment, and while not every situation is addressed by these rules, hikers can avoid problems by always practicing the Golden Rule of Trail Etiquette: *Common sense and courtesy are the order of the day.*

LOW-IMPACT CAMPING

Everyone loves to sit around a campfire, letting the orange flames hypnotize them and stir a wealth of thoughts and dreams. Unfortunately, if everyone who entered the wilderness built a fire, the campsites would be filled with charcoal, and the forests would soon be picked clean of dead wood, leaving the hordes of small critters with nowhere to scrounge for food (the insects that eat the dead wood provide meals for an army of birds and animals). So, fires should be left to the car campgrounds with their structured fire pits and readily available supplies of firewood. Backcountry campers should stick to small pack stoves, even when regulations technically allow campfires.

Hikers must also remember that anything that is packed in must be packed out, even biodegradable items like apple cores. The phrase, "leave only footprints, take only pictures," is a worthy slogan to live by when visiting the wilderness.

You should also give some thought to your campsites. When hardened sites are available, use them. Restricting campers to one or two sites around a lake prevents the entire shoreline from being trampled and stripped of its

Trail workers take a lunch break at Echo Mountain.

vegetation. If there is no established site, choose a rocky or sandy area where you won't damage fragile vegetation. If you must camp in a meadow area, choose a location with good drainage and restrict the time your tent is set up. Rather than pitch the tent immediately upon reaching your camp, leave it in its stuff sack until you are done with dinner, and then set it up. First thing next morning, break it down before breakfast—this prevents the plants under the tent from being smothered and, most of the time, even though they are a bit bent and crumpled, they'll spring back up again soon.

Keep in mind that you aren't the only hikers out enjoying the beauty of the wilderness. That rocky bench with a view of the mountains across the valley might seem like the perfect place for a tent. If you set up camp and someone comes along behind you and just wants to sit and enjoy the view for a few moments, chances are that they will feel uncomfortable stepping up for a look from your campsite. It's a much better idea to set up camp well back from the most scenic locations so that everyone can enjoy them.

The same goes for water. Keep your camp at least 100 feet away from lakeshores and stream banks. This not only lets other hikers—and animals—get to the water without having to bypass you, but it helps to keep the water clean.

Another important Leave No Trace principle focuses on taking care of personal business. The first rule of backcountry bathroom etiquette says that if an outhouse exists, use it. This seems obvious, but all too often, folks find backcountry toilets are dark, dank affairs, and they choose to use the woods rather than the rickety wooden structure provided by the land manager. It may be easier on your nose to head off into the woods, but this disperses human waste around the popular camping areas. Privies, on the other hand, keep the waste concentrated in a single site, minimizing contamination of area waters. The outhouses get even higher environmental marks if they feature removable holding tanks that can be airlifted out. These johns and their accompanying stack of tanks aren't exactly aesthetically pleasing, but having an ugly outhouse tucked into the corner of the woods is better than finding toilet paper strewn throughout the woods.

When privies aren't provided, the key factor to consider is location. You'll want to choose a site at least 200 to 300 feet from water, campsites, and trails. A location well out of sight of trails and viewpoints will give you privacy and reduce the odds of other hikers stumbling across the site after you leave. Other factors to consider are ecological: a good surrounding of vegetation, with some direct sunlight, will aid decomposition.

Once you pick your place, start digging. The idea is to make like a cat and bury your waste. You need to dig down through the organic duff into

Privy hidden in mossy forest in North Cascades National Park

the mineral soil below—a hole six to eight inches deep is usually adequate. When you've taken care of business, refill the hole and camouflage it with rocks and sticks—this helps prevent other humans, or animals, from digging in the same location before decomposition has done its job.

WATER

You'll want to treat your drinking water. Wherever humans have gone, germs have gone with them, and humans have gone just about everywhere. That means that even the most pristine mountain stream may harbor microscopic nasties like *Giardia* cysts, *Cryptosporidium*, or *E. coli*.

Treating water can be as simple as boiling it, chemically purifying it (adding tiny iodine tablets), or pumping it through one of the new generation of water filter or purifiers. (Note: Pump units labeled as filters generally remove everything but viruses, which are too small to be filtered out. Pumps labeled as purifiers must have a chemical element—usually iodine—that kills the

Hiker filtering water from Spray Creek (Hike 75), Mount Rainier National Park

viruses after filtering out all the other bugs.) Never drink untreated water, or your intestines may never forgive you.

CLEAN-UP

When it comes time to wash up, whether it's just your hands or your dinner pots, give a thought to what you want in the water you drink. You get your drinking water from the nearby lake or stream, right? Would you want to find someone's leftover macaroni and cheese in it? Or their soap scum? Of course not, and neither would other folks, so you need to be careful with your clean-ups.

When washing your hands, rinse off as much dust and dirt as you can in plain water first. If you still feel the need for a soapy wash, collect a pot of water from the lake or stream and move at least 100 feet away. Apply a tiny bit of biodegradable soap on your hands, dribble on a little water, and lather up. Use a bandanna or towel to wipe away most of the soap, and then rinse with the water in the pot. Follow the same procedure with your pots and pans, making sure you eat all of the food first (never dump left-over food in the water or on the ground. If you can't eat it, pack it into a plastic bag and store it with your other food—in other words, carry it out!).

BEARS

Speaking of food, you'll want to learn the proper method for bear-bagging your food and heavily scented clothing items (i.e., shirts with a lot of sweat and/or deodorant). There are an estimated 30,000 to 35,000 black bears in Washington, and the big bruins can be found in every corner of the state. The high, wild country around the Pacific Crest Trail is especially attractive to the solitude-seeking bears, and they can be found roaming every inch of the PCT in Washington. Watching bears graze through a rich huckleberry patch or seeing them flip dead logs in search of grubs can be an exciting and rewarding experience. Provided, of course, you aren't in the same berry patch. Bears tend to prefer solitude to human company, and will generally flee long before you have a chance to get too close. There are times, however, when the bears either don't hear hikers approaching, or they are more interested in defending their food source—or their young—than they are in avoiding a confrontation. These instances are rare, and you can take the following steps to further minimize the odds of an encounter with an aggressive bear:

■ Hike in a group, and hike only during daylight hours.
■ Talk or sing as you hike. If bears hear you coming, they will usually avoid you. On the other hand, bears feel threatened when surprised, and often go on the offensive in a surprise encounter, at least until they feel the threat is neutralized. So make noises that will identify you as a human—talk, sing, rattle pebbles in a tin can—especially when hiking near a river or stream (which can mask more subtle sounds that might normally alert a bear to your presence).
■ Be aware of the environment around you, and know how to identify "bear sign." Overturned rocks and torn-up dead wood logs are often the result of a bear searching for grubs. Berry bushes that are stripped of berries, with leaves, branches, and berries littering the ground under the bushes, show where a bear has fed. Bears will often leave claw marks on trees, and since they use trees as scratching posts, fur in the rough bark of the trees is a sign that says "a bear was here!" Tracks and scat are the most common signs of a bear's recent presence.
■ Stay away from abundant food sources and dead animals. Black bears are opportunistic and will scavenge food. A bear that finds a dead deer will hang around until the meat is gone, and it will defend that food against any perceived threat.

Opposite: *Black bear seen through forest trees, Olympic National Park*

- Keep dogs on leash and under control. Many bear encounters have resulted from unleashed dogs chasing a bear; the bear gets angry and turns on the dog; the dog gets scared and runs for help (i.e., back to its owner); and the bear follows right back into the dog owner's lap.
- Leave the perfume, hair spray, cologne, and scented soaps at home. Using scented sprays and body lotions makes you smell like a big, tasty treat.
- Never eat or cook in your tent. The spilled food or even food odors can permeate the nylon material, essentially making your tent smell, at least to a bear, like last night's dinner.
- Never clean fish within 100 feet of camp.
- Always store all your food and other scented items in their own stuff sacks when preparing to hang them.
- Always suspend your food bags at least 12 feet in the air and 8 to 10 feet from the nearest tree trunk. In some popular backcountry camps, the land managers provide wires, complete with pulleys, to help you do this, but you should know how to string your own rope to achieve these heights, too.

On the very rare occasion, hikers can do all the right things and a bear will still behave aggressively. It could be as simple as being in the wrong place at the wrong time—I found myself between a bear black sow and one of her cubs once simply because the cub had wandered downhill of the trail, while the sow was uphill of it. Fortunately, the youngster was a second-year cub and momma bear was ready to toss it out on its own at any time, so she barely looked up from her huckleberry dinner as I grouped the hikers behind me into a tight cluster and hustled everyone up the trail. But the bear could have turned aggressive. If you find yourself in that situation, here are some guidelines to follow in an encounter:

- Respect a bear's need for personal space. If you see a bear in the distance, make a wide detour around it, or if that's not possible (i.e., if the trail leads close to the bear) leave the area.
- If you encounter a bear at close range, remain calm. Do not run as this may trigger a predatory/prey reaction from the bear.
- Talk in a low, calm manner to the bear to help identify yourself as a human.
- Hold your arms out from your body, and if wearing a jacket hold the front open so you appear to be as big as possible.
- Don't stare directly at the bear—the bear may interpret this as a threat or challenge—watch the animal without making direct eye-to-eye contact.
- Slowly move upwind of the bear if you can do so without crowding the bear. The bear's strongest sense is its sense of smell, and if it can sniff you and identify you as human, it may retreat.
- Know how to interpret bear actions. A nervous bear will often rumble in its chest, clack its teeth, and "pop" its jaw. It may paw the ground and swing its head violently side to side. If the bear does this, watch it

closely (without staring directly at it). Continue speaking low and calmly.

■ A bear may bluff-charge—run at you but stop well before reaching you—to try and intimidate you. Resist the urge to run as that would turn the bluff into a real charge, and you will NOT be able to outrun the bear (black bears can run at speeds of up to 35 miles per hour through log-strewn forests).

■ If you surprise a bear and it does charge from close range, lie down and play dead. A surprised bear will leave you once the perceived threat is neutralized. However, if the bear wasn't attacking because it was surprised—if it charges from a long distance, or if it has had a chance to identify you and still attacks—you should fight back. A bear in this situation is behaving in a predatory manner (as opposed to the defensive attack of a surprised bear) and is looking at you as food. Kick, stab, punch at the bear. If it knows you will fight back, it may leave you and search for easier prey.

■ Carry a 12-ounce (or larger) can of pepper spray bear deterrent. The spray—a high concentration of oils from hot peppers—should fire out at least 20 or 30 feet in a broad mist. Don't use the spray unless a bear is actually charging and is in range of the spray.

COUGARS

Very few hikers see cougars in the wild. Not only are these big cats solitary and shy animals, but there are just 2500 to 3000 of them roaming the entire state of Washington. Still, cougars and hikers occasionally do encounter each other. In these cases, the hikers should, in my opinion, count their blessings—they will likely never see a more majestic animal than a wild cougar. To make sure the encounter is a positive one, hikers must understand the cats. Cougars are shy but very curious. They will follow hikers simply to see what kind of beasts we are, but they very rarely (as in, almost never) attack adult humans. If you do encounter a cougar, remember that cougars rely on prey that can't, or won't, fight back. So, as soon as you see a cat:

■ Do not run! Running may trigger a cougar's attack instinct.

■ Stand up and face the animal. Virtually every recorded cougar attack has been a predator/prey attack. If you appear as another aggressive predator rather than as prey, the cougar will back down.

■ Try to appear large—wave your arms or a jacket over your head. The idea is to make the cougar think you are the bigger, meaner beast.

■ Parents should keep their children within sight on the trail at all times—wildlife encounters are just one of many potential dangers of backcountry hiking.

■ Maintain eye contact with the animal. The cougar will interpret this a show of dominance on your part.

■ Do not approach the animal; back away slowly if you can safely do so.

If the cat acts aggressive:
- Do not turn your back or take your eyes off the cougar.
- Remain standing.
- Throw things, provided you don't have to bend over to pick them up. If you have a water bottle on your belt, chuck it at the cat. Throw your camera, wave your hiking stick, and if the cat gets close enough, whack it HARD with your hiking staff. (I know of two cases where women delivered good, hard whacks across the nose of aggressive-acting cougars, and the cats immediately turned tail and ran away.)
- Shout loudly.
- Fight back aggressively.

You can minimize the already slim chances of having a negative cougar encounter by doing the following:
- Do not hike or jog alone (in fact, don't jog at all—joggers look like fleeing prey to a predator).
- Keep children within sight and close at all times.
- Avoid dead animals.
- Keep a clean camp.
- Keep dogs on leash and under control. A cougar may attack a loose, solitary dog, but a leashed dog next to you makes two foes for the cougar to deal with—and cougars are too smart to take on two aggressive animals at once.
- Be alert to the surroundings.
- Use a walking stick.

Remember, above all else cougars are curious animals. They may appear threatening when they are only being inquisitive. By making the cougar think you are a bigger, meaner critter than it is, you will be able to avoid an attack (the big cats realize that there is enough easy prey and they don't have to mess with something that will fight back). Keep in mind that fewer than twenty fatal cougar attacks have occurred in the United States in the past 100 years (on the other hand, more than fifty people are killed, on average, by deer each year—most in auto collisions).

WEATHER
Mountain weather in general is famously unpredictable, but the Cascade Mountains stretch that unpredictability to sometimes absurd lengths. The high, jagged nature of the mountains coupled with their proximity to the Pacific Ocean makes them magnets for every bit of moisture in the atmosphere.

As the moist air comes rushing in off the Pacific, it hits the western front of the Cascades. The air is pushed up the slopes of the mountains, often forming clouds and eventually rain, feeding the wet rain forests that dominate the western slopes. By the time the airstream crests the Cascades and starts down the eastern slopes, the clouds have lost their moisture loads, leaving the east side dry and filled with open stands of drought-resistant pine.

Where east meets west the wet clouds hit the dry heat, often creating thunderstorms. Hikers on the trail must be aware of this potential, because the storms can brew up at any month of the year. They can also come up quickly, with little warning, and a hiker stuck on a high pass as a thunderstorm develops is a good target for a lightning bolt.

To reduce the dangers of being struck by lightning if thunderstorms are forecast or develop while you are in the mountains, do the following:

- Use a NOAA Weather radio (i.e., a radio tuned to one of the national weather forecast frequencies) to keep abreast of the latest weather information.
- Avoid travel on mountaintops and ridge crests.
- Avoid setting up camp in narrow valleys, gullies, or ridge tops. Instead, look for campsites in broad, open valleys and meadows, keeping away from large rock formations.
- Stay well away from bodies of water.
- If your hair stands on end or you feel static shocks, move immediately—the static electricity you feel could very well be a precursor to a lightning strike.
- If there is a shelter or building nearby, get into it. Don't take shelter under trees, however, especially in open areas.
- If there is no shelter available, and lightning is flashing, remove your pack (the metal stays or frame are natural electrical conduits) and crouch down, balancing on the balls of your feet until the lighting clears the area.

Of course, thunderstorms aren't the only weather hazard hikers face. A sudden rainsquall can push temperatures down 15 or 20 degrees in a matter of minutes. Folks dressed for hot summer hiking need to be prepared for such temperature drops and the accompanying soaking rain if they want to avoid hypothermia.

If the temperature drop is great enough, hikers can miss the rain and get hit instead by snow. I've seen snowstorms blow through the Cascades every month of the year, with as much as a foot falling on some routes in late August.

Besides fresh fallen snow, summer hikers need to be aware of snowfields left over from the previous winter's snowpack. Depending on the severity of the past winter, and the weather conditions of the spring and early summer, some trails may melt out in June while others remain snow covered well into August or beyond—some years, sections never melt out.

In addition to treacherous footing and difficulties in routefinding, these lingering snowfields can be prone to avalanches or slides.

GEAR

No hiker should venture far up a trail without being properly equipped. Starting with the feet, a good pair of boots can make the difference between a wonderful hike and a horrible death march. Keep your feet happy and you'll be happy.

But you can't talk boots without talking socks. Only one rule here: wear whatever is most comfortable unless it's cotton. Corollary to that rule: never wear cotton.

Cotton is a wonderful fabric when your life isn't on the line—it is soft, light, and airy. But get it wet and it stays wet. That means blisters on your feet. Wet cotton also lacks any insulation value. In fact, get it wet and it sucks away your body heat, leaving you susceptible to hypothermia. So leave your cotton socks, cotton underwear, and even the cotton tee shirts at home. The only cotton I carry on the trail is my trusty pink bandanna (pink because nobody else I know carries pink, so I always know which is mine).

Backpacker with tent set up on a sandy area to protect nearby vegetation

A good, three-season tent for shelter and a fluffy, lightweight sleeping bag—with a small pad (used as much for insulation from the cold ground as for padding)—are the primary items in your pack, along with your pack stove and food. Those are the big things, but there are a lot of little things that need to go into your pack, even on a day hike. Though every hiker must decide what gear they need and want with them on their outing, the folks at Washington Trails Association and I have put together checklists for day hikers and backpackers. These lists should by no means be considered the last word on what to take with you, but you can use them as general guidelines when loading up your pack. Lists available at *wta.org.*

While the list of what you pack may vary from what another hiker on the same trail is carrying, there are a few things each and every one of us should have in our packs. For instance, every hiker who ventures more than a few hundred yards away from the road should be prepared to spend the night under the stars (or under the clouds, as may be the case). Mountain storms can whip up in a hurry, catching sunny-day hikers by surprise. What was an easy-to-follow trail during a calm, clear day can disappear into a confusing world of fog and rain—or even snow—in a windy tempest. Therefore, every member of the party should have a pack loaded with the Ten Essentials, and a few other items that aren't necessarily essential, but are good to have on hand in an emergency.

The Ten Essentials:

1. Extra Clothing. This means more clothing than you would wear during the worst weather of the planned outing. If you get injured or lost, you won't be moving around generating heat, so you'll need to bundle up.

2. Extra Food. Pack enough so you'll have leftovers after an uneventful trip (those leftovers will keep you fed and fueled during an emergency).

3. Sunglasses. While necessary for most high alpine travel, they are absolutely essential when traveling on snow or exposed rock.

4. Knife. There are a multitude of uses, some come to mind easily (whittling kindling for a fire, first-aid applications) while others won't become apparent until you find you don't have a knife handy. A multi-tool is an even better option as the pliers can be used in repairs of damaged packs, stoves, and other gear.

5. First-aid Kit. Nothing elaborate needed—especially if you are unfamiliar with some of the uses. Make sure you have Band-Aids, a roll of gauze, some aspirin, etc. A Red Cross first-aid training course is recommended.

6. Fire Starter. An emergency campfire provides warmth, but it also has a calming effect on most people. Without it the night is cold, dark, and intimidating. With it, the night is held at arm's length. A candle or tube of fire-starting ribbon is essential for starting a fire with wet wood.

7. Matches. Can't start a fire without them. Pack in a waterproof container and/or buy the waterproof/windproof variety. Book matches are useless in wind or wet weather and disposable lighters are unreliable.

8. Flashlight/headlamp. If caught after dark, you'll need it to follow the trail. If forced to spend the night, you'll need it to set up an emergency camp, gather wood, etc. Carry extra batteries and bulb.
9. Map. Carry a topographic map of the area you plan to visit, and knowledge of how to read it.
10. Compass. Again, make sure you know how to use it.

In addition to these essentials, I add two small kit bags. One is a repair kit, containing a 20-foot length of nylon cord, a small roll of duct tape, some 1-inch webbing and extra webbing buckles (to fix broken pack straps), and a small tube of super glue. The other tiny package at the bottom of my pack is my emergency survival kit, which holds a small metal mirror, an emergency mylar "blanket," a plastic whistle, and a tiny signal smoke canister—all useful for signaling to search groups whether they are on the ground or in the air.

USING THIS BOOK

No guidebook can provide all the details of a trail, nor stay current with constantly changing conditions of trails, stream crossings, and access roads. So before any hike, you should call the land manager for the latest information on trail conditions—you'll find the phone numbers for each land manager in the Appendix.

You'll also find references to the Green Trails map quadrants covering the described hike. Green Trails, Inc., uses the standard 7.5-minute United States Geological Survey (USGS) topographical maps as their starting point, but where USGS maps may not have been updated since sometime in the 1950s, the Green Trails cartographers have researchers in the field every year, checking trail conditions and making updates. Many hikers still use USGS maps, and they work when you are looking at the mountains and contours since the natural features don't change rapidly. But the man-made features do change, and in my opinion, Green Trails does the best job of all the mapmakers in staying abreast of those changes.

The maps are available at most outdoor retailers in the state, as well as at many U.S. Forest Service offices.

When referring to the Hiking Time, please bear in mind that this is an estimation based on my experience on the trail and the speed with which I expect the average hiker to travel. You may find my estimates are too high or too low. I apologize in advance, and again encourage you to use my estimated time merely as a tool to help plan your hike and not as a gauge by which to measure your success or failure.

The Best Hiking Time listing is another subjective tool meant to be a guide and not an absolute. Some years (such as 1999) the heavy winter snowpack doesn't melt off the high country until early September. In other years—the drought year of 2001, for instance—the highest trails may be snow-free by the Fourth of July. Again, use this listing as a tool to help plan your trips, and then make sure to call the land manager to get the latest information on trail conditions.

Note that throughout this guide, the abbreviation "FS Road" is used in place of Forest Service Road.

VOLUNTEER TRAIL MAINTENANCE: VOLUNTEERS TAKE CARE OF TRAILS

As congressional budget allocations diminished throughout the 1980s and early 1990s, a nonprofit hiker's organization stepped in to pick up some of the slack. Washington Trails Association (WTA) had grown tired of watching our backcountry trails fall into disarray and, at times, disappear due to lack of maintenance. So WTA created a volunteer trail maintenance program to ensure that not another mile was lost to neglect. In less than a decade, the program grew from 250 volunteer hours a year to nearly 50,000 hours of volunteer trail maintenance time coordinated annually. Each year more than 1500 volunteers help maintain trails from the Columbia River Gorge to the Canadian border, from the rain forests of the Quinault to dry ridges of the Teanaway country. WTA teams have built sections of the world-renowned 95-mile Wonderland Trail that encircles Mount Rainier. They've also maintained largely unknown, but still spectacular, trails such as the Tinkham Mountain Loop near Snoqualmie Pass.

WTA's volunteer trail maintenance program is now responsible for much of the routine maintenance on hiking trails in Washington. They

A WTA volunteer work party learns about trail tools and their safe use.

work on trails governed by federal, state, and county agencies, and a few on private lands (when the trails are open and accessible to the public). Volunteers who participate in one day of trail maintenance on a U.S. Forest Service trail earn a free one-day NW Forest Pass. Two days of volunteer work earns you an annual NW Forest Pass. (Volunteer days need not be consecutive. When you have earned two day passes, you can trade them in to WTA for an annual pass.)

So what can volunteers expect when they join a work party? Here are some common questions and answers:

When do I work? On the average summer weekend there are as many as five separate work parties each day. The work starts at 8:30 A.M. and ends at 3:30 P.M. or sooner. There are also at least two work parties a week all winter long.

Where do I work? From the Olympic Peninsula to the Wenatchee National Forest, and from the Oregon boarder to North Cascades National Park.

How much experience do I need? No experience necessary, and you're guaranteed to have a good time.

How much time do I have to volunteer?

Front Country. If you're new to trail work join the work party on the trail in places like Tiger Mountain or Wallace Falls.

Backcountry. Backcountry trails need the most work. Join us for a day on a forest service trail and earn a free one-day NW Forest Pass.

Weekend. Join us on a weekend for 2 days of trail work with a potluck BBQ on Saturday night. Work both days or work 1 day and hike on the other.

Weeklong. Both the core trail volunteers and the first-timers will enjoy the weeklong backcountry "vacations." Choose from car camping or backpacking.

How do I volunteer? You can call the WTA office, (206) 625-1367, visit the Washington Trails Association's website, *www.wta.org*, or email *info@wta.org*.

ENJOY THE TRAILS

Above all else, I hope you can safely enjoy the trails in this book. These trails exist for our enjoyment and for the enjoyment of future generations. We can protect them as we use them if we are careful with our actions and forthright with our demands on Congress to continue and further the protection of our county's wildlands.

Throughout the twentieth century, wilderness lovers helped secure protection for the lands we enjoy today. As we enter the twenty-first century, we must see to it that those protections continue, and that the last bits of wildlands are also preserved for the enjoyment of future generations.

Please, if you enjoy these trails, get involved. Something as simple as writing a letter to Congress can make a big difference.

A NOTE ABOUT SAFETY

Safety is an important concern in all outdoor activities. No guidebook can alert you to every hazard or anticipate the limitations of every reader. Therefore, the descriptions of roads, trails, routes, and natural features in this book are not representations that a particular place or excursion will be safe for your party. When you follow any of the routes described in this book, you assume responsibility for your own safety. Under normal conditions, such excursions require the usual attention to traffic, road and trail conditions, weather, terrain, the capabilities of your party, and other factors. Keeping informed on current conditions and exercising common sense are the keys to a safe, enjoyable outing.

The Mountaineers Books

HIKES BY INTEREST

FEATURE	HIKE #	TRAIL NAME
Panoramic Views		
	17	Seven Pass Loop
	87	Snowgrass Flats/Goat Lake Basin
	72	Burroughs Mountain
Solitude		
	100	Aiken Lava Bed
	60	Koppen Mountain
	21	Reed Peak
Old-growth Forest		
	1	Mount Muller
	5	Sol Duc Hot Springs
	79	East Side Loop
Dog-friendly Trails		
	15	Ebey's Landing
	59	DeRoux Creek
	99	Bird Mountain Loop
Kid-friendly Trails		
	4	Sams River Trail
	69	Sand Creek
	80	Naches Peak
Wildflower Viewing		
	22	Horseshoe Basin/Windy Peak
	72	Paradise/Glacier Vista
	24	Schriebers Meadows

Waterfalls and Rivers

Lakes

Wildlife Viewing

Natural Splendor

1 MOUNT MULLER

Round trip ■	**12 miles**
Loop direction ■	Counterclockwise
Hiking time ■	8 hours
Starting elevation ■	1000 feet
High point ■	3748 feet
Elevation gain ■	2750 feet
Best hiking time ■	Early March to October
Map ■	Green Trails Lake Crescent, No. 101
Contact ■	Olympic National Park, Wilderness Information Center

Proof that fire marks a beginning and not an end awaits hikers along this route. The trail pierces deeply shadowed, wildlife-rich second-growth forests and crosses broad ridge-top meadows sporting colorful wildflower carpets and expansive views. But neither of these features would be present if not for the cleansing touch of wildfire in the early part of the twentieth century. Forest fires burned the old trees that once grew here. Vibrant stands of Douglas fir and western hemlock sprung up on the lower flanks of the mountain, while the ridge tops sport treeless meadows and broad clearings awash in wildflowers and native plants.

To get there, from Port Angeles drive west on U.S. Highway 101 past Crescent Lake and, about 3 miles west of Fairholm, turn right (north) onto FS Road 3071 and find the trailhead about 0.5 mile north at the end of the road.

The trail begins heading east along the valley bottom, gaining roughly 2700 feet to the summit of Mount Muller. The first 3 miles pierce moss-laden forest of towering Douglas fir and western hemlock. These aren't true old-growth stands—the forest here was cleared by wildfire in the early twentieth century, but the naturally seeded second growth has grown tall and strong since that fire. The trail climbs gradually through long, sweeping switchbacks through this forest.

At about 3 miles the trail leaves the timber and climbs through clearings and increasingly broad sidehill meadows to reach the ridge crest at about 3.5 miles. As the trail gains the ridge, the views expand outward. Following the ridge east, take in the sights of the Olympic Mountains towering off to the south, the mist-shrouded channel of the Strait of Juan de Fuca to the north, and the snowcapped cone of Mount Baker to the northeast.

Once on the ridge crest, the trail meanders along the undulating spine for another couple miles, passing through occasional stands of fir and hemlock. For the most part, though, the ridge walk sticks to sun-splashed meadows and stellar views. The panoramic scenery along the ridge makes the trip worthwhile, but the best views are found at the top of Mount Muller, about

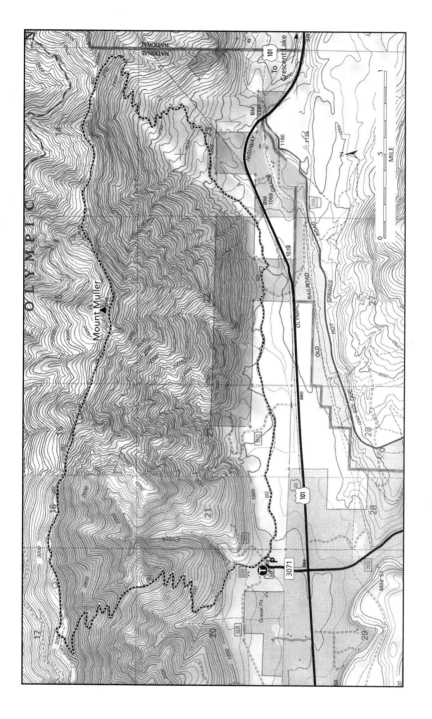

The trail to Mount Muller through lush forest, carpeted with plants

5.5 miles from the trailhead. From here, you enjoy the scenery you witnessed along the way, but you can also soak in the sights to the southeast. Peer into the deep green valley of the Sol Duc River, and up over its southern rim— the emerald crest of the High Divide, from Bogachiel Peak to the Bailey

Range. Behind this ridge looms the majestic summit of Mount Olympus.

From the top of Muller, the trail drops to the west and descends through another series of switchbacks into the forest, following a long contouring course back to the trailhead. Look for black-tailed deer and great horned owls along this section as both species lurk in these cool, dark forests—the deer foraging on the rich vegetation on the forest floor, and the owls plucking plump deer mice from the fallen trees and hidden nooks.

2 HEATHER PARK/LAKE ANGELES

Round trip	■	**12 miles**
Loop direction	■	Counterclockwise
Hiking time	■	8 hours
Starting elevation	■	1000 feet
High point	■	6050 feet
Elevation gain	■	2750 feet
Best hiking time	■	Early March to October
Maps	■	Green Trails Port Angeles, No. 103 and Mount Angeles, No. 135
Contact	■	Olympic National Park, Wilderness Information Center

Deep valleys filled with old-growth forest, steep sidehills covered with lush second-growth stands of timber, and broad ridge-top meadows painted with the vibrant colors of native wildflowers await hikers here. There are clear lakes to enjoy and expansive views to absorb. In short, this modest loop presents a taste of some of the best features found throughout Olympic National Park.

To get there, drive west on U.S. Highway 101 to Port Angeles. In town, turn south onto Heart of the Hills Road (signed as Hurricane Ridge, Olympic National Park) and drive south toward the park entrance. Just before entering the national park, turn right into the Heart of the Hills Campground, and park at the main parking area.

Two trails leave from the same parking lot: one to Lake Angeles, the other to Heather Park (and Mount Angeles). Take the right-hand trail to do the loop counterclockwise. You'll climb steeply away from the trailhead, piercing dense second-growth forest for the first 3 miles. The trail receives regular maintenance and plenty of use, resulting in a smooth, clear pathway.

At around 3 miles, the trail breaks out of the continuous forest and slides upward into forest clearings, and eventually into hillside meadows below the ridgeline between First Top and Second Top. At 4 miles, the trail enters

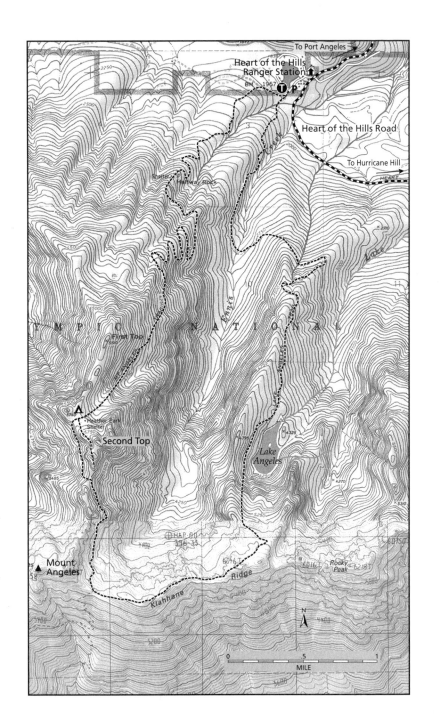

To Port Angeles

Heart of the Hills
Ranger Station

BM 1967

Heart of the Hills Road

To Hurricane Hill

Halfway Rock

Ennis

First Top

Heather Park
Shelter

Second Top

Lake
Angeles

O L Y M P I C   N A T I O N A L

HAP 60

Mount
Angeles

Rocky
Peak

Klahhane   Ridge

N

0   5   1
MILE

the lush meadows draped across the broad saddle between the peaks. This expansive field of flowers is Heather Park. To the north is a long straight ridge slanting gently downward to a prominent peak, First Top, at 5510 feet. To the southeast, at the other end of the ridge, is a more substantial peak, Second Top, at 6000 feet. Take a long rest in the meadows of Heather Park. Adventurous folks can scramble up a climbers' path to the top of Second Top before returning to Heather Park and starting south once more along the main trail.

In another mile, you'll climb into the subalpine environments of Klahhane Ridge and at 6 miles, you'll intercept the Lake Angeles Trail atop the rocky spine of Klahhane Ridge. Marmots and pikas can be seen and heard among the rock fields here, and some visitors even see the elusive mountain goats that caused such a political stir in the mid-1990s (the park wanted to shoot all the goats, which are an introduced species, to restore natural order to the park).

At the junction with the Lake Angeles Trail, turn east (left) and follow the ridge for a little over a mile. From this high route, you'll have 6218-foot Rocky Peak in your forward sights, and the tall spires of Elk Mountain

Blooming heather adds color to a foggy day in Heather Park.

(6729 feet) and Maiden Peak (6434 feet) on your right flank. To the north, you can peer out over the Strait of Juan de Fuca, and to the northeast—on clear days—you can see the shimmering white summit of Mount Baker.

Around the 7-mile point, on the flank of Rocky Peak, the trail hooks north and begins the long descent to the trailhead. But leaving the ridge doesn't mean the end of the scenery. At 8.5 miles, the trail passes the cold, blue waters of Lake Angeles. This is a fine place to camp or just rest and relax for a bit before continuing down through the cool, shady forests for the final 3.5 miles to the trailhead.

3 CAPE ALAVA

Round trip ■	**9.3 miles**
Loop direction ■	Counterclockwise
Hiking time ■	8 hours day hike or backpack
Starting elevation ■	80 feet
High point ■	500 feet
Elevation gain ■	420 feet
Best hiking time ■	Open year-round, best March to October
Map ■	Green Trails Ozette, No. 130S
Contact ■	Olympic National Park, Wilderness Information Center
Permits ■	Overnight campers require permits; advance reservations recommended, and required in busy summer months. **Contact** office listed above.

The coastal zone of Olympic National Park is a 62-mile strip of Pacific coastline with abundant wildlife. One of the most popular trails in Washington is the Cape Alava Loop Trail, taking hikers from Lake Ozette through the rain forest and to the ocean. This loop trail is actually a triangle. Visitors here will find ancient petroglyphs as well as excellent opportunities for encounters with marine wildlife. Look for sea lions on the offshore rocks (or even on the onshore rocks) and whales spouting in the surf. Eagles, ospreys, and terns glide overhead. Deer ramble around the forests at the end of the beach, and the occasional black bear lumbers through the trees and fishes in the tide pools. This hike is described counterclockwise, but can be traveled either way.

To get there, from Port Angeles drive west on U.S. Highway 101 to a junction with State Route 112. Drive north northwest onto SR 112 and continue through Clallum Bay to Sekiu. From the village of Sekiu drive about

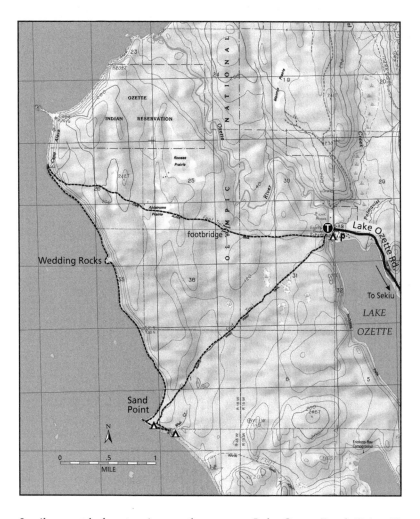

3 miles west before turning southwest onto Lake Ozette Road. Drive 21 miles to the Ozette Campground and Ranger Station. The trailhead is located next to the ranger station at the end of the road.

The first part of this hike journeys along 3.3 miles of a wooden plank-and-stair trail leading to Cape Alava, the westernmost point of the lower forty-eight. This cedar puncheon boardwalk is an example of the importance of the trail maintenance programs—hikers used to slog through muck before it was boarded over. The boardwalk can be slick when wet, and slippery when frosty, so exercise caution. At approximately the 2-mile mark you cross Ahlstroms Prairie, site of a long-abandoned farm. This area is a bog rather than a prairie. Lars Ahlstroms's barn and homestead have long

Huge starfish on the beach

since deteriorated. You can't help but wonder what this early Scandinavian farmer had in mind settling in this remote and boggy landscape. A few old fruit trees remain in tribute.

As we approached the Pacific Ocean, we heard the sea lions long before we saw them. Hundreds were basking in the sun on Ozette Island, producing a continuous cacophony of barking. Raccoons visited the beach to feast on crabs and fish, and they were not shy about picking through the backpacks outside tents at the campsites along the beach.

Cape Alava is near Ozette Village, a 2000-year-old Makah community that was buried in a mudslide 500 years ago. Excavated in the 1970s, the site is now closed to the public and marked by a memorial approximately 0.3 mile north of Cape Alava. Fascinating cultural artifacts from this native coastal people are housed at the Makah Cultural and Research Center located in the town of Neah Bay on the northern tip of the peninsula.

Follow the Pacific coast south along the rocky beach approximately 3 miles to Sand Point. The rocky beach makes for slow walking, and there is much along the way to distract. Watch carefully for Native American petroglyphs at Wedding Rocks, the first southern headland. Be sure to check the tide tables to time your beach walk with the outgoing tides. The ocean is abundant with life. Low tide reveals mussels, keyhole limpets, and goose barnacles clinging to rocks. Hermit crabs and anemones are visible in the tide pools.

At Sand Point there are campsites and a shelter among the trees. A turn inland leads back to Lake Ozette, another 3 miles along wooden-planked trails.

The campground is at Lake Ozette, the largest natural body of fresh water in Washington State. There are fourteen campsites, and the lake is ideal for canoeing and kayaking. Boaters have access to two additional campsites along the lake, and two other trails to the ocean. Avoid the high winds and rough waters that occur in the afternoon hours.

4 SAMS RIVER TRAIL

Round trip ■	2.7 miles
Loop direction ■	Clockwise
Hiking time ■	2 hours
Starting elevation ■	0 feet
High point ■	0 feet
Elevation gain ■	0 feet
Best hiking time ■	Open year-round, best from March to October
Map ■	Green Trails Kloochman Rock, No. 165
Contact ■	Olympic National Forest, Pacific Ranger District, Quinault Office

Ancient, interlocking branches of countless vine maple trees (bushes) create an interesting and unique feature on this short, but spectacular, loop trail. The web of branches creates an archway over the trail. Or rather, because of the length of the long tangle overhead, the interwoven maple limbs resemble a tunnel more than an arch. The path dives into this dark bramble of maple and rolls under it. Move quietly and slowly through the maple corridor and you might spot some of the resident deer and elk browsing on the far side. Look for these majestic beasts gliding silently through the wet, mossy forests around the trail.

To get there, drive on U.S. Highway 101 to its junction with Queets Valley Road, approximately 18 miles northwest of Lake Quinault or 7 miles southeast of Queets village on the Quinault Indian Reservation. Follow Queets Valley Road about 14 miles, passing the Queets Ranger Station, to the Queets Campground, situated on the banks of the Queets River. Note that this road can be very muddy and deeply rutted in spots.

The trail begins about 100 yards west of the entrance to the Queets Campground on the banks of the river. The melt-off from the glaciers and snowfields that encircle the Queets River basin combine as the source of the river. The bottomlands are lush with spruce and hemlock. The path

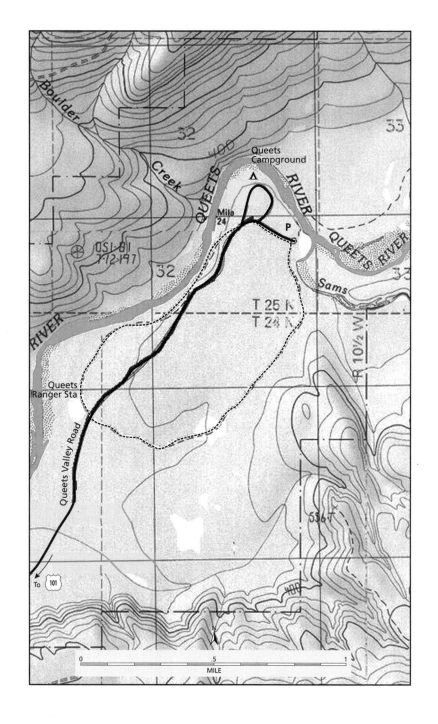

Boulder

Creek

QUEETS

RIVER

Queets
Campground

▲

Mile
24

P

QUEETS RIVER

QUEETS RIVER

Sams

OSI-BI
772-197

32

T 25 N
T 24 N

R 10½ W

33

33

32

RIVER

Queets
Ranger Sta

Queets Valley Road

536 T

To 101

0   .5   1
MILE

meanders through virgin forest, second-growth forest, and the vestiges of long-abandoned homesteads. The trail passes the ranger station, and as you cross the road you enter a forest of hemlock, spruce, and alder. There are many small creeks crisscrossing the areas that make for an interesting, but at times muddy, walk.

The path continues to a large meadow, filled with berry bushes and the interesting remains of an abandoned orchard. Deer and elk now visit this meadow. Old, weathered apple and cherry trees recall a time when homesteaders tried to domesticate this land; they stand in stark contrast to the rain forest evergreens encircling the meadow. Beyond the meadow is the highlight of this trail, a tunnel created by the branches of vine maple that elegantly arch over the trail, with streamers of moss hanging from the trees' canopies, forming an inviting pathway to the next vista of white-barked alders. The trail ends at Queets Valley Road. Queets Campground also serves as the jump-off point for a 16-mile trek following the Queets River into some of the most remote and beautiful areas of Olympic National Forest. This trail begins with the waist-deep fording of the Queets River, which can be quite dangerous depending on the water levels.

The beautiful fast-flowing springtime waters of Sams River along the trail

5 SOL DUC HOT SPRINGS

Round trip	■	**5.5 miles**
Loop direction	■	Counterclockwise
Hiking time	■	3 hours
Starting elevation	■	1650 feet
High point	■	1900 feet
Elevation gain	■	250 feet
Best hiking time	■	March through November
Map	■	Green Trails Mount Tom, No. 133
Contact	■	Olympic National Park, Wilderness Information Center

Here is a playful loop requiring a minimum of effort and time but with interesting waters at the start/finish and midway through. The walk upstream and back down along the musical and handsome Sol Duc River begins at the hot springs where, if it's to your taste, you can wallow in sulfur-enriched waters in the 98–106 degree range. Fees are in the ten-dollar range. For those who dislike the sulfurous aroma, a swimming pool may be more attractive. The Sol Duc Valley Hot Springs Resort, on a warm summer day, will be busy and noisy, with plenty of kids and families on holiday. Fear not—a peaceful stroll in superb forests awaits you.

To get there, from Port Angeles drive west on U.S. Highway 101, pass Crescent Lake, and watch for a left turn into Olympic National Park and the access road to the resort. To find the trailhead, pick up a local map at the registration desk at the resort. The trail, also called Lovers Lane (you and your sweetheart can walk much of it hand in hand), begins at the south end of the parking lot and heads up into the woods. Follow the trail westnorthwest, in an upriver direction (back toward the hot springs).

Moss above, moss below, a cushion for your footpath keeps your walking quiet and soft through most of this hike. Starting out in second-growth forest, you soon find towering virgin Douglas fir all around. The midpoint target is Sol Duc Falls, an impressive swirling cascade 3 miles out where the river slices through a rocky chasm with thunderous results. The falls is easily accessible by car on the other side of the river and may be busy with tourists. For a more meditative time by falling water, stop for a rest at the bridge over Canyon Creek, entering on the right, about 0.25 mile before Sol Duc Falls. Western hemlocks now mingle with the Douglas firs. Minutes beyond the creek, the side trail up to Deer Lake enters from the right. This would be a 5.8-mile round-trip add-on, rising to 3550 feet.

At Sol Duc Falls cross the river and head downstream…probably with a small crowd of visitors. The parking lot for the falls lies about 0.5 mile farther, and the footpath back to the resort may be tough to find. It branches

Tributary to the Sol Duc River

off, leftward, downhill toward the river about 500 feet before you reach the parking area. There is no trail sign.

A couple of pleasant miles are passed while you amble downstream in a forest of mixed hard- and softwood trees. The trail then somewhat ambiguously skirts the riverside edge of two auto-accessible campgrounds (Loops A and B), and then an area of RV sites before ending at the access road to the resort, leading back to the parking lot where you began, 5.3 miles ago. Maybe now that you're back at start, it's time for a soak in the magical waters to ease your tired muscles and soothe your achy joints. If that's not your style, how about a burger and a shake at the poolside canteen? It's a tough life, this hiking business. . . .

6 THE HIGH DIVIDE

Round trip ■	24 miles
Loop direction ■	Clockwise
Hiking time ■	2 to 3 days
Starting elevation ■	1600 feet
High point ■	4400 feet
Elevation gain ■	2800 feet
Best hiking time ■	Late July through early October
Maps ■	Green Trails Mount Tom, No. 133 and Mount Olympus, No. 134
Contact ■	Olympic National Park, Wilderness Information Center
Permits ■	Overnight campers require permits; advance reservations recommended.

This is a great 2- to 3-day backpacking trip. Follow a diverse trail through thick, meandering forests to serene meadows and spectacular views of Bogachiel Peak and Mount Olympus. Find lakeside camping at Deer Lake, in Seven Lakes Basin, and at Heart Lake.

To get there, from Port Angeles drive west on U.S. Highway 101, past Crescent Lake, and south onto Sol Duc River Road. (Hint: Look for brown Olympic National Park signs for Sol Duc Valley Hot Springs Resort.) Drive to the trailhead at the road's end, near the national park campground.

The most approachable way to do this loop trail, starting with a gradual increase in elevation, is to begin at the Sol Duc trailhead and follow the trail 0.8 mile to Sol Duc Falls reaching 2000 feet elevation. Follow the Sol Duc River Trail toward Appleton Pass. The junction is reached at approximately 4.8 miles. You'll see lupine and other wildflowers along the way. Once the trail crosses the river you'll start a steeper climb toward Heart

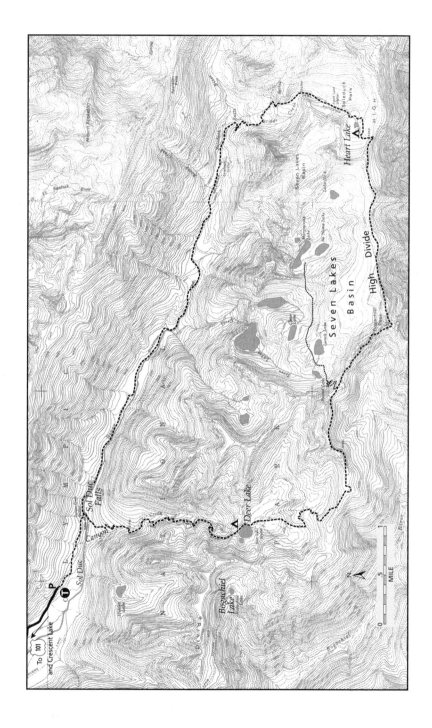

Lake through a gorgeous silver forest of trees until you've reached about 8 miles. Set up camp at Heart Lake and then continue on the trail slightly to the left on the side of Cat Peak. Follow the trail 3 miles in and you'll be rewarded with a fantastic up close and personal look at the Bailey Range and Mount Olympus. They're truly stunning, especially on a clear day. Three miles back out gives you a full day of hiking at about 14 miles.

Continue on the High Divide Trail toward Bogachiel Peak for approximately 2 miles at about 5400 feet and then on to the Lunch Lake trail junction (the lake is in the Seven Lakes Basin, where avalanche lilies often abound). There is usually snow on this part of the trail until mid-August and there are a lot of trail contours so caution is especially advised for less-experienced hikers. Along this ridge top you'll be able to see down to the lush, green Hoh Valley and across to magnificent Mount Olympus. A side trip to Lunch Lake is less than a mile one-way, but involves a steep descent.

You will start to hike down to about 3000 feet heading toward Deer Lake approximately 4.3 miles farther. Take a quick dip at Bogachiel Lake, a 2-mile (round trip) side trip east along the Little Divide Trail before Deer Lake. If you took the recommended hike for views of the Bailey Range and Mount Olympus you now have hiked about 20 miles. Deer Lake is your last camping option for the night and there is a ranger station located close by.

Hike out another 3 miles and down 1600 feet to finish the loop at Sol Duc Falls Trail.

Avalanche lilies (Erythronium montanum) *fill High Divide meadows as soon as the snow melts.*

1 OLYMPIC HOT SPRINGS/HAPPY LAKE RIDGE

Round trip	■	**18 miles**
Loop direction	■	Clockwise
Hiking time	■	1 to 3 days
Starting elevation	■	1700 feet
High point	■	5300 feet
Elevation gain	■	3600 feet
Best hiking time	■	Late July through early October
Maps	■	Green Trails Mount Olympus, No. 134 and Joyce, No. 102
Contact	■	Olympic National Park, Wilderness Information Center

This is a spectacular hike or overnight trip offering relaxing hot springs and stunning views of Mount Olympus (nestled behind Mount Fitzhenry), Mount Appleton, and Cat Peak to name a few. Beautiful lakes, creeks, small cascading waterfalls, wildflowers, and wildlife, including Columbia black-tailed deer and snowshoe hares, abound.

To get there, from Port Angeles drive west on U.S. Highway 101 and turn left on the Elwha River Road and into the northern entrance of Olympic National Park. Continue straight on this road to the end where there will be a parking area and trailhead signs.

There are four main parts to this hike: the Olympic Hot Springs, Boulder Lake, Happy Lake Ridge, and Happy Lake. If you want a more gradual elevation gain, start clockwise and head toward Olympic Hot Springs. The trail starts off really easy although there is a steeper incline about a third of the way in. The trail is paved for about 2 miles. You'll pass three small waterfalls and will see a lot of foxglove, some birchglade, and Indian paintbrush. At the 2.5-mile point, near the old Boulder Creek Camp, you'll find a junction. To the left is a short 0.5-mile trail leading to the hot springs. The trail is dotted with tiny, pretty, purple-blue forget-me-nots as you approach the hot springs and as you cross over a wooden footbridge, the violet-carpet extends under your feet. You're not far from the pools when you start to smell the sulphur. The main pool is just off to the right of the trail and is small and shallow with an even smaller, hotter pool adjoining in the back. (Clothes are optional.) There is a smaller, more concealed hot spring just after you cross the footbridge, and yet another past the main hot spring.

After a visit to the hot springs, head back to the trail junction, and go left. Campers will find sites available at the river just north of the springs, and the park service has provide several bear wires from which campers can hang their food bags at night (black bears are common in this valley). To continue the loop, move on past the camps and follow the trail up the

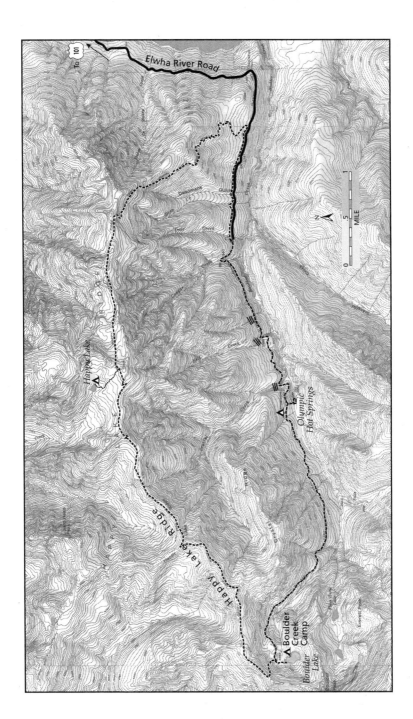

Morning sunbeams through cedar trees en route to Olympic Hot Springs

valley bottom. At 0.5 mile past Boulder Creek Camp, the trail splits. Stay right and begin the long, 3-mile climb to Boulder Lake. About 3 miles from the trailhead, the trail crosses a waterfall and, shortly after, the trail steepens. Midsummer hikers will find large, fragrant daisies at the lower parts of this trail section and as you near the lake; the trail is colored purple and fuchsia with the tall spires of lupine. If the lupine haven't bloomed yet, you might find the delicate white avalanche lilies in abundance.

Boulder Lake, at 6 miles, spreads out before you in all its glory as snowcapped peaks make a perfect backdrop to this absolutely stunning, dark-emerald green lake. There are five campsites; the quintessential spot is actually where the land juts out onto the lake. There is one smaller and one larger spot. Three other campsites are spotted around the lake, and there is a bear wire and toilet to the right of the trailhead sign upon entering. Many deer can often be seen browsing through this area.

From Boulder Lake, head northeast, climbing the steep flank of Happy Lake Ridge. In about a mile, the steep trail levels out atop the ridge, where it remains for another mile or so, providing breathtaking views. Look for Mount Olympus, Mount Fitzhenry, Mount Appleton, and Cat Peak. Continue for about 2 more miles to the Happy Lake trailhead sign. You'll go about a mile down a steep trail and pass over a creek on your way to the lake. There are just a few designated campsites to the right.

To close the loop trail you'll come back up from Happy Lake and continue another 4 miles. Before the trail really starts to wind down you should be able to see Port Angeles and Dungeness Spit. The last couple miles of this trail descend steeply. At the end, you'll come to the Elwha River Road and will have to walk about a mile to your right, back to the parking lot and the Olympic Hot Springs trailhead.

If you want a slightly more challenging hike, head to Happy Lake first. The advantage of starting this way is that you can relax at the hot springs toward the end of your hike.

8 ┆ LONG RIDGE/ELWHA VALLEY

Round trip ■	**33 miles**
Loop direction ■	Clockwise
Hiking time ■	2 to 3 days
Starting elevation ■	1198 feet
High point ■	5753 feet
Elevation gain ■	4600 feet
Best hiking time ■	Late July through early October
Maps ■	Green Trails Mount Olympus, No. 134 and Mount Angeles, No. 135
Contact ■	Olympic National Park, Wilderness Information Center

What a rewarding adventure this is! Bring your camera! Discover wonderful campsites in a gorgeous setting in the Elwha River valley, and panoramic vistas of the Olympics, in a historic area, full of wildlife. This loop is not for the casual hiker. Features include fording the Elwha River and gaining 4300 feet in a day. The best time to hike this loop is late July through early October, because of river and snow conditions.

The loop can be hiked up the Elwha River, returning on a gradual descent down Long Ridge. This option includes a steep uphill climb to Dodger Point in the middle. Hiking the opposite direction involves a gradual 11-mile hike up Long Ridge, which lacks water and campsites. The next leg is a steep downhill to the Elwha Ford, and then returns through the Elwha River valley.

To get there, from Port Angeles drive 8.5 miles west on U.S. Highway 101 to the Elwha River. Turn south on Olympic Hot Springs Road. In 4 miles, come to the Elwha Ranger Station. Just beyond, turn left onto a narrow, dirt road, and go 4.3 miles to road's end and Whiskey Bend trailhead with a large parking lot.

The well-maintained Elwha Trail begins at 1198 feet. It is open to stock and hikers. For several miles, hike through a Douglas fir and hemlock forest with little or no brush because of fire. The excellent trail gains 425 feet in the first 3.5 miles, straying from the Elwha to skirt Rica and Grand Canyons. The trail descends to reach well-developed Lillian River Camp at 4.6 miles. This area is pretty; however, it is shady, cool and damp, even on warm days. The trail climbs again and stays away from the river until

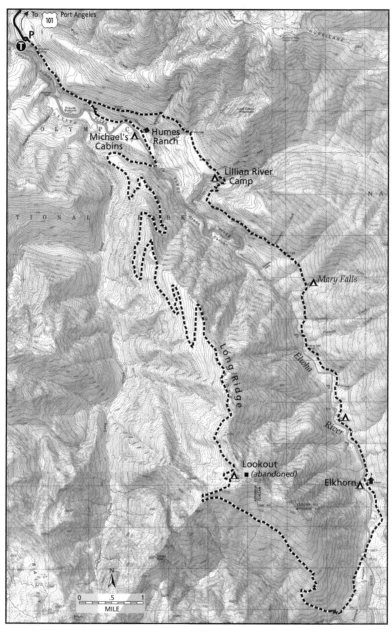

coming to Mary Falls Camp along the river at 8.6 miles. This is a beautiful setting with a view of a waterfall across the river flowing into the Elwha. Good campsites are found here, at Canyon Camp at 10.2 miles, and at

Elkhorn Ranger Station at 11.3 miles, as the trail hugs the river. Campsites are equipped with toilets and bear wires. Olympic National Park encourages the use of bear-proof containers in preference to hanging food, especially in areas above 4000 feet where trees are often not suitable for hanging food. The Wilderness Information Center provides new lightweight bear cans for a suggested donation.

There are two options for crossing the river. The first is a logjam at 12.3 miles. You then must hike 0.75 mile south through heavy brush to reach the start of Dodger Point Trail. The second option is to ford the river at 12.9 miles, just beyond Remanns Cabin, where the ford is well marked. This depends on river conditions. During periods of heavy rain or snowmelt, it may not be possible to ford the river.

Dodger Point Trail starts at 1450 feet and gains 4303 feet in 5.8 miles to

Leaves lay still on mossy rocks scattered throughout Elwha River.

an abandoned lookout. The trail is not regularly maintained but is in good shape. After climbing the first 4.8 miles from the Elwha, come to a junction with Long Ridge Trail at 5000 feet. An abandoned trail heads 1.3 miles southwest to Ludden Peak, an entrance to the Bailey Range. Just before this junction, find a pond and campsite. Insects flourish here until colder weather arrives.

The junction to Dodger Point is 0.5 mile northeast at 5200 feet. Take the 0.5-mile trail east, gaining 553 feet to the lookout. The highlight of this hike is a knock-your-socks-off 360-degree view of the Olympics at 5753 feet. To continue the loop, hike 10 miles downhill on a pleasingly gradual grade from the Dodger Point Junction. Water is scarce or nonexistent on Long Ridge Trail, except at Dodger Lakes with a campsite, a mile from the junction.

At the first junction after crossing the river, bear left and stay along the river for the shorter, easier, and more scenic route. Humes Ranch and Michael's Cabin are good sites to stop, drink some water, and read the historical information posted. From Michael's Cabin, retrace your steps 1.8 miles to Whiskey Bend trailhead.

While challenging many hikers, this loop offers mountain and valley beauty, with spectacular scenery in an area that is active with bear, elk, deer, and cougar.

9 GRAND LAKE/BADGER VALLEY

Round trip ■	8.5 miles
Loop direction ■	Counterclockwise
Hiking time ■	2 to 3 days
Starting elevation ■	6100 feet
High point ■	6500 feet
Elevation gain ■	2100 feet
Best hiking time ■	Late July through early October
Map ■	Green Trails Mount Angeles, No. 135
Contact ■	Olympic National Park, Wilderness Information Center
Permits ■	Overnight campers require permits; advance reservations recommended.

The Grand Lake/Badger Valley loop is perhaps one of the best overnight trips available in Olympic National Park, particularly if you take the time to detour up to Grand Pass. The Olympics have their own rain shadow, not as large or as well known as eastern Washington, but just as effective. Lying within a stone's throw of the coastal rain forest, this loop wanders

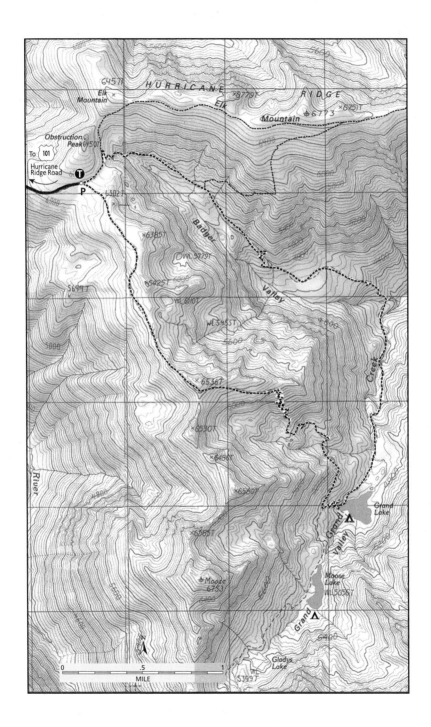

HURRICANE RIDGE

Elk Mountain

6451T

×9779T

Elk Mountain

×6773 ×6751T

Obstruction Peak 6450T

To 101

Hurricane Ridge Road

T

P ×6302T

×6385T

Badger

OWL 9779T

×5699T

×6425T

WL 8010T

WL 5345T

5600

Valley

×5906

5800

×6536T

Creek

×6530T

×6486T

River

×6580T

×6586T

Grand Lake

Grand Valley

Moose 6753

Moose Lake WL 5035T

Grand Valley

Gladys Lake

WL 5399T

N

0   .5   1
MILE

through parched hillsides that look more like the Pasayten than the Hoh. With wide-open hillsides, meadows full of wildflowers, and rugged views all around, this trip is almost 100 percent eye candy.

Like all backcountry trips in the park, this loop requires permits for overnight visitors, and a limited number are available. Make reservations, or take your chances at the park's Wilderness Information Center in Port Angeles. If you can't get a permit, the loop can easily be hiked in a day—but you lose the luxury of lingering and further exploration.

To get there, from U.S. Highway 101 in Port Angeles turn south onto the Hurricane Ridge Road and drive 17 miles, to the Hurricane Ridge Visitors Center parking lot. (Stop off at the base of the road at the Wilderness Information Center to get permits if you're overnighting.) The road to Obstruction Point is a hairpin reverse turn on the left just before the visitors center. The road—unpaved, narrow, and "scenic" (meaning sharp drop-offs)—proceeds for another 8.5 miles to the trailhead.

The trail begins at the Obstruction Point trailhead, accessed from the main road at Hurricane Ridge Visitors Center. From Obstruction Point, head south while looking west to dizzying views of Mount Olympus and company. Look while you can: the trail eventually descends to Grand Lake. There are a number of campsites around the lake, and it makes for a good spot to either set up camp or rest before detouring to Grand Pass.

Grand Lake is a pleasant little alpine pool, but it's the trail up through Grand Valley that earns the area its name. As the valley opens up more and more to marmot-strewn boulder fields, it becomes everything an alpine route should be. There are more campsites at Moose Lake, should you be inclined to spend an evening taking all this in.

The last stretch of trail, on the north side of Grand Pass, may remain snow-bound until late in the season. At the top, a quick scramble up to Peak 6701 reveals stunning views of the Elwha Valley and the High Divide, and to the south are a jumble of Needles and Brothers and other saber-toothed spires.

As difficult as it may be, you should resist the temptation to scramble on. Why? Well, while Cameron Pass looks like an adventure from this vantage point, the trail plummets rapidly down to Cameron Creek, so you should carefully analyze the costs and benefits of the return trip.

Make a note to yourself: "Must return someday," and proceed back down the valley to Grand Lake. Camp here, or follow Grand Creek down to Badger Valley. This 1.5-mile leg of the trip is an easy downhill slog. The fancy masonry and fine trail construction of the route to Grand Lake is replaced by over-impacted mud. But the forest adds shade and diversity to a hike that might otherwise be too heavy on the eyes.

The trail turns left up Badger Valley, and after some stiff switchbacks the forest opens up into meadow. Wildflowers! You're back in the cradle of the mountains. If you start to itch to be on top of the world again, a spur trail just before the head of the valley will carry you up to the flanks of Elk Mountain. The climb is steep, dusty, and shadeless, and the trail is all but

Grand Creek en route to Badger Valley

washed out in places, requiring hikers to scamper up and down through dusty gullies. But it's worth the climb for a last set of outstanding views, including some new ones to the as-yet unseen Puget Sound and our neighbors to the north. And once at those heights, you're high and free for the entire 2-mile ramble back to the trailhead.

10 ┊ GRAY WOLF/LOST PEAK LOOP

Round trip ■	**46.5 miles**
Loop direction ■	Clockwise
Hiking time ■	2 to 3 days
Starting elevation ■	2500 feet
High point ■	6500 feet
Elevation gain ■	4000 feet
Best hiking time ■	Late July through early October
Maps ■	Green Trails Mount Angeles, No. 135 and Tyler Peak, No. 136
Contact ■	Olympic National Park, Wilderness Information Center

No wolves roam this deep, forested valley anymore, but the country remains wild and untamed, and some folks hope to see wolves returned someday. In the meantime, they live on in name along this picturesque route, and other wildlife species abound in the cathedral forests and high alpine meadows found on this loop. Black-tailed deer browse through the emerald forests, marmots and pikas scurry and whistle among the rocks of the talus slopes, cougars prowl unseen and unheard throughout the region, and black bears lumber up and down the mountains looking for grubs, berries, and roots to consume. As you hike up the trail, you may not see all of these shy creatures, but even if no wildlife it spotted, you'll enjoy the stunning scenery around you. Crystal waters of the Gray Wolf

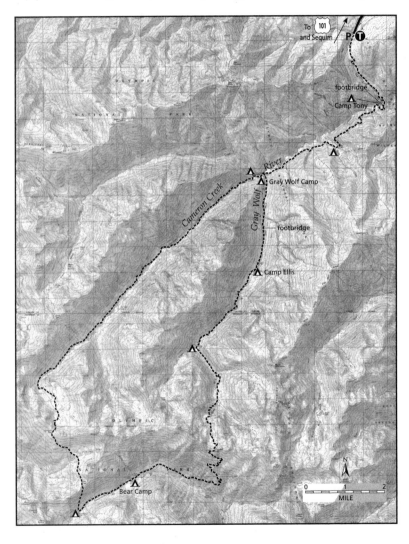

Black bear peering through grasses

River cascade over jagged rocks, burble through tight fissures, and flow through gravelly pools and basins under the green limbs of the forest.

The trail climbs from this river valley to high alpine pastures under the craggy summits of the Olympic Mountains, looping through a pair of high passes on the flanks of Lost Peak and Cameron Peak before descending into another quiet river valley for the return.

To get there, from Sequim drive west on U.S. Highway 101 about 2.5 miles and turn left onto the Taylor Cutoff Road. Follow Taylor Cutoff Road to its junction with FS Road 2870 and continue straight ahead on Road 2870. Turn right onto FS Road 2875 and drive to Slab Camp, found near a sharp hairpin turn near the boundary of the Buckhorn Wilderness.

The trail descends from Slab Camp along the Slab Camp Creek for about 3.1 miles. Along this stretch, the trail pierces old second-growth forest and some stands of old growth, with the pretty little creek heard, if not seen, in the valley to the west. At 3.1 miles, the trail crosses the Gray Wolf River on a scenic wooden footbridge, and then intersects the Gray Wolf Trail on the south side of the river. You'll find good camping here, at Camp Tony, at 1600 feet and immediately adjacent to the trail junction.

Turn right (west) onto the Gray Wolf Trail and head upstream, following this noisy, churning river less than 0.25 mile before the trail angles up onto the valley wall, leaving the river below. The sound of the river can still be heard, but now it's a muffled purring sound as the forest smoothes out the roar of the crashing waters. At 5.4 miles from the trailhead, the trail hooks sharply south and plunges into Slide Creek Canyon briefly before crossing the creek and turning back north to exit this deep, narrow side canyon. At the creek crossing stands another good camping option—Slide Camp—and from here is a faint climbers' path leading up Slide Creek to a climbers' route up Mount Baldy to the south.

The jag into Slide Creek Canyon covers less than 0.25 mile, then the trail continues west along Gray Wolf River, staying well above the river most of the time, to reach the Gray Wolf Camp at 8 miles. Here is the start of the true loop. Turn south here and continue upstream on the main branch of the Gray Wolf River. The forest now is primarily old-growth Douglas fir, with some hemlock and western red cedar stands scattered throughout. This is also good bear habitat, and blackies have been known to prowl Gray Wolf Camp in search of poorly hung food bags and packs of careless hikers. In other words, when staying here, make sure to properly bear-bag your food and any scented items, and never cook or eat in your tent.

At about 9.5 miles, the trail crosses the river on a rustic footbridge and at 10.7 miles, you'll find Camp Ellis. Camp Ellis provides good access to the river, plenty of places to sit out and enjoy the afternoon sun, and some wonderful places to set up a tent for maximum scenery and minimum bugs (i.e., facing the river for views and a bug-clearing breeze).

About 2.5 miles upstream from Camp Ellis, the trail again crosses the river, this time on a broad foot log. Take your time and watch your footing on this (and subsequent) crossings because the logs can be a bit slippery when wet, and there are no handrails. In the next 4 miles, the trail climbs ever higher, crossing the dwindling river twice, and finally climbs to the high basins that are the headwaters of the river. At 17.5 miles, the trail crests Gray Wolf Pass. This 6200-foot pass sits midway along the east-west ridge running from Mount Deception, 7789 feet, to the east, to Mount Cameron, 7190 feet, in the west. Snow lingers in the pass, and along the trail on the north slope as you approach the pass, well into the summer most years, so be prepared for some slick conditions.

The trail drops from the pass in a steep 3.5 miles to intercept the Dosewallips River Trail near the 3600-foot level. Turn right (west) and hike upstream along the Dose for another 2 miles to reach Bear Camp. An old three-sided shelter stands near the camp, but it's best left to its rodent inhabitants while you pitch your tent in one of the sun-filled camps above the river. From Bear Camp, continue up the Dose Trail 1.7 miles to a junction with the Lost Pass/Cameron Creek Trail at Dosewallips Meadows, about 24.7 miles from the trailhead. Turn right (north) and climb this brushy, steep trail a mile—gaining 1100 feet—to Lost Pass at 5600 feet. From Lost Pass continue upward through heather meadows and wildflower fields another 2 miles to Cameron Pass, 6500 feet, on the flank of Cameron Peak. From here, a steep, rocky descent of 2 miles gets you to the headwaters of Cameron Creek. Continue northeast along the creek for another 8.5

miles to reach Gray Wolf Camp at about 38.5 miles from the start of your hike. From here, simply return to the trailhead via 8 miles down the Gray Wolf and Slab Creek Trails.

11 ┊ MARMOT PASS

Round trip ■	**20 miles**
Loop direction ■	Counterclockwise
Hiking time ■	2 days
Starting elevation ■	1700 feet
High point ■	6100 feet
Elevation gain ■	4400 feet
Best hiking time ■	Late July through early October
Map ■	Green Trails Tyler Peak, No. 136
Contact ■	Olympic National Park, Wilderness Information Center

This hike offers an opportunity to camp overnight in a completely undeveloped alpine meadow where, if you're lucky with the weather, you will see a huge star-filled sky wrapping around you for 360 degrees. But there is a price to pay. The footpath up to the meadow at Marmot Pass and then beyond it for the next day's walk is arid. You will have to carry every drop of water you will need for a half-day's hiking and a full night's stay. The panoramic views westward from Marmot Pass across the Dungeness River valley toward the Needles make the effort entirely worthwhile. An added bonus up high here is the likelihood of near-solitude.

To get there, from U.S. Highway 101 at Sequim Bay State Park turn left onto Louella Road. Drive 0.9 mile to Palo Alto Road, which becomes FS Road 28. At 7.4 miles from US 101, keep right and follow FS Road 2860. Watch for sign of possible washouts requiring the use of alternate FS Road 2880. Follow FS Road 2860 to Royal Basin trailhead.

Trail 833 is also called Dungeness River Trail, and it starts at the Royal Basin trailhead (on FS Road 2860) across the road from the smallish River Campground (with outhouse). The trail follows the river on slowly rising, smooth terrain under cooling shade all the way to Camp Handy, off the right side, at about 3.5 miles. Rest up here, for now the climb begins. Camp Handy is an idyllic riverside meadow, with a lean-to and plenty of space for tents. It's a good target if you want to be out overnight but can't do the climbing this hike requires. Refill your water here; creeks beyond this point are not reliable in summer.

The trail rises now at a steep, unrelenting grade to accomplish 3500 feet by the time you reach Marmot Pass. You'll want to rest at Boulder Camp,

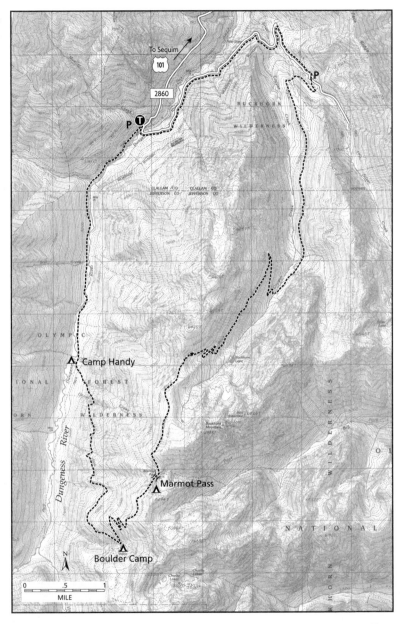

around 6.4 miles from the trailhead where there may be water, before huffing and puffing up the switchbacks to the pass. Ascending, take breathers to look west across the valley to grand views of Mount Mystery, Mount Deception, Mount Clark, and others. As you climb the terrain dries out so that by the

time you reach the pass the soft cushion of needles and moss you enjoyed in the valley is replaced with talus, crumbing soft rock, and parched dirt.

Marmot Pass stands at 6100 feet, 8.2 miles from the start. We spent 8 hours getting here, without pushing ourselves. Downhill to the right, just over the pass, a broad alpine meadow opens before you. Although there were no apparent sources of water here, it served as a magnificent campsite (near a cluster of scrubby conifers in the middle). A few other campers used sites in the woods on the meadow's perimeter, but we barely heard or saw them. No outhouse here, you're on your own. With luck this meadow may provide good sightings of elk on their journey through and raptors soaring on the thermals from the valley to the west, but we saw more marmots than anything else. Two travelers on horseback ambled through, looking like true cowboys of the distant past. On a clear night the meadow affords a huge 360-degree sky view and a billion stars.

A note about camping at this altitude and about dehydration: one member of our party awoke around midnight with a disturbingly bad headache. Tylenol did the trick after about a half hour's discomfort and worry. We wondered, is the air thin enough at 6000 feet to cause the onset of altitude sickness for some people, or could it have been the consequences of dehydration during a hot day's climb on a largely exposed trail? In either case, be forewarned. Bring a first-aid kit and drink a lot of water.

The second day begins following Trail 840 from Marmot Pass, heading generally northwards, with a continuation of the climb, for another 1.5 hours toward the hike's high point on the barren shoulder of Buckhorn Mountain. The peak is up to your right at 6956 feet, but this is more of a giant block of stone than it is a spiky mountaintop. The trail slices through talus with occasional small patches of ground-hugging plants (some appeared to be succulents) that have adapted well to constant wind, baking sun, and raw winters. Footing can be dangerous here, especially if there have been washouts. Trekking poles or a hiking stick will help you to keep your

Tiger lilies (Lilium columbianum) *color the trail orange in June.*

balance when vertigo wants to pull you down the barren mountainside.

On the far north side of Buckhorn, the trail switchbacks downwards through more talus and eventually reaches a grassy area, then scrub pines, and, finally, the shelter of taller trees—a huge relief after several morning hours in the full sun. The first water was a full 4 hours from Marmot Pass. So, harbor your overnight supplies cautiously.

By now Trail 840 has taken you to the upper reaches above an impressively steep valley where Copper Creek flows at the bottom. Before descending to the valley floor, however, Trail 840 marches a good distance northwards, often on a jarring, rocky footpath, again exposed to the elements. The drop to the valley floor comes on a long series of switchbacks, with the sound of running water wafting up through increasingly tall and dense conifers. Where the trail crosses Copper Creek, the old Tubal Cain Mine is hidden in the woods to the southeast, and the trail takes its name from this mine.

The rest of the hike is a breeze, basically flat though winding and dark, amidst dense rhododendron forest, ending at FS Road 2860 in the parking lot for the Silver Creek Campground, approximately 17 miles from yesterday's start. You're now faced with a walk of 3 miles along the road back to Royal Basin trailhead, but some judicious hitchhiking can take the edge off that requirement.

12 ANDERSON PASS/MARMOT BASIN

Round trip ■	**41.3 miles**
Loop direction ■	Clockwise
Hiking time ■	4 or 5 days
Starting elevation ■	1600 feet
High point ■	5566 feet
Elevation gain ■	4000 feet
Best hiking time ■	Late July through early October
Map ■	Green Trails Mount Steel, No. 167
Contact ■	Olympic National Park, Wilderness Information Center

Incredible vistas and mountain scenery await you here, but so too do encounters with wildlife. Our researcher spent one night listening to the haunting calls of bugling elk while camped in the river valley and later spotted five black bears during a two-hour period along the valley trail. Keep your eyes open and you might enjoy such wonderful luck, too. (Also, make sure to take proper precautions in bear country—hang your food and any scented items every night, at least 12 feet off the ground, 10 feet from any tree trunk, and 100 feet from camp.)

To get there, from Brinnon drive north on U.S. Highway 101 and turn west on Dosewallips River Road (FS Road 2610). Continue after the road becomes gravel at 4.7 miles to the end at the Dosewallips Ranger Station (15 miles from US 101). Note: Road was washed out. Call Ranger Station for current condtions.

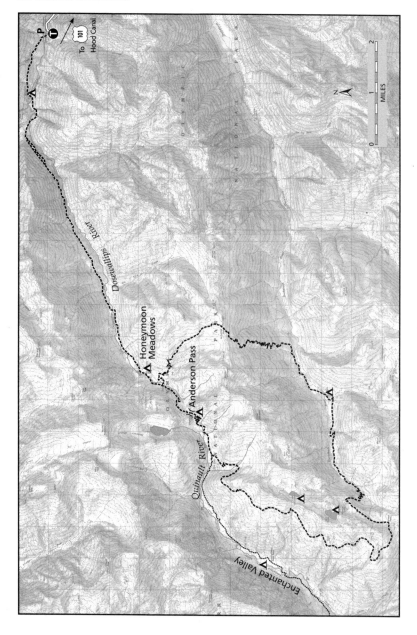

Deer grazing in the meadows just before Anderson Pass

This loop trip has it all. A forest approach, climbs in the alpine zone to passes with grand views, lakes, wildlife, views down long valleys, views of a glaciated peak, and wonderful camps. The loop begins after a 9.1-mile walk, but it is worth every mile of repeated trail, and then some. Consider the extra hiking part of your commute to the "trailhead."

Begin at the Dosewallips Ranger Station by paying fees and picking up the Olympic National Park map. It has good information on camp locations. Hike up the easy Dosewallips Trail 1.4 miles to a junction. Take the left junction heading up the west fork of the Dosewallips River toward Dosewallips Forks. Cross a high bridge later, enjoy the mossy trail, and pass more camps in the forest at 4.2 and 6.8 miles. Continue to Honeymoon Meadows at 9.1 miles. It's good to camp here since the next camp is considerably farther.

Turn left at Honeymoon Meadows, and follow lonelier tread toward LaCrosse Pass. It climbs up and up, finally breaking out into grand views of meadows of grass, fields of blueberries, and populations of grasshoppers. Continue up to LaCrosse Pass at 12.2 miles and 5566 feet. Note how the vegetation changes on the other side of the pass—less lush in the drier microclimate. But lower down the trail it becomes a little more brushy if not recently maintained. Descend to the junction with the Duckabush River Trail at 15.5 miles and turn right. There is a good camp 1.8 miles farther. If energy permits, more scenic camps are 3.4 miles farther, but 1800 feet higher. Or camp here, and plan an extra day in the playgrounds beyond.

Be sure to turn right on the trail toward Marmot Lake after fording the

Duckabush River. The way climbs gradually, and then switches back to glorious high views. Good camps are at Marmot Lake and Hart Lake. It is mandatory to play in the lakes and graze for blueberries with the bears, which frequent this area. Besides, the next camp is quite some distance.

After romping in the gardens, continue to O'Neil Pass at 21.9 miles and 5000 feet. Then traverse across steep meadows for several miles. Elk frequent the area below the trail. Views abound and the trail gradually descends making for fun progress to the junction at 30.5 miles.

Energetic hikers can take a side trip down to the 1930 chalet in the Enchanted Valley (add 6.4 miles and 900 feet for the round trip). The trail has views of waterfalls across the valley, and the world's largest western hemlock. There is good camping in the valley.

Turn right toward Anderson Pass (32.2 miles, 4460 feet) and views of Mount Anderson and its glacier. A short side trail heads toward the glacier. A half-mile beyond the pass is a good camp. And another mile beyond that is Honeymoon Meadows, the end of the loop and begin of your commute through the mossy easy trail 9.1 miles to the trailhead.

13 STAIRCASE RAPIDS LOOP

Round trip ■	**2.5 miles**
Loop direction ■	Counterclockwise
Hiking time ■	3 hours
Starting elevation ■	900 feet
High point ■	1000 feet
Elevation gain ■	100 feet
Best hiking time ■	Year-round
Map ■	Green Trails Mount Steel, No. 167
Contact ■	Olympic National Park, Wilderness Information Center

This is a perfect outing for the family, or for anyone with a few hours to enjoy a glorious hike alongside a gin-clear mountain stream, under the cool eaves of an emerald forest. Hikers can often see sleek torpedoes flashing through the deep pools of the river—rainbow trout hunt the cold depths devouring insects which live and breed in the waterways. Overhead, kingfishers, bald eagles, and ospreys are frequently seen as they patiently hunt the trout. In the brush along the riverbanks, black-tailed deer and large Roosevelt elk browse. All of these critters, and a slew of small species, provide ample opportunities for hikers to enjoy a wildlife encounter along this quiet, gentle loop.

To get there, from U.S. Highway 101 in Hoodsport turn west onto Lake

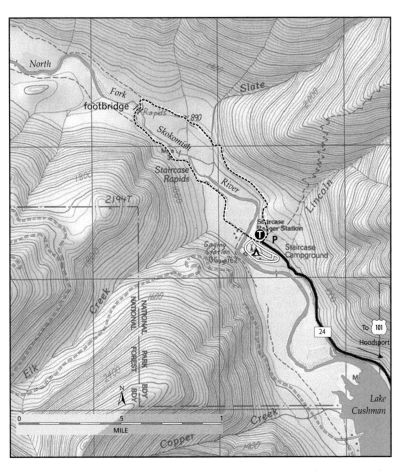

Cushman Road. Follow this road, which becomes FS Road 24, past Lake Cushman and into Olympic National Park. The road ends at the Staircase Ranger Station and Campground. Park in the lot near the ranger station, and find the trailhead to the right (north) side of the building.

The trail heads up into the forest behind the ranger station and then angles west along the bottom of the hillside. You'll cross a couple of small side streams and then find a broad trail angling west up the North Fork Skokomish River valley. The trail was once a road used by early park visitors to drive deep into the park. But the forest has largely reclaimed the road, and all that's left is a hikers' path bordered by wildflowers and young trees. For more than a mile, the trail follows this old roadbed, passing through an old forest fire area midway along its length. Look for deer and elk browsing the rich vegetation of

Opposite: *Feeder stream in the Skokomish Valley*

this hillside "meadow," and listen for the head-jarring pounding of woodpeckers as they pry insects from the still-standing dead trees.

At 1.1 miles, the trail reaches a junction. To the left, a small trail weaves down to the river shore. Follow this trail and you'll find a new footbridge over the icy waters of the North Fork Skokomish. The bridge sits upstream from Staircase Rapids, so named because of the broad shelves—or steps—that the water tumbles over. The bridge provides a good vantage point from which to observe spawning fish (large trout from Lake Cushman will migrate up the river to spawn in the early summer). Or, if the fish aren't in evidence, just let yourself succumb to the hypnotic quality of moving water.

After enjoying the river view from the bridge, continue across, and find the trail on the far (south) side. Turn left and proceed downstream. This side of the river bears little resemblance to the north side. Here, the forest is old, untouched by fire or roads, and the feeling is one of walking through a cathedral. The trail rolls along under huge old trees, and stays always close to the cool, shady river. There are ample opportunities to drop down onto the rocks along the river to splash your feet or even drop a fishing line.

Continue down the trail and, at about 2.4 miles from the start, you'll find yourself at the Staircase Campground, crossing a broad bridge back over the river to get to your starting point.

14 QUINAULT RAIN FOREST LOOP

Round trip ■	**4 miles**
Loop direction ■	Clockwise
Hiking time ■	2 to 4 hours (leave extra time for the kids to explore)
Starting elevation ■	300 feet
High point ■	400 feet
Elevation gain ■	100 feet
Best hiking time ■	Year-round (best March through October)
Map ■	Green Trails Quinault Lake, No. 197
Contact ■	Olympic National Forest, Pacific Ranger District, Quinault Office

The lush, humid temperate weather zone of the Pacific Northwest is home to a vast integrated "web of life" that comprises the rich ecosystem of the coniferous rain forest. A series of looping hikes in this area, ranging from 0.5 mile to 4 miles, to as much as 8 miles if you cover the entire area, allow ample opportunities to explore.

The Civilian Conservation Corps constructed the Quinault Loop Trail in 1935, two years before President Franklin D. Roosevelt visited the still-present Lake Quinault Lodge.

This short, gentle loop explores the essence of the ancient rain forests of western Washington. The path weaves among towering cedars and firs, with some of the most massive specimens of Sitka spruce found anywhere in the world. Between the massive trees stretches an emerald green blanket of life. Mosses, lichens, and ferns cover every surface, from the duff-rich soil to the life-giving nurse-logs to the ancient trees that reach to the skies. Moving silently across this living carpet you'll find the uniquely beautiful Roosevelt elk that evolved in this rain forest environment. Visit in the autumn, and you might hear their haunting calls echoing through the cathedral woods. Birds swoop and dive through the gray/brown trunks of the trees. The rare and endangered marbled murrelets live here, as do owls (spotted, great horned, and barred), and an array of twittering songbirds. In short, this is a path short in distance but long on natural history and ecological wisdom. Bring the kids, and plan on spending hours moving slowly through this magical world.

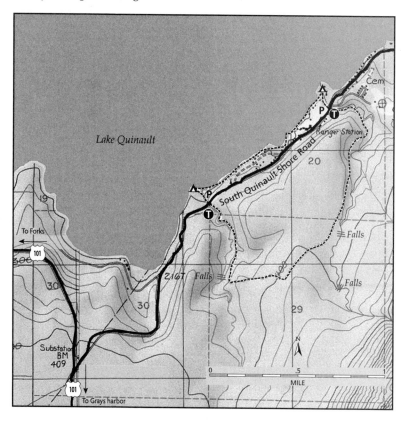

To get there, from Forks drive south on U.S. Highway 101 and turn east onto South Shore Road. Continue 1.6 miles to the ranger station. You can park at the Quinault Ranger Station and begin your loop hike.

Hike approximately 0.4 mile to Cascades Falls, a lovely, gentle waterfall enveloped in the gray-green colors of the forest. In another 0.6 mile, you will encounter another waterfall at Falls Creek. The forest floor is covered with a carpeting of moss, sword fern, lady fern, deer fern, and oxalis. Travel another 0.5 mile to a cedar bog, with many healthy specimens of skunk cabbage and their bright yellow flowers.

After another 0.1 mile or so through the forest, at about 1.6 miles, you'll find a waterfall at Willaby Creek. In addition to the wealth of plants, the rain forest is host to a range of birds and mammals. The marbled murrelets are spring and summer visitors, nesting on the long horizontal branches high in the upper canopy. They travel 50 miles from their ocean habitat to nest. The forest contains an abundance of fungi, including yellow chanterelle mushrooms. Under the ground next to the large rain forest trees are Oregon white truffles. Northern flying squirrels live high in the canopy and come down to feed on these delicacies. The rain forest trees have an incredibly shallow root system relative to their large size and height, and are very vulnerable to the wind. More than 80 percent of downed trees are due to wind damage. Colonnades of trees stand in rows, the result of getting their start in life on nurse logs, long since decayed over time.

A side trail allows you to take an optional half-mile detour along the Rain Forest Nature Loop. You can take a left and then connect back to the main trail, or continue straight ahead. The interpretive trail is great for engaging children in the wonders of this ecosystem. Connect back with the

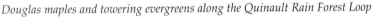

Douglas maples and towering evergreens along the Quinault Rain Forest Loop

main trail and cross under South Shore Road. The trail continues along Lake Quinault, past cabins and Lake Quinault Lodge, ending at the Quinault Ranger Station.

15 EBEY'S LANDING

Round trip ■	**5 miles**
Loop direction ■	Clockwise
Hiking time ■	4 hours
Starting elevation ■	50 feet
High point ■	300 feet
Elevation gain ■	250 feet
Best hiking time ■	Year-round
Map ■	USGS Whidbey Island
Contact ■	Washington State Parks

Isaac N. Ebey filed claim to this area in 1850—an action not particularly appreciated by the local native inhabitants. As a result of this and other landgrabs by European settlers, the natives and the newcomers came to blows repeatedly and with horrendous results. Some of the evidence of those wars between settlers and native tribes still stand. Log forts, or block-houses, stand at Ebey's Landing, and some of the headstones in the adjacent cemetery reach back to those wars.

The park is peaceful now. The area is mostly public, thanks in part to the purchase, and subsequent donation to the state, of several parcels by the Nature Conservancy. Hikers will find quiet pebbly beaches to stroll along and great views from the 250-foot bluffs above the shore. They may see seals and sea lions bobbing in the gentle waves off shore, and black-tailed deer browsing through the native grass prairie atop the bluff. Shorebirds soar and dip in the waters, and swallows dip and dive along the cliffs.

To get there from the north, drive State Route 20 south from Anacortes, crossing the Deception Pass Bridge to Whidbey Island. Continue south toward Coupeville. From the south, take the Mukilteo Ferry to Whidbey Island and drive north on SR 20 to Coupeville. Just north of Coupeville, turn west onto Terry Road. Continue west until Terry Road turns southward at a junction with Ebey's Landing Road. Stay right (i.e., straight ahead) onto Ebey's Landing Road and follow it to Ebey's Landing, about 2.1 miles.

From the parking area, head to the shoreline, turn right (north) and start walking along the pebbly strand. With Admiralty Inlet on the left, and the high cliffs of Peregos Bluff on your right, you might feel hemmed in. Just keep walking, but while you walk keep one eye on the cliffs and another on the water. Not because there's danger—no, keep your eyes out for birds on the cliffs and sea mammals in the surf. Seals, sea lions, and even orcas frequently can be seen in the rich waters of Admiralty Inlet, and an array of birds make their homes on the steep walls of the bluff.

After about 1.7 miles of walking, you'll reach Perego's Lagoon—a pool of brackish seawater trapped by a high sand spit. Most of the year, the spit is a continuous wall, turning the lagoon into a lake, but following heavy storms, the spit is sometimes breached. Do not attempt to cross the outflow from the lagoon if there is a breach in the spit—walk around the inland side of the lagoon instead.

After passing the lagoon—which is home to an array of waterfowl and shorebirds—continue north another 0.1 mile to find a trail climbing a steep gully in the bluff face. Climb this short trail—less than 0.25 mile—to the top of the 250-foot bluff, and then stop, turn, and stare. From this height, you can gaze across the inlet into the heart of the north

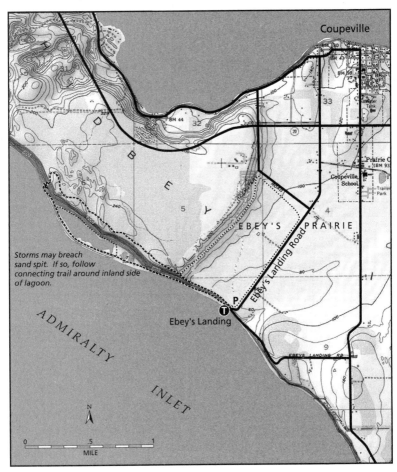

Hiker on bluff trail high above the open waters at Ebey's Landing

sound. On clear days, look west to the Olympic Mountains, northwest to Vancouver Island, and southwest to the islands of central Puget Sound. From here, head south along the lip of the bluff. You'll pass the Fort Ebey cemetery—worth a long, lingering stop to examine the headstones and feel the history of this place—before descending along the sloping bluff back to the trailhead at Ebey's Landing.

16 ┋ LITTLE/BIG BEAVER CREEK

Round trip	▪	**30 miles**
Loop direction	▪	Counterclockwise
Hiking time	▪	3 days
Starting elevation	▪	1600 feet
High point	▪	3600 feet
Elevation gain	▪	2000 feet
Best hiking time	▪	July through mid-October; wildflowers typically at their peak in late July
Maps	▪	Green Trails Ross Lake, No. 16 and Mount Challenger, No. 15
Contact	▪	North Cascades National Park
Note	▪	Call Ross Lake Resort (206-386-4437) to arrange for a water taxi up Ross Lake.

This trip is not about grand vistas and bagging peaks but is rather a long contemplative walk in the woods, a woods so mature that it feels like a park. If hikers want sure views of the Pickets, they need to plan according to the weather. There are well-maintained campsites with easy access to water, except for the camp at Beaver Pass. (In August and September a short hike may be in order to find water on the south side of the pass. In the fall, water may be scarce in sections between camps.) Fall brings out beautiful colors, and vast quantities and varieties of mushrooms.

To get there, from Bellingham drive east on State Route 20 (North Cascades Highway) to Colonial Creek Campground and continue another 4 miles east. Park at the trailhead for the Ross Dam Trail, on the north side of the highway.

From the Ross Dam parking lot, walk 0.8 mile downhill. At the bottom of the hill turn right and walk east on gravel road to the telephone and dock for the Ross Lake Resort and water taxi.

This trail was hiked counterclockwise, beginning with Little Beaver

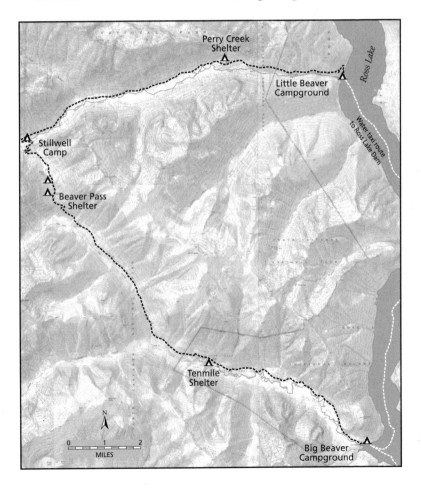

Creek. The water taxi stops at the mouth of Little Beaver Creek, the site of a camp with a bear box. The trail promptly begins climbing in switchbacks, gaining 600 feet as the trail first heads north up Ross Lake and then switchbacks south and west with a view of Ross Lake and Ruby Mountain. Begin with what will be many miles of walking through mature forests of cedar, hemlock, fir, alder, birch, and maple. The trail parallels first Little Beaver and then Big Beaver Creek, waterways almost always within earshot but seldom within sight.

After 4.5 miles of up and down trail is Perry Camp, with campsites on the creek to the left and a shelter at the trail. Cross the many branches of Perry Creek on bridges and logs, passing marshes packed with skunk cabbage. At 9 miles cross the delta of Redoubt Creek with views upvalley to Mount Spickard and Mount Redoubt. At 11.5 miles is the junction with the Big Beaver Trail. Turn right and cross the suspension bridge to Stillwell Camp at 12 miles.

The Douglas squirrel is native to the Northwest's coniferous forests.

After Stillwell Camp begin steady switchbacks to gain 1200 feet and Beaver Pass. At 3 miles from Stillwell Camp is the Beaver Pass backpacker camp on the left and in an additional 200 yards, an emergency shelter. On the left in another 0.1 mile is a packers' camp. A seasonal creek is found draining south to Big Beaver Creek. If weather permits, hike east from the pass, gaining elevation and views of the Picket Range.

From Beaver Pass begin the descent down into the Big Beaver drainage. At 6.7 miles from Stillwell Camp is Luna Camp on the right side. There are two campsites and a pit toilet. About 2 miles from Luna Camp, the trail turns southeast and enters a wider valley of even larger trees. At 11 miles from Stillwell is 39 Mile Camp. The last remaining 5 miles to Big Beaver Camp takes you past large specimens of cedars, alongside the murmuring Big Beaver Creek. Big Beaver Campground has numerous campsites, and all are equipped with bear boxes.

17 SEVEN PASS LOOP

Round trip ■	27 miles
Loop direction ■	Clockwise
Hiking time ■	3 days
Starting elevation ■	6200 feet
High point ■	6800 feet
Elevation gain ■	2000 feet
Best hiking time ■	Mid-July through September
Maps ■	Green Trails Washington Pass, No. 50 and Pasayten Peak, No. 18
Contact ■	Okanogan and Wenatchee National Forests, Methow Valley Ranger District

This route offers the best kind of alpine hiking—you start high and stay high, over most of the route. You leave from the highest drivable road in the state and follow the long, high path of the Pacific Crest Trail for half of the loop. You can expect to find a plethora of wildflowers, wildlife, and wild country here, without the effort of hiking from the lowlands to the high alpine world crossed by this trail. The reason is simple: the trailhead is at Harts Pass, and from there, you amble north on the PCT, which keeps you near the 6000-foot level. Along the way, you'll cross rocky alpine meadows in the shadow of jagged granite spires. You'll hike under the boughs of old larch forests—venture up here in September to enjoy the awesome splendor of the larch as they don their golden mantles of autumn—and wander through broad fields of wildflowers.

To get there, drive east on State Route 20 (North Cascades Highway) east of Rainy Pass to the small community of Mazama and turn left, cross the river, and turn left again on Harts Pass Road (FS Road 5400) at the Mazama Country Inn. Follow the road about 20 miles to its end at Harts Pass. Park in the trailhead parking lot near the crest of the pass.

Heading north, the trail climbs modestly for the first 2 miles, ascending to the 6800-foot level on Slate Peak before easing into a long traverse around the peak's flank. In another mile, cross the first of the six passes you'll hike over (the seventh being Harts Pass where you started the journey). Buffalo Pass is a low divide on the ridge separating Benson Creek basin from the West Fork Pasayten. There are some fine views west into Allen Basin Park and down the Benson Creek valley, as well as fabulous meadows to enjoy in the pass itself.

The next pass to get past is Windy Pass on an east-reaching ridge of Tamarack Peak. Windy offers incredible views of the North Cascades spires and peaks. Rounding the eastern flank of Tamarack Peak, the PCT continues

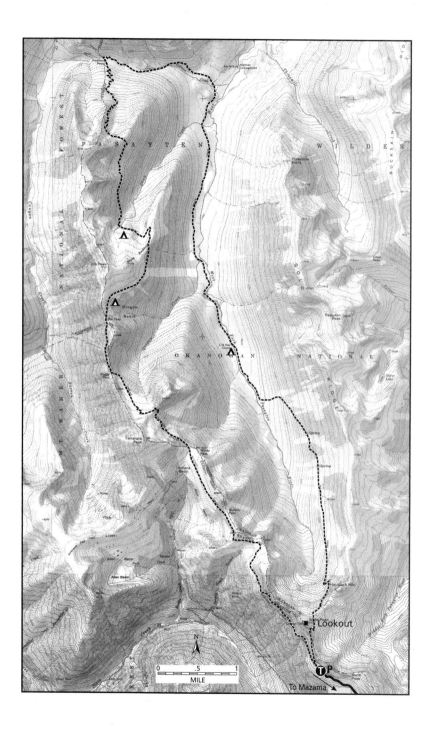

north on the ridge above the West Fork Pasayten River. As the trail approaches Jim Peak, it drops through the saddle of Foggy Pass and, just a mile later, Jim Pass before cruising through deep green meadows in the Oregon Basin. Campsites here are spectacular.

Now on the flank of Jim Peak, the PCT cuts east to avoid the jagged line of rock known as the Devil's Backbone, before slanting west once more around the north side of Jim. Campsites are found here as the trail crosses the headwaters of Shaw Creek near the 5300-foot level.

A steep climb to the ridge top at 6100 feet is followed by another descent through a long series of forested switchbacks to Holman Pass, 14 miles north of the trailhead at Harts Pass.

You'll leave the PCT at Holman Pass by turning right onto a side trail (Trail 472A) and descending along Holman Creek to its junction with the West Fork Pasayten River. In 2 miles, turn right on the West Fork Pasayten River Trail 472 and hike upstream, heading south, alongside the stream. The trail climbs past several excellent campsites located near the trout-filled river.

After you've traveled about 7 miles from Holman Pass, the trail crosses the river and begins a long climbing traverse of the east valley wall. The

Larches dot the Pasayten high country around Harts Pass.

trees give way to meadows, and then the meadows give way to trees. You'll pass several good water sources and fine campsites along the hillside as you approach the 6400-foot level of Haystack Mountain at the head of the West Fork Pasayten River valley. Hugging the rocky slopes below the summit, the trail climbs around the west side of the peak and follows the ridgeline south to Slate Peak just 0.5 mile south. You'll find an old dirt road leading to the fire lookout site at the top of Slate Peak. Follow this about a mile down, going through Slate Pass, to a trailhead at a large left-hand switchback. Jump off the road onto this trail and drop a few yards west to the Pacific Crest Trail. Turn south and hike the final 1.5 miles to the trailhead at Harts Pass.

18 ┊ MAPLE PASS LOOP

Round trip ■	7 miles
Loop direction ■	Counterclockwise
Hiking time ■	5 to 6 hours
Starting elevation ■	4800 feet
High point ■	6970 feet
Elevation gain ■	2170 feet
Best hiking time ■	Late July through early October
Maps ■	Green Trails Washington Pass, No. 50 and Mount Logan, No. 49
Contact ■	Okanogan and Wenatchee National Forests, Methow Valley Ranger District

Hikers venturing out along this route will find unmatched views of alpine splendor for more than 2 miles along the crest of the Cascades between Heather Pass and Maple Pass. During this high, lonesome walk, revel in views of Lake Ann and all of the Washington Pass peaks to the north (including, Whistler Mountain, Cutthroat Peak, and even the mountains toward the Harts Pass region) while to the west and south gaze out on Black Peak, Fisher Peak, Corteo Peak, and Lewis Lake by Heather Pass. The trail pierces a plethora of foliage that, come fall, is a bonanza of colors. The open slopes along the ridge crest are strewn with vine maples, huckleberry bushes, and Sitka mountain ash—with a few larches dotting the slopes here and there. That bounty, though, comes with a price. The grinding climb is more moderate when the loop is approached counterclockwise—our route researcher nearly lost his mind, and his lungs, when trudging up the other way (gaining more than 2000 feet in less than 2 miles). On the other hand, a descent that steep can do

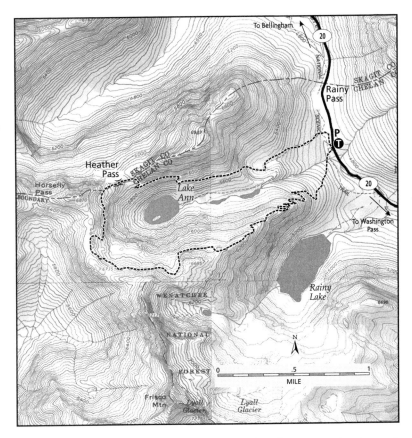

horrible things to your knees. The path must be taken—you simply need to decide whether to push your knees or your lungs.

To get there, drive east on State Route 20 (North Cascades Highway) to Rainy Pass near milepost 157, and turn into the Rainy Pass rest area. The parking lot is also signed for the Rainy Lake/Lake Ann Trails. Drive back into the rest area 0.1 mile and find a place to park. There are toilet facilities available at the trailhead.

From the trailhead, start north along the trail. The first 1.6 miles of the hike climbs gently through beautiful old pine and fir forests. A few sidehill meadows break the forest monotony now and then, offering sweet huckleberries to travelers in late summer and startling fall colors soon after.

The route forks at 1.6 miles. To the left is the Lake Ann Trail. Stay right. Just past the junction, the trail turns a bit steeper as it angles up to Heather Pass. As you near the pass, the trail opens onto rocky slopes with excellent views down to Lake Ann and southwest to the cut of Maple Pass. The trail continues upward through a series of switchbacks, finally cresting Heather

Pass at 2 miles from the trailhead. Autumn hikers will find stunning colors gracing the foreground, with awesome craggy peaks punctuating the horizon in all directions.

From this point until leaving the ridge about 2 miles later the views are constant. In the fall, larch trees glow and dot the rocky meadows as you look down upon Lake Ann. And once hitting the top of the ridge at Maple Pass the views open up south and westward as well. Black Peak and Corteo Peak are stunning and tempting to explore. I was occasionally hiking in drizzle across this area, but the peaks remained in view the entire time! The mile or so across the ridge from Maple Pass until you hit the high point above 6900 feet at times has a mix of trails that are somewhat confusing or faint, but by simply remembering that you need to keep gaining altitude and heading south you can't get lost. There are no trees to block the view so it was easy to regain the "main" trail within moments at all times.

Descending from the high point back to the trailhead required 2 grueling miles that were hard on the knees (if you have those types of problems). The ridge dropping down toward Rainy Lake at the close of the loop sported groups of blue grouse, and uncommon pine grosbeaks were found just before intersecting with the Rainy Lake Trail. I saw only two people hiking up this steep grade, and while this is a popular area in the fall for the larch trees and views, I didn't see more than ten people all day on a prime fall Saturday!

Lake Ann and surrounding mountains

19 ⋮ DOLLAR WATCH MOUNTAIN

Round trip	▪	**41 miles**
Loop direction	▪	Clockwise
Hiking time	▪	3 to 5 days
Starting elevation	▪	4800 feet
High point	▪	7679 feet
Elevation gain	▪	2880 feet
Best hiking time	▪	Late July through early October
Maps	▪	Green Trails Pasayten Peak, No. 18 and Billy Goat Mountain, No. 19
Contact	▪	Okanogan and Wenatchee National Forests, Methow Valley Ranger District

If the North Cascades are socked in and soaked, consider this drier, east-slope alternative. Follow a river deep into the Pasayten Wilderness and climb a peak for sweeping views of North Cascades and Canadian mountains. This loop takes a popular trail to low-elevation First, Middle, and Big Hidden Lakes and then continues in more lonely territory over three passes and though several river drainages. You'll understand why this is horse country: miles of rolling trails take you away from roads and civilization and a horse can get you even farther—all the way to Canada if you want.

To get there, from Winthrop's town center on State Route 20 (North Cascades Highway) follow the East Chewuch River Road signed for Perrygin Lake. Pass the road for Perrygin Lake State Park on the right and in 6.9 miles cross the Chewuch River to reach a junction with West Chewuch River Road. Turn right. Alternately, from SR 20 just east of Winthrop, at the Methow Valley Visitor's Center, turn left onto West Chewuch River Road. West Chewuch River Road becomes FS Road 51 9.5 miles from the Winthrop town center. At 10 miles, turn left onto FS Road 5130 (also Eightmile Creek Road), signed "Billy Goat, 16 Miles." Drive 16.4 miles to the road's end and the Billy Goat Corral trailhead for hikers (there is a horse trailhead 0.8 mile earlier).

Hidden Lakes Trail 477 begins as a wide old road, but it soon narrows to trail and in 0.25 mile reaches a junction with your return route on the right (Trail 502A). Head left and climb through Douglas-fir forest to Eightmile Pass at about 1.5 miles. Moving on, you'll reach a well-used camp at 4 miles at Drake Creek. This is the last reliable water for the next 6 miles.

The trail from here climbs steeply to Lucky Pass (5800 feet) in 1.4 miles. About halfway to the pass you begin hiking through an old burn that continues all the way to the pass. For a good break spot, continue about 0.25 mile from Lucky Pass to an opening that provides views north up Lost River, with

Lost Peak and Rampart Ridge rising steeply from the river's west side.

Reach a waterless, well-used camp at 8 miles from the trailhead, hidden on a knoll to the right above the trail—look for a side trail heading up. The camp is exposed, with little tree cover, but has a fantastic open view of Rampart Ridge and the Lost River valley. Or, if you prefer a "wet" camp, leave the views and descend to reach Diamond Creek at about 9.5 miles,

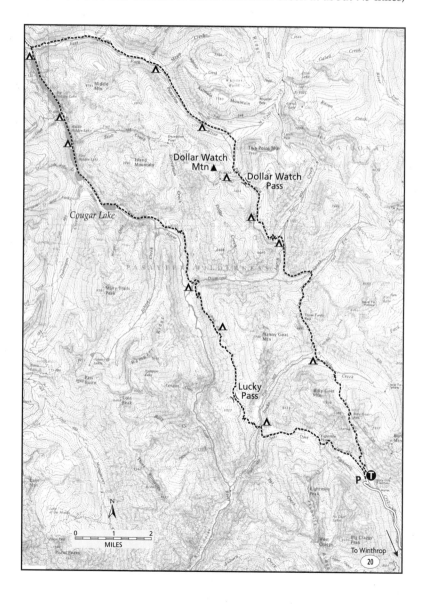

where there is a large camp. At about 12 miles, you'll finally drop onto the banks of Lost River, which is lined with large Douglas firs. Pretty and grassy Cougar Lake is at about 13.2 miles. Two miles farther, you'll find the Hidden Lakes. Walk along the shores of First Hidden Lake and at about 15.6 miles at the northern end of the lake, come to a hikers' camp with a shelter and separate horse camp. There is a guard station that was built in 1954 and is staffed by volunteers because of forest service budget cuts. This is a high-use area, but open views of the lake, with ridges rising on both sides, make it a pleasant spot. The lakes (First, Middle, and Big) have native fish populations of Dolly Varden, rainbow, and brook trout. Many hikers make this their destination and enjoy fishing and day trips to Dollar Watch or the Tatoosh Buttes.

Proceed along the eastern shores of Middle Hidden Lake and, north of the lake, browse thimbleberries in forest openings and even wild raspberries along rocky sections of the trail. Reach Big Hidden Lake in almost 1 mile, at about 16.6 miles.

Just past 18.5 miles, reach a shelter amid bare ground and lodgepole pines. There is a decrepit pit toilet behind the shelter. Soon after, come to a junction with the East Fork Pasayten Trail (Trail 451) at 4400 feet. Straight ahead leads deeper into the Pasayten and to the Canadian border—a trail sign says it's 5 miles to the Pasayten River but the Green Trails map say 3.7 miles. Go right on Trail 451 toward Bunker Hill. Walk a sandy trail through spruce and lodgepole pine with some Douglas fir. Hear the East Fork Pasayten but never see it as you climb gradually through a several-year-old burn and open forest. Reach the junction with the trail to Bunker Hill (Trail 456) in 1.8 miles.

At about 24.25 miles from your car reach a junction at 5700 feet with Trail 548 that heads up Ashmola Mountain to Sand Ridge. There are finally glimpses through the trees of Two Point Mountain and the north side of Dollar Watch. Reach McCall Gulch in about 0.15 mile—closer than on the Green Trails map. A bit of bare ground above and before the stream would make an okay camp if you've had it for the day.

Better to press on to meadows. Contour around the base of Two Point Mountain. The trail becomes eroded and steep as it climbs to Dollar Watch Pass. The main trail continues up while several side trails branch in this area and head right to Dollar Watch's summit. There may be a cairn up the main trail marking the most-used route to the peak. Follow one of the side trails and head for the notch to the southwest. You will inevitably intersect the most worn trail to Dollar Watch (unmaintained Trail 462), which, after traversing meadows and spotty forest, climbs steeply to a bench below the mountain. This is an excellent place for a high camp (no water) with views west and south of surrounding peaks. This bench is about 0.5 mile from where the side trail leaves the main trail.

Opposite: *Dense forest near Dollar Watch Mountain*

The trail continues from the bench and meets up with the Stub Creek Trail (Trail 458). Follow the trail and take a right on well-traveled but unmaintained Trail 462A to climb steeply above tree line and across broad grassy slopes another 0.5 mile to the summit of Dollar Watch, the high point of your trip at 7679 feet. After visiting the summit, return to the main trail and continue to Dollar Watch Pass at 7000 feet. Take in views as you descend to meet Tony Creek and a forested, protected camp about 0.75 mile from the pass. This is the first real camp below the pass, and the first reliable water. The trail continues down to Larch Creek and a large camp at about 5500 feet, 2.5 miles from pass and 31.7 miles from your trip's start.

The trail drops into Diamond Creek valley, then climbs up and over Three Fools Pass (6000 feet) to an unlabeled junction with Trail 502A at 5700 feet and 36 miles. Meet up with Drake Creek, pass a forested camp, and ascend through meadows and spruce forest to a wide-open camp below craggy Billy Goat Mountain. Continue climbing another mile to dry Billy Goat Pass, at 6600 feet and 38.15 miles. No more climbing! Begin your final descent on steep sections of trail and switchbacks, with views of hills to the south and glimpses of Big Craggy Peak. At 2.7 miles below the pass, reach a junction with your original Hidden Lakes Trail. Turn left and return the final 0.25 mile to your car for a grand total of 41 miles.

20 ∶ EIGHTMILE/BURCH MOUNTAIN

Round trip ■	**11 miles**
Loop direction ■	Counterclockwise
Hiking time ■	6 hours
Starting elevation ■	4900 feet
High point ■	7400 feet
Elevation gain ■	2500 feet
Best hiking time ■	Late July through early October
Maps ■	Green Trails Billy Goat Mountain, No. 19 and Mazama, No. 51
Contact ■	Okanogan and Wenatchee National Forests, Methow Valley Ranger District

An old lookout sits atop Burch Mountain, attesting to its spectacular views. Yet, as is common with fire lookouts, the trail to the top is steep and rough, and in this case, somewhat indistinct and hard to follow. But even if the summit is bypassed, the loop route around the flank of Burch offers a stunning exploration of eastern pine forests and sun-dappled meadows, both of which are full of wild birds and beasts.

To get there, from State Route 20 (North Cascades Highway) in Winthrop, turn north onto Chewuch River Road (FS Road 51). Continue north to FS Road 5140 and turn left (west). Drive to the trailhead at road's end.

From the trailhead, start northwest up the trail through a thin pine forest, and in about 0.75 mile, you'll notice a faint way trail into the trees

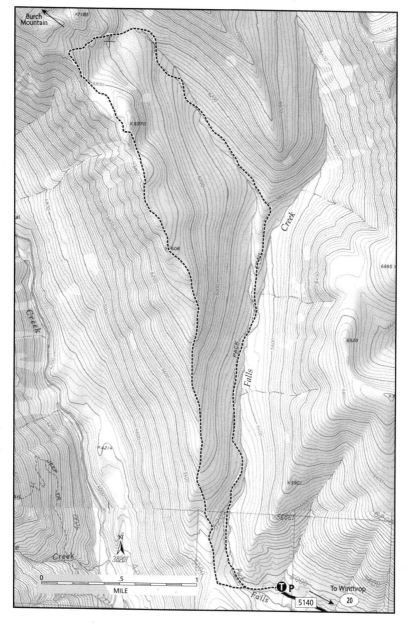

Clark's nutcracker in search of its main food source: seeds from ponderosa pines

off to the left. This is where you'll close the loop on your return. Stay right and continue up the Falls Creek valley as the trail climbs alongside the noisy, splashing creek. Black bears are common here, as are mule deer—and the Pasayten mule deer can grow to nearly elk-stature. But it's far more likely you'll encounter the resident avians, including an assortment of flicker and woodpecker species that busily hammer the pines in search of juicy beetles.

At 2.8 miles from the trailhead, the creek splits and the trail angles modestly up the low ridgeline between the two creek forks. In another mile, the trail hooks to the west and follows the west branch of Falls Creek to its headwaters on the flank of Burch Mountain. The trail traverses around the head basin of the creek valley, then ends at a junction with Eightmile Trail at 6.4 miles from the trailhead. Here, at 7400 feet, you stand on open grass and wildflower glades on the flank of Burch Mountain.

To get to the summit, look for a faint side trail just to the north of this trail junction. It climbs a steep half-mile to the summit of Burch Mountain, 7782 feet.

The loop route can be completed by turning left at the trail junction. From here you descend gradually along the crest of Eightmile Ridge, popping in and out of forest, with intermittent panoramic views of the eastern Pasayten peaks. To the west is the craggy Eightmile Peak at the north end of Isabella Ridge, and sitting just east of that ridge is Big Craggy Peak, 8479 feet.

The trail stays tight to the crest of the ridge, dropping 2100 feet in 3.5 miles from the trail junction to the 5300-foot level. Pay attention here and you'll find a faint boot-beaten path on the left. Follow this and in less than 0.25 mile, you'll be back on the Falls Creek Trail. Turn right and you'll find the trailhead in 0.75 mile. If you have trouble with the side trail, just walk due west from the Eightmile Ridge Trail at the 5300-foot level—the Falls Creek Trail parallels the Eightmile Ridge Trail and is no more than 0.3 mile away throughout this entire section.

21 REED PEAK

Round trip ■	**17 miles**
Loop direction ■	Clockwise
Hiking time ■	2 days
Starting elevation ■	3100 feet
High point ■	7523 feet
Elevation gain ■	4400 feet
Best hiking time ■	July through early October
Map ■	Green Trails Coleman Peak, No. 20
Contact ■	Okanogan and Wenatchee National Forests, Methow Valley Ranger District

Stunning dry-side river valleys, high peaks capped with alpine meadows and dazzling fields of wildflowers, and endless opportunities to meet and see wildlife await you here.

To get there, from State Route 20 (North Cascades Highway) in Winthrop turn north onto West Chewuch River Road (becomes FS Road 51). Continue north to Camp Four Campground. The road continues north from here as FS Road 5160, still following the Chewuch River. Drive to the Andrews Creek trailhead and park.

The trail leaves from the north side of the road and climbs steeply for the first 0.5 mile. Actually, there are two trails here, rolling about 0.1 mile apart (at most) but at 0.5 mile they diverge. Stay left to climb along the eastern side of the Andrews Creek valley. The trail dips to the creekside at 1.5 miles, then hugs the creek for the next 4 miles. Several campsites can be found along this stretch, nestled in the cool pine forests alongside the tumbling water. But unless stress and fatigue overcome you, push on. The best camps are found farther along the trail.

At 5.5 miles, the trail forks. Turn right and begin sweating. That's right, this is where the work starts. In that first leg of the journey, you climbed a mere 1500 feet in 5.5 miles. In the next 2 miles, you'll gain more than 1700 feet. After the trail splits, you start climbing a long series of tight switchbacks, staying well above a faint unnamed creek as you head northeast. In about

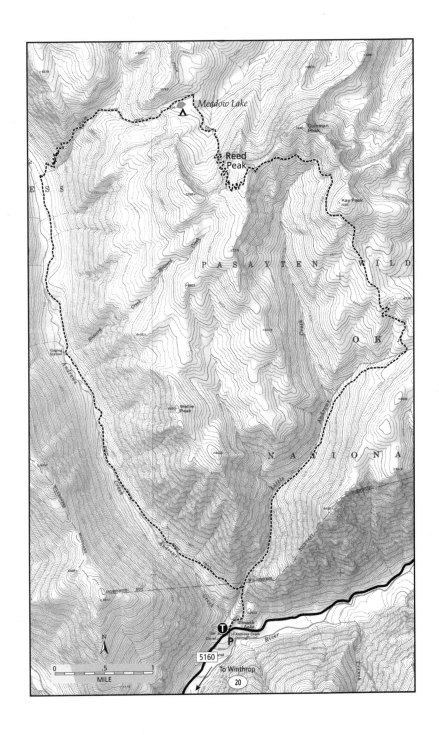

Meadow Lake

Coleman Peak

Reed Peak

Kay Peak

E S S

P A S A Y T E N   W I L D

O K

Gaging Station

Wallie Peak

N A T I O N A

T

P

5160

N

0   .5   1
MILE

To Winthrop

20

1.5 miles—7 miles from the trailhead—the switchbacks give way to a long, climbing traverse to the east. The trail exits the head basin of the valley and climbs to a small bench topped with a grassy meadow. In the midst of this field of green is a sparkling blue jewel—Meadow Lake, at 8.1 miles from the trailhead. You'll find great campsites near this lake. The sites on the north and northeast sides provide the best views.

Just 0.1 mile past the lake, the trail forks again. Turn right here and start south, climbing evermore steeply until you reach the summit ridge of Reed Peak at 7523 feet, around 9.4 miles from the trailhead. At the top, enjoy views of nearby Coleman Peak and Kay Peak, as well as the more distant, but also more stunning, Remmel Mountain (8685 feet) to the north, and Black Lake Ridge (7828 feet) to the west.

At the top of Reed, the trail bears east and swings into a long traverse along the west flank of Coleman Peak, then drops to the south to cut across the upper slopes of Kay Peak at 11 miles, before dropping gradually into the pine forests of Little Andrews Creek valley. Once at the creekside, follow the trail on the valley floor all the way back to the trailhead, at 17 miles.

Small creek waterfall in spring, along the trail toward Reed Peak

22 HORSESHOE BASIN/WINDY PEAK

Round trip ■	14.4 miles minimum, 20+ potential
Loop direction ■	Counterclockwise
Hiking time ■	2 days, though an extra "lay-over" day for basin exploration is recommended
Starting elevation ■	6000 feet
High point ■	7800 feet (summit scramble to 8334 feet)
Elevation gain ■	1800 feet
Best hiking time ■	July through early October
Map ■	Green Trails Horseshoe Basin, No. 21 (USGS Horseshoe Basin)
Contact ■	Okanogan and Wenatchee National Forests, Methow Valley Ranger District

This trail takes you through the varying climatic zones of the Pasayten Wilderness: from lodgepole pine, sagebrush, and bluebirds through subalpine meadows of wildflowers to the desolate Windy Peak and ptarmigans. Be prepared for unpredictable weather and know where the snow level is. The trail is rather "horsey." Since the drive is so long and the area so beautiful, it's best to allow 3 or more days for exploration and rambling. The trail was hiked counterclockwise. All major trail junctions are well signed.

To get there, from Loomis drive 2.1 miles north on the Loomis-Oroville Road and turn left on Toats-Coulee Road (FS Road 39). At 15.8 miles turn right onto gravel FS Road 500, signed "Road not maintained for cars or campers." At the time of this writing the last 3 miles of the road was very bad, but with patience it can be negotiated by cars with moderate clearance. At 21.6 miles reach the Iron Gate trailhead, 6100 feet.

The first 0.75 mile descends on an old mining road to the junction with the Clutch Creek Trail 343 and is repeated on the return trip. The trail begins in lodgepole pine, sage, lupine, and cinquefoil with an impressive vista of land you'll cover in this hike: Windy Peak and in the far distance, Horseshoe Basin. Hiking counterclockwise, the trail continues on the old roadbed. The first water is encountered at about 1.5 miles at Clutch Creek, which also hosts a small campsite. A larger campsite is just around the bend. From Clutch Creek the trail begins a gentle climb through gradually thinning woods to a meadow with views west to Windy Peak and Pick Peak and north to Sunny Pass. There are numerous campsites on the approach to Sunny Pass at 5.2 miles.

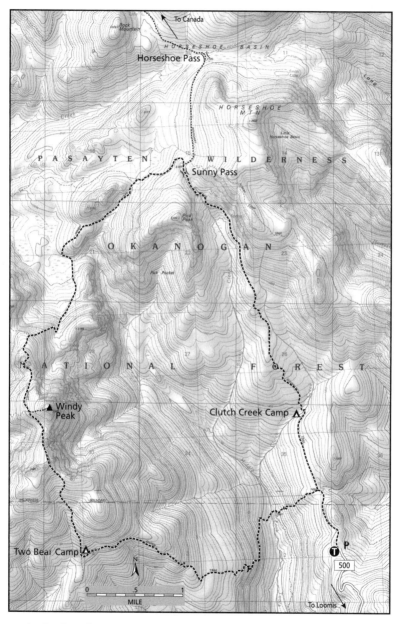

At the broad, grassy pass take in the lovely views of the expansive, tundra-like basin that beckons you to ramble. The right fork will lead in a few hundred feet to the cairn-marked junction with Horseshoe Mountain Trail, another possible loop back to the Iron Gate trailhead (adds nearly 6

U.S.-Canadian border from Armstrong Mountain. (Photo by Hally Swift)

miles to loop distance). Continuing on the right fork leads to heart of Horseshoe Basin with camps at Horseshoe Pass. There are many peaks to walk and scramble up, including Armstrong Mountain with a view of a slim clear-cut as far the eye can see to the east and its two markers indicating the U.S.–Canadian border.

The left fork at Sunny Pass starts the return trip. The trail skirts the southwest edge of the basin, surging up and down over a series of small hillocks. For each climb, though, there is a longer descent as the trail falls to a camp at the headwaters of the Middle Fork Toats Coulee River (6500 feet). Camping here makes for a reasonable day's hike back to the trailhead. From here the trail works to regain all of the elevation just lost and more. The trail climbs steeply up the north flank of Windy Peak and at 7000 feet crosses the creek from Windy Lake, the last water until Queer Creek. The trail breaks out into a sparse forest of subalpine larch, with stunning views to the north and west of the North Cascades including Jack Mountain and Cathedral Peak. The trail weaves a lazy S through a saddle between two knobs on the north side of Windy Peak, a beautiful but stark area populated with black lichen-covered boulders. The trail traverses the west side of Windy Peak to an intersection (7800 feet) with a trail that scrambles to the summit, the site of fire lookout built in the 1930s.

Continue traversing to the saddle on the south shoulder and begin descending to the headwaters of Queer Creek, following numerous cairns that mark the trail through sandy soil and meadows. When the trail enters the woods, watch for the Clutch Creek Trail on the right. The Clutch Creek Trail 343 traverses through verdant meadows that strive to reclaim it, making for a faint path. After traversing for about 2.5 miles, the trail switchbacks steeply down through meadows and beautiful groves of aspen, leveling again as it reenters the forest. At 3.2 miles from the junction with Trail 343, the Middle Fork Toats Coulee River is crossed, and the trail switchbacks a steep half-mile to meet up with the Boundary Trail. At the Boundary Trail, turn right for the short leg back to the trailhead.

23 BELL PASS (PARK BUTTE) LOOP

Round trip ■	15 miles
Loop direction ■	Counterclockwise
Hiking time ■	8 hours
Starting elevation ■	3100 feet
High point ■	4400 feet
Elevation gain ■	2300 feet
Best hiking time ■	Late July through early October
Map ■	Green Trails Hamilton, No. 45
Contact ■	Mt. Baker–Snoqualmie National Forest, Mount Baker Ranger District

The trail climbs along the mountainside, which sweeps up to your left and down to your right, through cool green forests with Douglas fir, red huckleberry, and ferns. It crosses waterfalls and mud bogs, several of which necessitated the building of wooden boardwalks. In late September the wildflowers have finished blooming for the most part, but there are trillium plants in abundance. Several varieties of ferns, thrive: sword

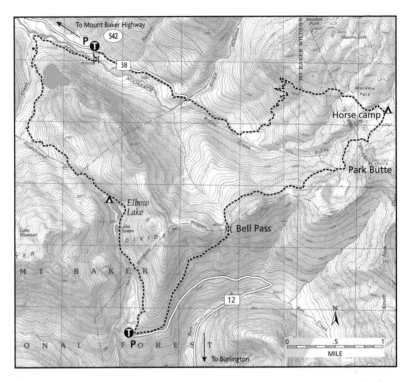

ferns, deer ferns, and maidenhair. The trail climbs through densely forested areas, fern meadows, and clearings loaded with big leaf maple and huckleberry. It tops out in a large open meadow, where there is a lean-to with a concrete bench in front of it.

To get there, from Everett drive north on Interstate 5 to the Burlington/ Anacortes exit. Turn right off the ramp and follow State Route 20 east to Sedro-Woolley. Stay on SR 20, heading east for about 16 miles to Baker Lake Road (just after milepost 82). Turn left and continue on Baker Lake Road for about 12 miles to FS Road 12. Turn left. After the sign at the turn, the road isn't well marked and is not paved. There are potholes and washboards, which make the going fairly slow. Follow FS Road 12 for about 17 miles to the trailhead. Plan on about an hour and a half from the Burlington turnoff to the trailhead. There is an unpaved parking lot at the end of FS Road 12.

The ranger at the Sedro-Woolley station said this trailhead would be preferable to starting at the Middle Fork Nooksack River trailhead. You would have to stop and park about 0.5 to 0.75 mile from the start of that one (where FS Road 38 meets Trail 697) because the bridge at Wallace is washed out.

From the trailhead at the parking lot, hike in about 0.25 mile. There is a junction where Trail 697 and Trail 603.3 meet. Trail 697 goes toward Lake Doreen and Trail 603.3 stays right and heads for Bell Pass. The signs are very clear. Head towards Bell Pass.

The trail gains 1000 feet in about 1.8 miles to reach Bell Pass at 4100 feet. Broad meadows and wildflower fields line the wide pass, and the trail continues through meadows and sparse forest for another 2-plus miles as the path traverses along the ridge toward Park Butte.

A trailside tributary creek seen en route to Bell Pass

At about 4 miles, the trail passes under the summit of Park Butte, and at an established and official horse camp, a faint secondary trail drops to the west into Ridley Creek basin. This side trail isn't maintained, and in mid-summer can be quite brushy and hard to find. If the route is impassable, it may be necessary to abandon the loop and return the way you came. But if the trail (Trail 696) can be found, descend from the horse camp into the headwater basin of Ridley Creek, cross to the north side of the valley (crossing the small creek in the process), and traverse west down the valley, staying well above the creek level as you go.

About 5 miles after leaving the horse camp (9 miles from the trailhead) Trail 696 ends at the Middle Fork Nooksack River Road. Hike west (downstream) 1.6 miles along this road, then turn left on a small side road. Follow this short road 0.1 mile to its end, ford the Middle Fork Nooksack and start a climb on Trail 697 toward Elbow Lake and Lake Doreen. At 14.2 miles, the trail passes Lake Doreen, and in another mile, reaches your starting point.

24 SCHRIEBERS MEADOWS

Round trip ■	**8 miles**
Loop direction ■	Clockwise
Hiking time ■	8 hours
Starting elevation ■	3300 feet
High point ■	4700 feet
Elevation gain ■	2300 feet
Best hiking time ■	Late July through early October
Map ■	Green Trails Hamilton, No. 45
Contact ■	Mt. Baker–Snoqualmie National Forest, Mount Baker Ranger District

This loop is best when hiked clockwise, especially when an early morning start can be had. This puts you in the meadows with a soft morning sun to illuminate the brilliant fields of wildflowers throughout these sprawling alpine meadows. The meadows, rich in flora, are also home to an assortment of wildlife, from whistling marmots to majestic black-tailed deer. The flowers, small ground-hugging blueberries, and taller, bushy huckleberry shrubs provide sweet fruit for hungry birds, bears, and hikers.

To get there, from Burlington drive east on State Route 20 for 22.7 miles. Turn left onto Baker Lake Road and continue about 12 miles. Here, turn left onto FS Road 12 (this road junction is found just after the Baker Lake Road crosses a bridge). At 3.6 miles, turn right onto FS Road 13 and

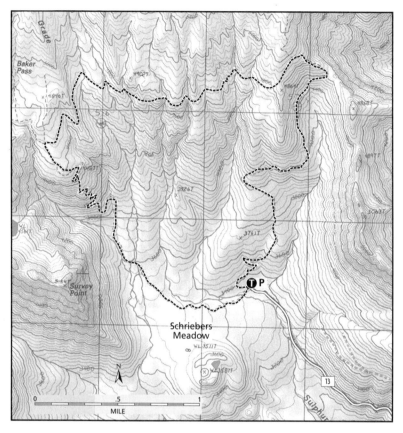

continue another 5.1 miles to the road's end and a large parking area.

From the trailhead, find the trail on the left to complete the route in a clockwise direction. The trail climbs 1400 feet in 2 miles, slicing upward through old-growth forest to reach alpine meadows at a junction with the Scott Paul Trail (Trail 603). Turning left here leads to Park Butte and side trails to High Camp on the south flank of Mount Baker. Either of these destinations makes a fine option for folks looking to extend their trip. But to stick with the basic loop, stay right at the junction, and follow Trail 603 east along the flank of Mount Baker for about 1.5 miles, before the trail turns south and descends from the high meadow country, then drops in a fast decent back to the trailhead through forest. Take time along this steep trail to enjoy grazing on the huckleberries adjacent to the path (season of ripeness is typically late August through September). If the berries aren't ripe, you can feast on the fantastic views presented whenever the ancient forests open onto broad meadows and sun-filled glades.

Fun suspension bridge near Schriebers Meadow

25 STILETTO PEAK VIEW LOOP

Round trip ■	**12 miles**
Loop direction ■	Counterclockwise
Hiking time ■	8 hours
Starting elevation ■	3900 feet
High point ■	6100 feet (summit scramble to 7300-foot level of 7660-foot peak)
Elevation gain ■	2200 feet
Best hiking time ■	Mid-July through September
Maps ■	Green Trails Washington Pass, No. 50 and Stehekin, No. 82
Contact ■	Okanogan and Wenatchee National Forests, Chelan Ranger District

Feel free to customize your outing along this route. If you prefer to keep it easy and light, skip the climb to Stiletto Peak and instead simply enjoy the scenic, easy loop around the pretty Bridge Creek valley. You'll find open, ancient forests with massive Douglas firs towering overhead, and fruit-rich huckleberry bushes scattered between the trees.

To get there, drive State Route 20 (North Cascades Highway) 1.5 miles east of Rainy Pass and park at the Bridge Creek trailhead.

The small trail leads south from the trail and intercepts the Pacific Crest Trail in just a few hundred yards. Turn left onto the PCT and follow the wide valley of Bridge Creek. Looking up through the trees, try to spot Frisco Mountain to the west and, directly behind you, enjoy good views of Whistler Mountain (take a just few peeks back as you head out, knowing you'll be able to completely enjoy the view on the return).

About a mile south of the trailhead, the trail forks. Stay right on the PCT and cross the tumbling waters of Bridge Creek on, appropriately enough, a well-made bridge. For the next 3 miles, you'll follow the creek south and west as it contours around the base of Frisco Mountain. The trail stays in the trees but frequently comes within sight and sound of the creek.

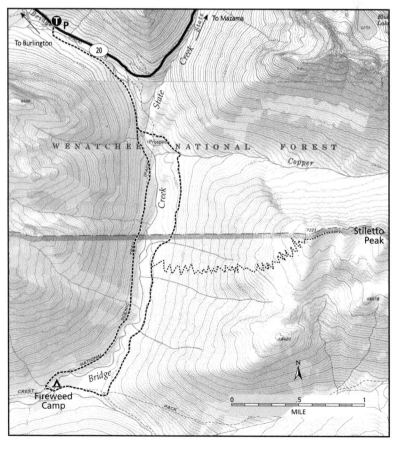

A blue grouse darts across the trail up Stiletto Peak.

Four miles from the trailhead, you'll find another junction at Fireweed Camp. This is a fine place to camp, and the short, easy hike to the camp makes it a good choice for a backpacking trip with youngsters.

At the junction, leave the PCT by turning left onto McAllister Creek Trail. You'll pass three or four more camps in the next 0.5 mile before hitting another trail fork. Go left again, this time on the Stiletto Peak Trail and start heading north along the Bridge Creek valley, this time on the east side of the creek. After a mile of forest hiking, it will be time to make a decision. Stroll on back to the trailhead in the cool, refreshing forest. Or trudge up a steep, 3-mile trail for unbelievable views of the North Cascades peaks from a vast meadow on the flank of a mighty mountain.

The Stiletto Peak Spur Trail cuts east from the main trail, climbing 2100 feet in 3 miles of nonstop switchbacks. The trail leaves the forest and enters a broad sweep of meadows as it nears the upper end of the path, and finally the meadows give way to fields of rock as the trail ends directly below the 7660-foot Stiletto Peak. Looking out from the mountain, enjoy views of Frisco, Hock, Whistler, and Twisp Mountains, among a score of other unnamed peaks. When you've had your fill and used up the last of your film, descend the spur trail back to Bridge Creek and turn right (north) to return to the PCT junction a mile south of the Bridge Creek trailhead.

26 ┊ HOCK MOUNTAIN/CRESCENT MOUNTAIN

Round trip ■	**25 miles**
Loop direction ■	Counterclockwise
Hiking time ■	2 to 3 days
Starting elevation ■	3300 feet
High point ■	6000 feet
Elevation gain ■	2700 feet
Best hiking time ■	Mid-July through September
Map ■	Green Trails Stehekin, No. 82
Contact ■	Okanogan and Wenatchee National Forests, Chelan Ranger District

Four river valleys, two high passes, a couple of sparkling alpine lakes, and endless variety in topography, flora, and fauna all await you here. The trail pierces ancient pine forests—far different from the lush, emerald cathedrals of old-growth forests in western Washington, but by no means less impressive. Hikers can see tiny bundles of feathers—juncos, sparrows, nuthatches, and more—and scurrying bundles of fur fill the valleys. These furry critters range from chipmunks, deer mice, weasels, martens, and marmots to cougars, coyotes, and black bears. White-tailed and mule deer browse the river valleys and mountain goats navigate the craggy peaks towering over the route. But even without the wildlife, there's plenty to see and experience along the trail.

To get there, from Twisp drive northeast up the Twisp River Road (FS Road 4440) and find the trailhead near the Road End Campground at the road's end. The trailhead parking area is located about 0.25 mile before the campground. Park here and find the trailhead on the north side of the parking area.

From the trailhead, start up the trail, heading west along the North Fork Twisp River. You'll pass the Road End Campground in about 0.3 mile, and then cross into the Lake Chelan–Sawtooth Wilderness Area at 0.5 mile. The trail stays fairly straight and relatively level until you reach a trail junction at 1.6 miles—you gain a mere 800 feet in that distance.

At the trail junction, elevation 4400 feet, turn left and climb the pine-studded slope on the south side of the valley and then traverse around the nose of the ridge below Lincoln Butte to view the entire South Fork Twisp River valley. The trail never dips close to the river, so make sure you fill your water bottles at the trail junction.

After an initial steep climb away from the North Fork Twisp River, the trail enters a long, moderate climb around the flank of Lincoln Butte and, at 4.1 miles, crosses the low saddle of Twisp Pass at 6100 feet. The pass seems low, even at 6100 feet, because it is shadowed by Lincoln Butte, 7068

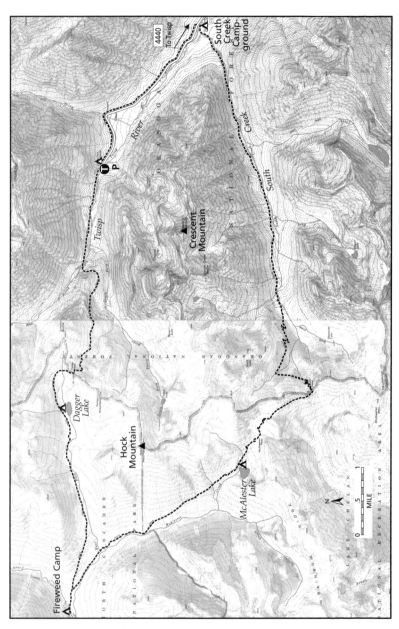

feet, on the north, and Twisp Mountain, 7161 feet, to the south. The pass offers a good place to stop, rest, and enjoy the views of the big peaks to the sides, and the bright flowers around your feet.

From Twisp Pass, the trail drops into the basin that forms the head of

East Fork Twisp River. The trail swings around the circular headwater basin, and in just a mile from the pass, the trail cuts along the shoreline of Dagger Lake. Wonderful camps—for both hikers and horse packers—are available here and from the camps on the north shore of the lake, campers can relax and enjoy the sunset as it colors the high peaks of Lincoln Butte and Twisp Mountain, as well as the neighbor to the south, Hock Mountain (7750 feet).

From the lake, continue down the East Fork valley, descending from alpine meadows and open stands of larch and fir, into the deeper, denser forests full of ponderosa pine. At 3.5 miles from the lake (8.6 miles from the trailhead) you'll encounter not just a trail fork but also a trail intersection. This four-way corner is marked by the Fireweed Camp. The trail heading due west leads to the Pacific Crest Trail. The northern branch leads to Stiletto Peak. That leaves the trail you came in on, and the one to the south. Therefore, turn south (left) and hike up the McAlester Creek valley. This trail begins near the creek, but after just 1.5 miles, climbs steeply away from the creek and, at 12.7 miles from the trailhead, rolls into camps on the shore of McAlester Lake, a pretty blue pool set below the steep slopes of Rainbow Ridge.

From the lake, it's another mile (maybe a little less) to the 6000-foot McAlester Pass. If you are looking for solitude, skip the lakeside camps and come on up to the pass to stay at High Camp, found on the west side of the pass near the headwaters of McAlester Creek.

From the meadow-filled cut of McAlester Pass, the trail stays high, traversing along a high ridgeline above tree line for most of the 1.4 miles to South Pass, which separates McAlester Mountain and Hock Mountain.

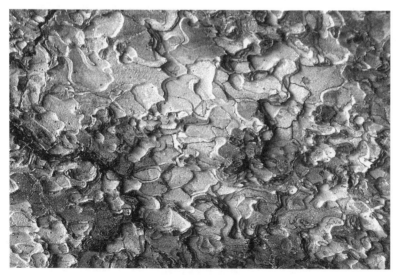

Ponderosa pine tree bark peels off in puzzle-like pieces.

South Pass leads into South Creek, and the trail drops steeply into the valley and flows west along the creek for 4.8 miles to a trail junction. The trail on your right (heading south) leads to Louis Lake—this is a good side trip for those with the time to explore a stunning alpine lake with great alpine scrambling opportunities.

If you don't have the time or inclination to explore, stay on the main trail, heading west down South Creek to the South Creek Campground (22 miles from the start) on Twisp River Road.

Here, you have a choice—hike up the road and hope for a ride, or cross the road to find Twisp River Trail and follow it up the valley parallel to the road. (No chance of catching a ride, but the trail is more scenic and far less dusty). You'll reach your starting point in about 3 miles, making for a 25-mile loop.

27 OVAL PASS

Round trip ■	**19.5 miles**
Loop direction ■	Clockwise
Hiking time ■	2 days
Starting elevation ■	4000 feet
High point ■	7700 feet
Elevation gain ■	3700 feet
Best hiking time ■	Mid-June through October
Map ■	Green Trails Milk Butte, No. 83
Contact ■	Okanogan and Wenatchee National Forests, Methow Valley Ranger District

The Lake Chelan portion of the Lake Chelan–Sawtooth Wilderness Area gets a lot of press, for wilderness enthusiasts who know the area will be quick to tell you that the true majesty of the wilderness area lies not in the lake but in the Sawtooth. That is, the ragged, jagged ridgeline that cuts the sky to the east of the long, deep lake. This loop explores a portion of that mighty ridgeline, as well as some of the most impressive old-growth forests on the dry side of the state. No towering cedars or Douglas firs here—well maybe a few Dougs—but you will find mammoth orange-skinned ponderosa pines, feathery-needled larch (locals call them tamaracks, though true tamaracks are actually a different species of tree than these western larch), and dark stands of white pine, red fir, and blue spruce.

To get there, from Twisp drive northeast up the Twisp River Road to FS Road 4430, found just 0.5 mile past War Creek Campground. Turn left onto FS Road 4430 and, after crossing the river, turn left again onto FS Road

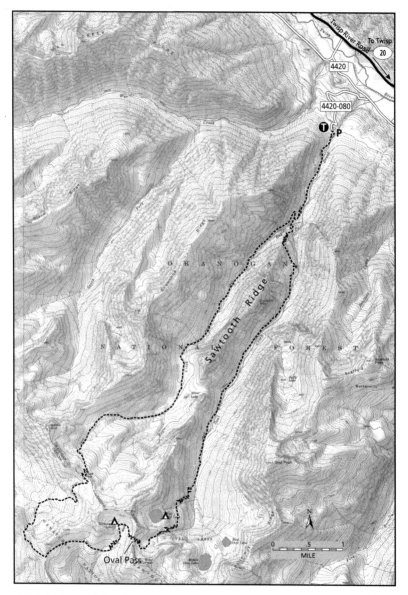

Oval Pass

4420. In about 0.7 mile, turn right onto FS Road 4420-080 and drive to the road's end and trailhead.

From the trailhead, hike south along Eagle Creek Trail 410 for 1.5 miles as it climbs gradually through heavy, pine forests alongside the creek. At 1.5 miles you'll cross the wilderness boundary and find a fork in the trail.

A large raptor sits atop a dead snag at Oval Pass.

You can head up either direction, but the recommended route is to stay left. Cross Eagle Creek and start a steep switchbacking climb up the snout of Duckbill Mountain. After gaining more than 600 feet in something like a 0.5-mile, the trail tapers into a gentle traverse around the east flank of the mountain and rolls into the Oval Creek valley, reaching the creekside at about 2.5 miles. For the next 3.5 miles, the trail climbs through open, sun-filled forests, hugging the west side of the creek most of the way. The tumbling waters provide gentle music to accompany your climb, helping speed the time as you ascend gradually toward the spine of the Sawtooth.

At about 6 miles, the trail angles up the slope west of the creek and shortly after that, begins switchbacking up the ever-steeper hillside. In about 0.8 mile of thigh-busting climbing, the trail finally moderates for 0.5 mile before climbing an even steeper 0.5-mile of switchbacks to a trail junction at 7000 feet, about 7.4 miles. Turning right here leads you to a fantastic campsite at West Oval Lake, about 0.25 mile and 100 feet lower, to the west. The broad lake is nestled in a rocky cirque below Gray Peak (8082 feet) to the south.

Camp here, or if there is still strength in your legs and light in the sky, push on for an even more impressive alpine camp a bit farther.

From the junction at West Oval Lake, turning left leads in a gradual 0.5-mile climb through stunning alpine meadows full of wildflowers to another junction, 7500 feet, on the flank of Gray Peak. Turn right and follow a faint track through the rock, heather, and snow to the northeast. Rock cairns help mark the trail in this rugged alpine world. In just 0.25 mile, cross Oval Pass at 7700 feet and descend into the remarkably beautiful and appropriately named Horseshoe Basin. At about 9 miles, the trail touches the shores of the tiny tarn called Tuckaway Lake (7500 feet). Again, an appropriate name—the folks who named the geographic features of this part of the country seemed to feel the obvious names were the best names—and we couldn't agree more!

Camp at Tuckaway or just enjoy a snack and a picture break at the tiny pond set like a jewel in a circular setting of towering stone. Moving on, you'll continue south from the lake, descending another 0.3 mile to another trail junction. Turn right here and loop southwest out around a long finger of the Sawtooth Ridge, staying in the alpine meadow country of this glorious wilderness, and in 1.7 miles, find another junction (11 miles from the trailhead). Turn right once more and climb a steep 1.2 miles (gaining 900 feet) to Eagle Pass, on Sawtooth Ridge between Gray Peak and Battle Mountain. Cross the pass and start a long, slow descent around the head basin of Eagle Creek valley. In about 2 miles, you'll be back alongside Eagle Creek proper, and for the next 3.8 miles, you'll follow the creek north back to the start of the loop at the mouth of Oval Creek valley.

There, continue down the Eagle Creek Trail the last 1.5 miles to the trailhead.

28 : SKYLINE TO LAKESHORE LOOP

Round trip ■	**25 miles**
Loop direction ■	Clockwise
Hiking time ■	3 to 4 days
Starting elevation ■	1200 feet
High point ■	6800 feet
Elevation gain ■	5600 feet
Best hiking time ■	Mid-June through October
Maps ■	Green Trails Stehekin, No. 82 and Lucerne, No. 114
Contact ■	Okanogan and Wenatchee National Forests, Chelan Ranger District

The peaks visible from this route have been called the Alps of America, so stunning, sheer, and picturesque are they. This trail provides an immersion into the majestic world of those mountains. You'll climb high into the granite and heather meadows of the alpine world, stroll through cool forests, and follow the shore of the cold lake.

To get there, from Chelan take the Lady of the Lake ferry to travel up Lake Chelan to the town of Stehekin. The trail begins near the ranger station. You might consider spending the night at the Stehekin Campground so you can get an early start on the trail—the first leg of the hike is slow going.

At Stehekin, tighten your bootlaces, fill your water bottles, and strip off any extra layers of clothing—the work begins nearly with the first step up the trail. The Purple Creek Trail climbs ruthlessly from the 1200-foot shoreline at Stehekin, to the high flower-filled Purple Pass at 6800 feet. This 5600

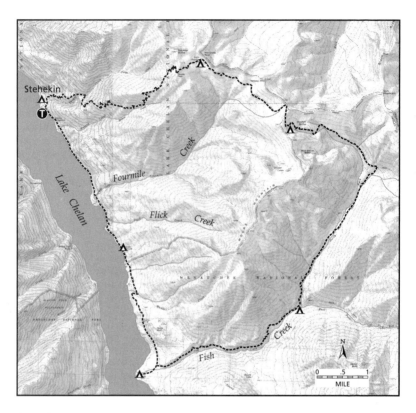

feet of elevation gain comes in a thigh-burning 7.5 miles. The path crosses Purple Creek a couple times, but mostly stays high on the forest-covered ridgeline as it stretches up, up, and up. Finally, high above the headwaters of Purple Creek, the trail reaches Purple Pass on the flank of Boulder Butte. If there is any feeling left in your legs, drop your pack at the pass and scramble up the 0.5-mile trail to the summit of the butte (7400 feet) for unmatched views.

If you've had all the climbing you can tolerate, though, skip the summit journey and just enjoy the almost-as-good views from the pass. You can look up on to Boulder Butte, back down the valley to the north end of Lake Chelan, and south and east to Twin Peaks and Splawn Mountain.

From Purple Pass, the trail slants slightly downhill for 0.5 mile to Lake Juanita, 8 miles from the trailhead. This is a perfect place to camp—good water, great views, and it sits at the end of a long, grueling climb.

On the east side of the lake, turn south onto the Summit Trail and enjoy a long rambling stroll along the crest of the ridge below Splawn Mountain. You'll end up with a net gain of 500 feet in the 2.5 miles from the lake to the crossing of a ridge separating Fourmile Creek basin from Fish Creek basin. Enjoy the views, and then drop into the meadow basin near Deephole Spring and start down the valley. At 13.2 miles from the trailhead, turn right onto the North Fork Fish Creek Trail and follow this creek southwest back to the lake.

At 16.3 miles, you'll pass another trail junction. Continue straight on the main route (the trail to the left climbs the East Fork valley) and at 17.5 miles, a faint side trail leads off to the left, climbing to Round Lake. Ignore that path too and keep moving straight ahead to skirt Round Mountain and attain the Lake Shore Trail at 19 miles. Turn right (north) onto the Lake Shore Trail and at 21.5 miles, you'll come to Flick Creek Camp at the water's edge. Camp here, or push on to Stehekin, found 3.5 miles farther north, at the end of the 25-mile loop.

An old sign showing evidence of where bark has overgrown it

29 GOAT LAKE/ELLIOTT CREEK LOOP

Round trip ■	**10 miles**
Loop direction ■	Counterclockwise
Hiking time ■	5 to 6 hours
Starting elevation ■	1900 feet
High point ■	3200 feet
Elevation gain ■	2300 feet
Best hiking time ■	Mid-June through October
Map ■	Green Trails Sloan Peak, No. 111
Contact ■	Mt. Baker–Snoqualmie National Forest, Darrington Ranger District

Because the trail starts at a relatively low elevation, it loses its snow cover early in the summer, presenting some stunning mountain hiking in June and July. Visiting the area in the early season allows hikers to trip through a landscape rich in color as the forest is blanketed with trillium, yellow violet, bunchberry, wild ginger, and starflower. The local residents take full advantage of the rich vegetation, too. Douglas squirrels dance and chitter in the trees and deer browse through the lush ground cover. Black bears are also common here thanks to the plethora of native bulbs and tubers, not to mention berries and assorted creepy crawly critters in the slowly rotting logs that litter the old forest.

For pure scenic splendor, hikers can enjoy thundering waterfalls. There's a particularly nice falls on the Goat Lake outlet stream; and a standout falls just below that, found by a little off-trail hiking shortly before reaching the lake.

To get there, from Granite Falls drive east on the Mountain Loop Highway about 30 miles to Barlow Pass. Continue northeast on the Mountain Loop Highway (it becomes a gravel road at Barlow Pass) another 3.5 miles (8–10 minutes) to the side road, marked Elliott Creek, leading off to the east. Near the road junction, you'll also see an old, weathered sign "Goat Lake Trail 647." Continue up this somewhat steep, rough road 0.75 mile to the road's end and trailhead.

The Elliott Creek Trail immediately drops about 200 feet from the parking area down to the creek. The trail is constantly in range of the roar of Elliott Creek with spectacular views dotting the trail at least every 0.5 mile. About a mile in (30 minutes), find one particularly fun area where you can go down to the creek for access to views of rapids and mossy rocks. After about 2 miles of great creekside hiking, the trail leaves the creek and over the next mile slowly climbs through open forest and brush slopes to meet up with the main Goat Lake Trail. This is an old roadbed as far as the wilderness boundary, so the hiking is relatively easy.

Once in the wilderness, the trail immediately passes through huge old-

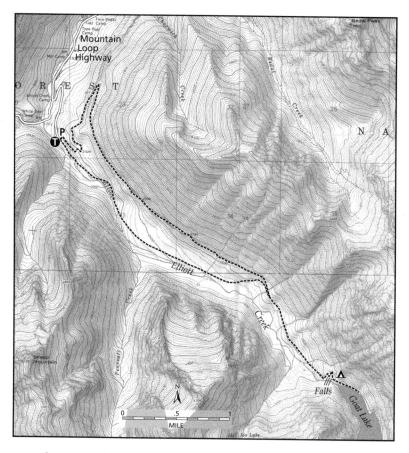

growth western hemlock and cedar trees and begins the last mile of switchbacks to the lake. This is the only steep portion of the entire hike. At the last switchback before the lake listen to the roar of water—this is the massive waterfall of Elliott Creek! An equally beautiful waterfall sits at the lake outlet—look and listen for it as you arrive at Goat Lake.

Goat Lake (4.6 miles from the trailhead) is breathtaking. Signs lead you to the established camps and toilet area north of the lake. Enjoy grand views of the rugged peaks south of the lake, especially Foggy Peak still completely covered in winter snow. Here, farther up lake, early spring waterfowl migrants can be seen—birds such as red-breasted mergansers, buffleheads, and hooded mergansers.

The hike back out to complete the loop is again splendid hiking through wilderness old growth. The last 4 miles back to the trailhead are on what used to be an old road that led almost to Goat Lake. This very flat and easy grade winds around through mostly deciduous trees and brush. Not the

Elliott Creek falls at Goat Lake outlet

most exciting trail, but if hiked in early spring it offers a couple of nice waterfalls in side tributary creeks and a carpet of early spring wildflowers to keep your mind on the beautiful aspects of this trail section.

30 WHITE PASS/KODAK PEAK

Round trip ■	**29 miles**
Loop direction ■	Clockwise
Hiking time ■	2 to 4 days
Starting elevation ■	2100 feet
High point ■	6000 feet
Elevation gain ■	3900 feet
Best hiking time ■	Mid-July through early October
Maps ■	Green Trails Sloan Peak, No. 111, Glacier Peak, No. 112, and Benchmark, No. 144
Contact ■	Mt. Baker–Snoqualmie National Forest, Darrington Ranger District

Some of the most spectacular high alpine country in Washington is found along this route. Glorious alpine meadows awash in wildflowers—from heathers to huckleberries, paintbrush to phlox—cover vast tracts of the trail. Elsewhere, the path pierces deep, rich old-growth forest, exploring ancient living cathedrals along rushing mountain rivers. Likely hikers will also experience an assortment of wildlife since literally hundreds of bird and animal species call this area home.

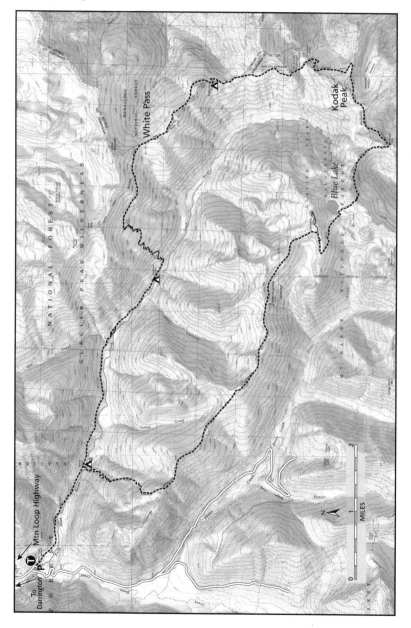

To get there from Darrington, turn south onto the Mountain Loop Highway and drive to the junction with North Fork Sauk River Road (FS Road 49) found near the North Fork Guard Station. Turn left (east) and follow the North Fork Road to Sloan Creek Campground. Turn left at the campground and find the North Fork trailhead.

Start up North Fork Trail 649, as it pushes up the lush valley of prime old-growth firs, hemlocks, and cedars—the forest walk extends more than 5 miles up the valley and offers a relaxing, stress-busting start to your hike.

At 2 miles from the trailhead, you'll pass a trail junction on your right. This is where you will close your loop. At about 4 miles, you have to ford Red Creek—early in the summer this creek can be fast and cold, but there are generally solid logs on which to cross. If no logs exist, you'll have to wade the creek. Just a mile past Red Creek, find Mackinaw Shelter, an old wooden shack inhabited by mice. If you are planning to stay here, pitch a tent rather than sleeping in the rodent hotel. With no official camps set along the route, hikers are free to pitch their tents wherever they end the day.

From the shelter, the trail climbs 3000 feet in 3 miles to reach the Pacific Crest Trail at 8 miles from the trailhead. Now, you're deep into alpine meadows, sprawling across the lower flank of Glacier Peak. Pink heathers, blue lupine, and soft white phlox fill the meadows, and between the flowers are clumps of low bush blueberries. Whistling marmots and pikas prance in the rock piles, and deer browse through the rich vegetation.

Turn south on the PCT and in 0.7 mile, cross the flower-filled saddle of White Pass, 5904 feet. Enjoy glorious views of Glacier Peak, Sloan Peak, and Indian Head Peak from the pass. Continuing past White Pass, the trail climbs along a long ridgeline, and at 11 miles, reaches a tiny meadow pond, known as the Reflection Pond. What does it reflect? Walk around it and watch as the reflection changes with the light and the angle of viewing—Indian Head Peak can sometimes be seen, as can Glacier Peak. Just 0.1 mile beyond the pond is a trail junction. Stay to the right and drop slowly to Kids Pond in 0.5 mile, then reach Indian Pass, 5000 feet, at 13 miles. Here you'll find another trail junction. Stay right once more and continue south, climbing the east flank of Kodak Peak. In just a mile from Indian Pass, you'll crest Wenatchee Ridge (5700 feet) above Meander Meadows and below the summit of Kodak. Enjoy the views—and plan on using a lot of film (it doesn't have to be Kodak brand, of course) to capture the stunning beauty of the area.

At the top of Wenatchee Ridge, turn west (a faint side trail leads east along the top of the ridge) and cross high above the green fields of Meander Meadows to Sauk Pass, 15 miles from the start. From Sauk Pass, drop south to Dishpan Gap (5600 feet), and then turn north at a four-way trail junction to traverse around toward Blue Lake on the flank of Johnson Mountain. Blue Lake (5625 feet) is reached at 17.5 miles from the trailhead.

The trail leaves Blue Lake and continues down the long spine of the ridge angling east from Johnson Mountain. At 27 miles, after 8 miles of forest travel, the trail drops back to the North Fork Sauk River Trail. Turn left and hike the 2 miles back out to the trailhead.

31 MILK CREEK AND MINERS RIDGE

Round trip ■	**35 miles**
Loop direction ■	Counterclockwise
Hiking time ■	3 to 5 days
Starting elevation ■	1600 feet
High point ■	5600 feet
Elevation gain ■	4000 feet
Best hiking time ■	Late July through early October
Map ■	Green Trails Glacier Peak, No. 112
Contact ■	Mt. Baker–Snoqualmie National Forest, Darrington Ranger Disrict

This loop trip has a variety of terrain, from rain forest valleys with large trees to alpine meadows with low heather and blueberry cover. From the high route along the Pacific Crest Trail, the views of the north side of Glacier Peak are superb. But beware, the biting insects can be fierce on Milk Creek in summer. Campsites are plentiful along the route, with fine riverside camps placed every 3 or 4 miles along Suiattle River and others located along Milk Creek, Milk Ridge, and Vista Ridge.

To get there, from Seattle drive north on Interstate 5 to the Arlington/State Route 530 exit. Turn east onto SR 530, heading to Darrington, and continue northeast on SR 530 through town. About 7 miles north of Darrington, just after crossing the Sauk River, turn right onto Suiattle River Road (FS Road 26). Drive about 23 miles to the trailhead at road's end. Note that this road is paved for about half of its length, with the final 12 miles rough gravel.

Begin with nearly a mile of easy walking along Suiattle River Trail 784 to the junction with Milk Creek Trail 790. Turn right onto Trail 790 and cross the fuming Suiattle River on a large bridge. The trail angles up in several switchbacks, and then traverses high above the Suiattle. In 2 miles the way levels out with large Douglas fir monarchs shading the way. This easier section lasts for several miles, and has good views of Lime Ridge and Glacier Peak towering above. There are several camps along the way. The trail crosses Milk Creek about halfway to the Pacific Crest Trail.

The trail climbs on switchbacks a mile before reaching the PCT at 7.3 miles. There is a camp at a right turn, down the PCT at its Milk Creek crossing. But turn left on the PCT, and climb through dry forest and avalanche paths via almost forty switchbacks. Mercifully, the climbing eases off shortly before cresting Milk Ridge about 10 miles from the trailhead at 5600 feet elevation. Here are some camps with water through midsummer.

For better camps and grand views across wide meadows, continue on the northbound PCT. An excellent camp is found near the East Fork Milk Creek at 12 miles. A scant mile farther on, find a junction with the Grassy Point Waytrail. This is a lovely side path that wanders the aptly named grassy ridge. Scramble up more than 1000 feet to the high point at 6596 feet for outstanding views of Miners Ridge, Lime Ridge, Glacier Peak, the Suiattle River valley, and the Milk Creek valley. You can see most of this trip from Grassy Point.

Once you've explored the views, continue north on the PCT, passing a horse camp on Vista Ridge at 14.5 miles. Take a good look at Gamma Ridge, Gamma Peak, and Glacier Peak, and then descend gentle switchbacks for several miles down to Vista Creek. There are a few camp possibilities in the forest at 18.5 miles before crossing Vista Creek on a bridge. A good camp is just across the bridge.

The rest of the trail is nearly flat to a junction with the Upper Suiattle and Gamma Ridge Trails, and then descends down to the Suiattle River at 21.3 miles. Cross the long bridge to a camp on the Suiattle River. This river has a lot of glacial flour, so to save your water filter, find water a bit farther downstream at Miners Creek.

The Suiattle River Trail is an easy but long walk back to the trailhead. One camp en route is at the junction with the Miners Ridge Trail. It's 10.8

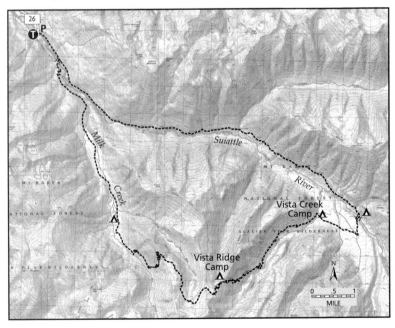

Milk Creek Trail passes by enormous old-growth trees, some long since downed.

more miles of nice forest to the parking area. Look for trees as large as you found them on the Milk Creek Trail.

32 LARCH LAKE/COW CREEK MEADOWS

Round trip ■	**18 miles**
Loop direction ■	Counterclockwise
Hiking time ■	2 to 3 days
Starting elevation ■	3100 feet
High point ■	6500 feet
Elevation gain ■	3400 feet
Best hiking time ■	Late June through early October
Map ■	Green Trails Lucerne, No. 114
Contact ■	Okanogan and Wenatchee National Forests, Entiat Ranger District

You might have to tolerate motorcycles along the first few miles of the trail, but even if the first few miles were on a motorcycle racecourse, the loop portion would make the journey worthwhile. But there is no racecourse. Because the trail leads straight up to the wilderness boundary in just a few miles, few bikers ride this way—they prefer longer routes that let them take advantage of their off-road vehicle's greater speed and range.

So ignore the few motorcycles you might see and instead enjoy the great landscape. Great fields of huckleberries stretch through the open pine forests along the valley bottom portions of the hike, and as you climb the ridges, you'll find yourself in broad, sweeping meadows, beside gin-clear alpine lakes, and

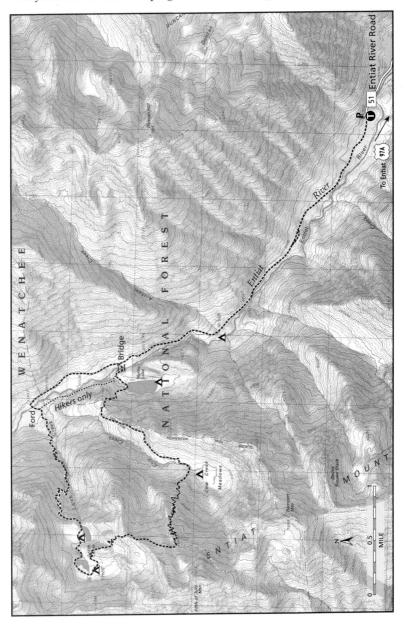

atop windy ridges and peaks with panoramic views spread before you.

To get there, from Wenatchee drive north on U.S. Highway 97A (west side of the Columbia River) to Entiat. Turn left (west) on Entiat River Road (FS Road 51) and drive to the trailhead at the road's end, just 0.25 mile past the Cottonwood Campground.

Head west from the trailhead, following the Entiat River valley upstream—the trail stays well clear of the river most of the way as it pierces the pine and fir forests of the valley bottom. The trees are well spaced, providing ample sunlight to filter through to ripen the fruit found on the vast expanses of huckleberry bushes throughout the forest. By early August, the lower elevation berries are beginning to ripen.

At 2.2 miles, you'll pass a faint, brush-covered trail on the right. This is the Anthem Creek Trail (see Hike 34). Continue straight ahead, staying on the Entiat River Trail. About 0.5 mile past the trail junction, you'll cross Anthem Creek itself. There are some nice campsites here, but you'll want to push on—the best is yet to come. About a mile past the creek, at 3.6 miles, another junction is reached. You have a choice here.

You can continue straight ahead up the Entiat River Trail and enjoy smooth, well-graded tread for another mile to the Larch Lakes Trail, then ford the ice-cold waters of the Entiat River—it can be a difficult ford early in the summer, but generally is only knee deep by midsummer. Or you can turn left at this junction, cross the river on a stout new bridge, and about 0.5 mile up the trail on the other side, find a faint, hiker-only trail heading north along the west side of the Entiat River. You avoid having to ford the river this way, but the path from the bridge to the Larch Lakes Trail tends to be brushy and poorly maintained. The distance is about the same either way.

Regardless of your choice, once on the west bank of the Entiat at the bottom of the Larch Lakes Trail—about 4.8 miles either way—head west and almost immediately start a long, steep climb up the valley wall. You'll gain 2000 feet in just over 2.5 miles to get to the upper lake. There are some nice campsites in the meadows around the lower lake, but this pretty fish-filled pond is also more sheltered, and therefore harbors a bigger population of mosquitoes. Keep moving and 0.5 mile farther up the trail—and about 300 feet higher in elevation—you'll reach the broad, upper Larch Lake at 7.6 miles. Huge fields of heather, Indian paintbrush, lupine, and elephant's head flowers surround this big lake, and the flanks of the walls circling the lake basin are covered in forests of western larch. Visit in September and you'll miss the flower blooms, but there will be shimmering stands of gold as the larch lose their green and go for the gold.

Best camps are along the south and west sides of the lake. Look for the house-sized rock in the meadow south of the lake—this makes a great wind block for your camp and serves as a perfect perch on which to doze in the sunshine.

From Larch Lake, the trail hooks around a north-reaching arm of Fifth of July Mountain and begins a moderate climb up the side of that peak. Gain a comfortable 700 feet in 2 miles to a larch meadow at the 6500-foot

Hiker in Cow Creek Meadows

level of the mountain. (Note: the "larch meadow" is a sidehill meadow studded with tall larch trees every few yards. It's not quite a forest, not quite a meadow—but its 100-percent stunning!)

At this point, 9.6 miles from the trailhead, find a trail junction and turn left. You'll descend steeply for the next 2 miles through increasingly dense forest until you find a broad side trail on your right. Turn here and walk the couple hundred yards into Cow Creek Meadows. This is a broad circular grass meadow ringed by a wall of sheer granite—a cirque below Rampart Mountain. A small pond anchors the north end of the meadow, and a clear streams meanders through the meadow itself. Marmots whistle and pikas chirp from the rocky tailings at the bases of the cliffs, and deer browse along the edges of the thin forests on the north and east flanks of the basin. There are some wonderful campsites here.

Leaving the meadows, continue down the trail and in another 2 miles— 13.6 miles from the trailhead, pass the long, forest-rimmed Myrtle Lake. There is a luxury camp—two actually—on the south end of the mile-long lake, with rustic picnic table and benches built quite ingeniously from old logs. From Myrtle it's a short 0.5 mile down to the Entiat River bridge you encountered earlier in the hike, and then the final 3.6 miles back down the Entiat River valley to the trailhead.

33 ENTIAT MOUNTAIN RAMBLE

Round trip ■	**45 miles**
Loop direction ■	Counterclockwise
Hiking time ■	3 to 5 days
Starting elevation ■	3100 feet
High point ■	6800 feet
Elevation gain ■	3700 feet
Best hiking time ■	Late June through early October
Maps ■	Green Trails Lucerne, No. 114, Holden, No. 113, and Plain, No. 146
Contact ■	Okanogan and Wenatchee National Forests, Entiat Ranger District

Valley-bottom forests, ridge-top scrambles, meadow walks, riverside strolls, and—glory of glories, vast fields of purple gold, the delectable huckleberry. What's more, this long, rambling route can be shortened or lengthened by using any of the numerous connector trails between the ridge top and the valley bottom.

To get there, from Wenatchee drive north on U.S. Highway 97A (west side of the Columbia River) to Entiat. Turn left (west) on Entiat River Road

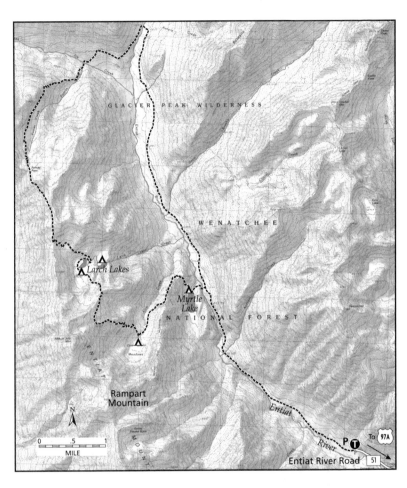

(FS Road 51) and drive to the trailhead at the road's end, just 0.25 mile past the Cottonwood Campground.

From the trailhead, follow the Entiat River upstream 13 miles, passing into the Glacier Peak Wilderness at 4.2 miles. This trail pierces open pine forests blanketed in huckleberries and provides numerous quality campsites along the river. At about 12 miles, the forest along the river begins to open up, and at 12.5 miles, the long fields of the Entiat Meadows begin. Look for deer and elk in these broad fields pierced by the bright waters of the river. Above the meadows to the south stands the spires of North Spectacle Butte while to the north is Buckskin Mountain. At 15 miles, turn left and cross the river, then turn left again and start climbing Trail 1431, heading up the flank of North Spectacle Butte. As you swing around the east face of the peak, you'll top out at 6600 feet—about 17.3 miles—before beginning a long descent down Coal Creek back toward the Entiat River. The trail actually swings down to the west bank of the Entiat—nearly within shouting distance of the outward leg of the loop. Indeed, at 20 miles, a short connector trail leads east across a broad ford of the Entiat to reach the Entiat River Trail in 0.25 mile (you could use this connector to knock 10 miles off the loop if you prefer).

From the junction with this connector, stay right and angle up Ice Creek valley for a mile, reaching yet another junction. Turn left and climb Pomas Creek valley to Pomas Pass, 6800 feet, on the flank of the Entiat Mountains. From Pomas Pass, traverse a broad, steep meadow on the upper slope of the ridge, before dropping to upper Larch Lake at 26 miles (see Hike 32) where you'll find good campsites for the night. From Larch Lake, climb the north flank of Fifth of July Mountain, enjoying great views of the glacier-carved Entiat River valley. At 28 miles, you have one more choice to make. At a trail junction, you can turn left and descend past Cow Creek Meadows and Myrtle Lake to rejoin the Entiat River Trail to head back to the trailhead. Or you can push on, staying to the right and traverse around the northwest flank of Rampart Mountain and

Sweeping views of the Chelan Mountain group seen along Entiat route

Garfield Peak. This leg of the journey slices through forests, meadows, and ridge top promontories with stunning views. At 37.4 miles, you'll find a small spring and a campsite at the head of Shetipo Creek valley. Turn left at the trail junction here and descend 4.7 miles on the Shetipo Creek Trail back to the Cottonwood Campground and the trailhead, for a loop of about 45 miles.

34 ⋮ BOREALIS PASS

Round trip ▪	**27 miles**
Loop direction ▪	Clockwise
Hiking time ▪	2 to 3 days
Starting elevation ▪	3100 feet
High point ▪	7600 feet
Elevation gain ▪	4500 feet
Best hiking time ▪	July through early October
Map ▪	Green Trails Lucerne, No. 114
Contact ▪	Okanogan and Wenatchee National Forests, Entiat Ranger District

The Entiat watershed contains some of the most primitive, remote wilderness in the state, and this route makes the most of it, exploring the diverse ecosystems and wildlife habitats that make this region so special. There are fine campsites throughout the loop, scattered along the Entiat River, in the side valleys, and on the ridge top. Take your pick.

To get there, from Wenatchee drive north on U.S. Highway 97A (west side of the Columbia River) to Entiat. Turn left (west) on the Entiat River Road (FS Road 51) and drive to the trailhead at the road's end, just 0.25 mile past the Cottonwood Campground.

Fewer folks hike this route than some of the other wonderful loops in Entiat country, but that doesn't mean it's any less spectacular—just less known. Start up the Entiat River Trail, and at 2.2 miles take note of the trail climbing through a bramble of huckleberries to the right. This is the Anthem Creek Trail—your return route. Keep moving up the Entiat River Trail now, however, passing the Myrtle Lake–Cow Creek Meadows Trail on your left at 3.6 miles, and the Larch Lakes Trail ford at 4.7 miles. About 1.5 miles past the Larch Lakes Trail, you'll find another trail junction on the right. If time is short, you can cut about 8 miles off the loop by turning up this trail and climbing 1.4 miles to a junction with the other side of the big loop. But while this shortcut saves time, it also cuts off the most impressive parts of the trail.

Better to press on up the Entiat River Trail another 1.8 miles to the Borealis

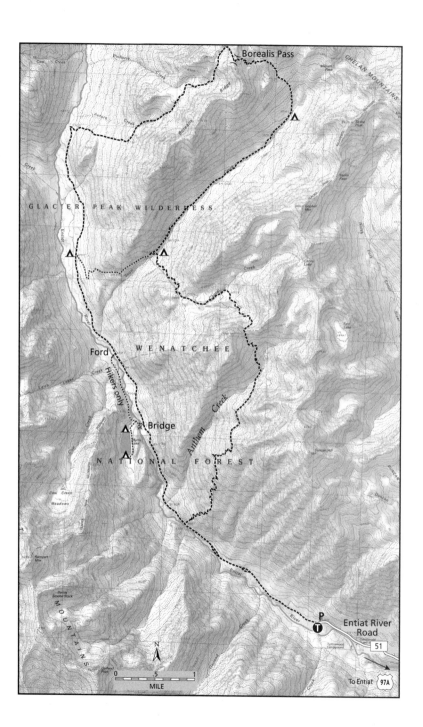

Hikers near Borealis Pass

Pass Trail 1432 found on the right, about 8 miles from the trailhead. You can camp near the trail junction and get an early start on the long, steep trail which ascends from the Entiat River, around the south flank of Borealis Mountain, and finally through Borealis Pass (7600 feet) at about 12 miles. As you climb from the valley to the pass, you'll move through thick forest into increasingly open country, until the trees give way to expansive wildflower meadows as you approach the pass.

From the pass, descend east about a mile to junction with the Brushy

Creek Trail. Turn right and head downstream along the creekside trail. Ignore the side trail found 0.5 mile down the valley (it leads to Saska Pass and high into the Chelan Mountains) and instead look for a junction 2.7 miles downstream, about 15.7 miles from the trailhead. This is where that shortcut would have brought you. If you are tired and don't want to bother with another climb, head straight down to the Entiat River Trail and out to the trailhead. But for another modest climb to stellar views, turn left up this track and climb southward up Choral Creek valley, gaining some 1800 feet in 3.5 miles from the junction to an unnamed pass (6800 feet) on a spur ridge of Gopher Mountain.

From this pass, 19.2 miles from the start, drop into the Anthem Creek valley and follow the Anthem Creek Trail down a steep, switchbacking route for 5.6 miles to rejoin the Entiat River Trail. Turn left on the Entiat River Trail and stroll the last 2.2 miles back to the trailhead, for a loop of 27 miles.

35 PUGH RIDGE

Round trip ■	14 miles
Loop direction ■	Clockwise
Hiking time ■	2 to 3 days
Starting elevation ■	3900 feet
High point ■	6600 feet
Elevation gain ■	2600 feet
Best hiking time ■	July through early October
Map ■	Green Trails Lucerne, No. 114
Contact ■	Okanogan and Wenatchee National Forests, Entiat Ranger District

Birds abound along this route as the rich forest ecosystem supports a myriad of species, from nutcrackers to eagles. The eastern side of the ridge is blanketed in larch trees, making this a grand option for autumn hiking—the larches will shimmer gold by late September. But even if the fall colors aren't out, the route provides plenty of visual delights, with great views of the assorted peaks in the Entiat and Chelan Mountains! Pyramid, Cardinal, Duncan Hill, Devil's Smoke Pipe—the list goes ever on.

To get there, from Wenatchee drive north on U.S. Highway 97A (west side of the Columbia River) to Entiat. Turn left (west) on the Entiat River Road (FS Road 51) and drive up the Entiat River valley. About 3 miles past Silver Falls Campground, turn right onto FS Road 5606 (note: if you reach the North Fork Campground you've gone about 0.5 mile too far). Drive up FS Road 5606 and continue about 2.5 miles north to the end of the road and the trailhead.

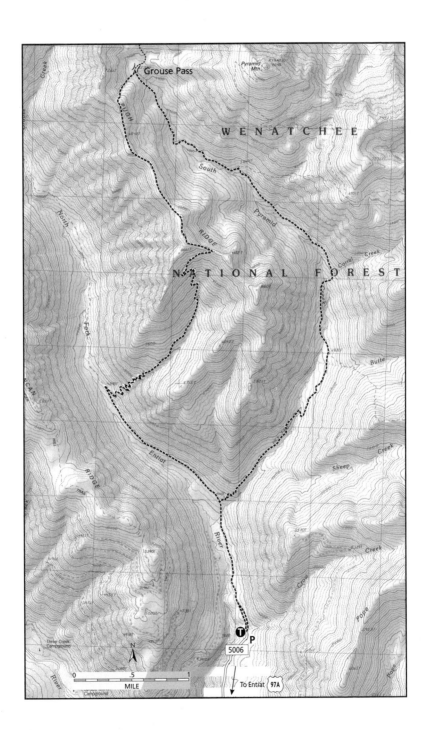

Grouse Pass

Pyramid Mtn.

WENATCHEE

South

Pyramid

RIDGE

NATIONAL FOREST

North

Fork

Butte

Entiat

RIDGE

Sheep

Creek

Creek

River

Crow

Creek

Pope

T

P

5006

Three Creek Campground

N

Pope

Campground

River

0   .5   1

MILE

To Entiat 97A

Start up the North Fork Entiat Trail, passing under some surprisingly large trees in the cool, pleasant forest alongside the river. This route is outside of designated wilderness, but even without that protection there is some remarkable old growth here. (There are also some fine campsites throughout the loop—along the Entiat River, in side valleys, and on the ridge top.) You'll cross a well-built bridge over Pyramid Creek at 1.2 miles and at 2.7 miles, you'll find a trail junction. Turn right here and climb up the steep Pugh Ridge Trail 1438. The next 2 miles ascend 2500 feet in elevation. The steep climb helps fight off early morning chills during early season, or late autumn, hikes, but will push a heavy sweat when the weather is warm.

At 4.7 miles, the trail finally tapers into a gradual climb as it's now atop Pugh Ridge, 6600 feet. From here, enjoy amazing views of the Entiat and Chelan Mountain Ranges (to the southwest and northeast, respectively). The trail continues north another 2.9 miles, rolling up and down now, along the ridgeline to intersect Trail 1433 just below Grouse Pass, at 7.6 miles.

Turn right at the junction and head east along Trail 1433 for 1.4 miles, descending some 700 feet, to find a junction with Pyramid Creek Trail 1439 on the lower flank of Pyramid Mountain. Turn right once more and descend Pyramid Creek Trail for 4 miles, rejoining the North Fork Entiat Trail at 13 miles. Keep an eye out for birds on this leg of the loop as vast numbers of Clark's nutcrackers have been seen swooping and diving around the headwaters of Pyramid Creek.

On the North Fork Entiat Trail once more, turn left and descend the last 1.2 miles to the trailhead.

Hiker crossing Pugh Ridge meadows

36 : SILVER FALLS

Round trip ■	**2 miles**
Loop direction ■	Counterclockwise
Hiking time ■	1 to 2 hours
Starting elevation ■	2600 feet
High point ■	3100 feet
Elevation gain ■	500 feet
Best hiking time ■	June through early October
Map ■	Green Trails Plain, No. 146
Contact ■	Okanogan and Wenatchee National Forests, Entiat Ranger District

This gentle forest walk is perfect for families or for those who simply don't have time to tarry on longer outings. The trail pierces beautiful old-growth forest, provides a great opportunity to see and hear songbirds of the forests, and leads to a stunning waterfall. All in just 2 miles.

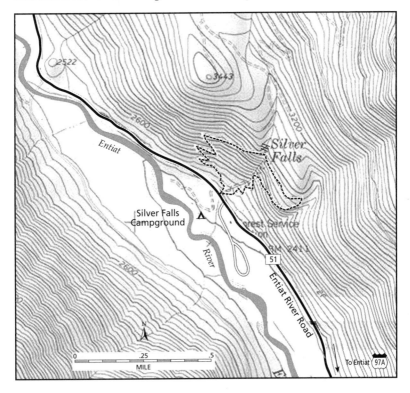

Spring snowmelt feeder stream near Silver Falls

To get there, from Wenatchee, drive north on U.S. Highway 97A (west side of the Columbia River) to Entiat. Turn left (west) on the Entiat River Road (FS Road 51) and drive up the Entiat River valley to Silver Falls Campground. The trailhead is found on the north side of the road.

You can hike in either direction, but by staying right at the fork, you gain elevation at a more modest pace. The trail sweeps north and east for 0.5 mile or so, slanting ever upward through the fragrant pine forests before hooking back to the northwest to reach Silver Falls in about a mile. This tumbling waterfall provides a refreshing spot to stop for a few pictures and a snack. Sit quietly and listen to the birds twitter and tweet as they snatch up insects living in the water below the falls or watch them nibble seeds from the assortment of bushes and flowers that thrive in this creek valley.

Once you've had your fill—or run out of time—push on past the falls and begin a gradual traverse along the steep hillside to the west of the falls. In about 0.3 mile, the traverse ends and the trail drops into a series of modest switchbacks, leading you back down the slope to the trailhead.

37 HORSETHIEF BASIN

Round trip	■	**14.5 miles**
Loop direction	■	Clockwise
Hiking time	■	9 hours, day hike or backpack
Starting elevation	■	6600 feet
High point	■	7600 feet
Elevation gain	■	1900 feet
Best hiking time	■	July through September
Map	■	Green Trails Prince Creek, No. 115
Contact	■	Washington State Parks

Perhaps the namesake of this basin got away, but as Horsethief Basin sits below Deadmans Pass, perhaps he didn't. Then again, perhaps the pass was named after someone else entirely. Regardless, the past is past, and despite the dire names, this area provides a gloriously peaceful adventure into some of the most beautiful country in Washington. This loop swings through a broad forested valley, across seemingly endless meadows of wildflowers, and along jagged ridges graced with mind-numbingly gorgeous panoramic views. Turn this day hike into a 2-day adventure by spending the night in the meadows below Deadmans Pass.

To get there, from Chelan drive north on North Shore Road (State Route 150) past the small town of Manson and turn right (northeast) onto Grade Creek Road (FS Road 82). Continue along this road to the South Navarre

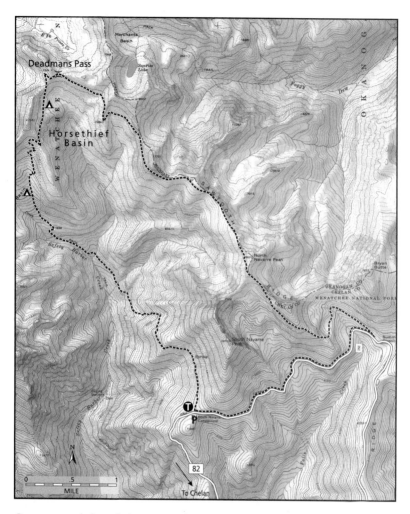

Campground, found about 38 miles out of Chelan. The trailhead is on the north side of the road, opposite the campground.

Some hikers fear to tread here simply because the trails are open to horses, mountain bikes, and even motorcycles, but the beauty of the region makes up for any inconvenience of sharing the trails. Indeed, the paths are open to other users, but few folks of any type venture here and the route is generally only lightly used.

From the trailhead, hike north through sun-filled forests along the western side of South Navarre Peak, crossing several avalanche chutes—filled with colorful fireweed, vine maple, and columbine—in the first mile, before dropping to a junction with the Safety Harbor Creek Trail at

A knot creates a swirling effect in this tree trunk seen along the trail.

2.4 miles. Turn right onto the Safety Harbor Creek Trail and, in less than 0.5 mile, the trail leaves the creekside and begins a gruelingly steep climb up a ridge spur jutting out in front of Miners Basin—a deep circular valley full of grassy meadows. Look for deer in the forest fringes and eagles in the air overhead. At 4.2 miles, the trail reaches another junction at 6500 feet. Stop here and soak in the views of Ferry Peak (7777 feet) to the west, high above Miners Basin.

Once you've caught your breath and gotten your fill of the views, turn right at the junction and continue climbing, now sweeping northeast around the head of Horsethief Basin. You'll gain 900 feet in 1.5 miles from the junction as you move through great fields of heather and wildflowers. The meadow carpet stretches right up to Deadmans Pass at 6 miles (7400 feet).

This is where the truly stunning views are found. You've enjoyed great views in bits and snatches along the trek to this point, but now you can stop and really take in the amazing landscape before you. The emerald green meadows and forest groves in Horsethief Basin nestle below your feet, while the skyward arms of the Sawtooth peaks stretch north and south like the serrated edge of a ragged saw blade.

From Deadmans Pass, turn south (right) and follow the ridgeline 2.4 miles to a junction with the Foggy Dew Trail. You'll lose just 100 feet in this stretch of trail, and you'll enjoy awesome views from the ridge-top meadows every step of the way. At the Foggy Dew Junction (8.4 miles from trailhead), stay right and climb southward another 1.5 miles along the high flank of North Navarre Peak, getting to about the 7600-foot level on the 7963-foot mountain, before dropping 2 miles to a junction with FS Road 82, at 12 miles. Turn right onto the road and follow it about 2.5 miles back to the South Navarre Campground and the trailhead.

38 WALLACE FALLS LOOP

Round trip ■	6.5 miles
Loop direction ■	Clockwise
Hiking time ■	4 hours
Starting elevation ■	250 feet
High point ■	1500 feet
Elevation gain ■	1250 feet
Best hiking time ■	Year-round
Map ■	Green Trails Index, No. 142
Contact ■	Washington State Parks

This route makes for a great winter outing, family outing, or both. In addition to the multiple viewpoints overlooking the thundering falls, there are ample opportunities for hikers to see the tumbling river and enjoy the beautiful birds and wildlife in the forest. American dippers can be seen from the bridge crossing the North Fork Wallace River. I've seen mergansers and buffleheads flying down the Wallace River. And wood ducks have been sighted on the North Fork Wallace River. The trail itself is a gem, thanks to the work of the Washington Trails Association. Their volunteer crews have spent the past two years making the 2.75-mile hike up to the Upper Falls splendid!

To get there, from Monro drive on U.S. Highway 2 (Stevens Pass Highway) east to Gold Bar. Once in Gold Bar, turn left onto First Street, and in 0.4 mile reach a four-way stop. Turn right onto May Creek Road (signed for Wallace Falls State Park) and continue along this road. Follow the signs to the park, about 1.5 miles farther on.

From the trailhead, hike up the service road under the powerlines. Not the most spectacular scenery here, but a host of birds call this area home, and the hike under the lines can be passed quickly while watching the many species of sparrows and towhees, and about a million robins in the bushes lining the path.

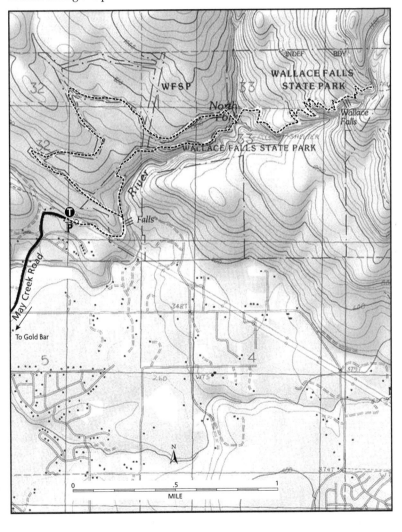

Tributary creek to Wallace River

Once past this first short section, enter the forest to a greeting of the roar of the Wallace River. Massive amounts of water pour down this river year-round, creating an impressive sight and sound. The loop begins here on the Woody Trail, which leads down to the river level. As you near the river, take the time to hike out the short (0.1 mile) side trail—built by an Eagle Scout working under the direction of WTA in 1995—leading to the most photogenic waterfall in the park.

Back on the Woody Trail there are numerous overlooks of the roaring Wallace River. When I hiked it, the river was lined with bright yellow Douglas maples in fall color making the scenes even more peaceful. At about 1.5 miles the trail crossed the North Fork Wallace River on a sturdy bridge, and here the roaring waters were hypnotic. American dippers were flying back and forth under the bridge, stopping on the mossy rocks and diving into the roaring waters.

After crossing the river the trail becomes quite steep, but the course of the next mile of switchbacks takes you past three incredible overlooks of waterfalls on the Wallace River. Lower Wallace Falls has a picnic spot and shelter and very open views of a wide torrent of water. Middle Wallace Falls is a good resting spot at 1200 feet and a view of the largest falls with a drop of more than 250 feet! The last 0.3 mile to Upper Wallace Falls is the roughest portion of the trail and is obviously still being worked on, but being the steepest part of the hike does make it worthwhile—the Upper

Falls is certainly the most spectacular as it forms a slight double-falls with a turn in the river in the middle.

From here, hike down the trail to the crossing of the North Fork Wallace River, and just past look for a signed trail leading 0.5 mile to a junction with the Old Railroad Grade path. Follow this downhill to return to the trailhead. These last 2.5 miles are easy and still beautiful as the former railroad route cuts through a mix of deciduous and conifer forest. About one mile from the trailhead is the signed junction with the Department of Natural Resources trail leading to Wallace Lake, still another 4 miles one way from this point. The service road connects the loop at the beginning of the Woody Trail, followed by a nice jaunt back out under the powerlines.

39 BALD EAGLE MOUNTAIN/ SKYKOMISH RIVER

Round trip ■	**24.4 miles**
Loop direction ■	Clockwise
Hiking time ■	2 to 3 days
Starting elevation ■	2500 feet
High point ■	6300 feet
Elevation gain ■	3800 feet
Best hiking time ■	Late July through early October
Maps ■	Green Trails Monte Cristo, No. 143 and Benchmark Mountain, No. 144
Contact ■	Mt. Baker–Snoqualmie National Forest, Skykomish Ranger District

This hike should be planned carefully to get good camps with water. Much of the trail can be dry late in the season, because it follows ridges. However, these ridges provide excellent scenic views of the Monte Cristo Peaks, Glacier Peak, Sloan Peak, and thousands of other mountaintops.

To get there, from Everett drive about 40 miles east on U.S. Highway 2 to the turnoff for Index, on the North Fork Skykomish River Road (FS Road 63). Follow it for 15.3 miles on pavement. Where the pavement ends, continue straight on FS Road 63. At 17.3 miles, continue straight (do not take the left turn for the Blanca Lake Trail). At 19.8 miles from US 2, park at the Quartz Creek and West Cady Ridge trailheads. The drive from Index takes 30 to 40 minutes. A pit toilet (no walls) is near the parking area. (The road continues straight to the North Fork Skykomish Trail about 1.5 miles, which you will walk at the end of the trip. Option: you can drop your packs and drive the rough road to the Skykomish River trailhead, then walk back.)

Quartz Creek Trail 1050 begins on well-maintained tread up the creek drainage. While you can see and hear Quartz Creek, you are not hiking right

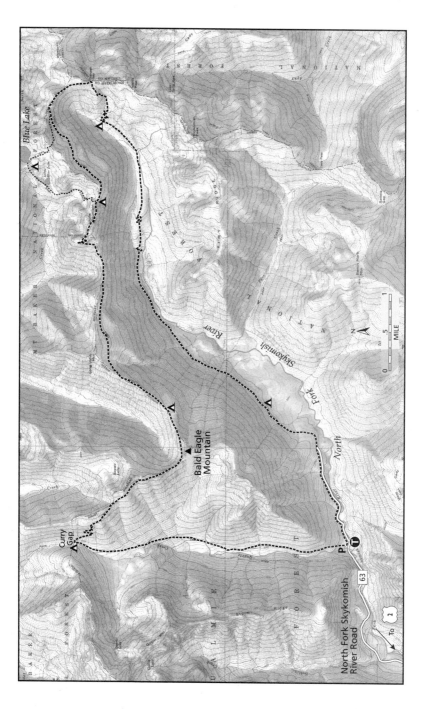

next to it. Fishers will have to walk down through relatively light brush to access the creek. The trail passes several creeks and climbs at a very reasonable rate to Curry Gap (4 miles, 2 hours), where there are several campsites.

Bald Eagle Trail 650 heads to the right at Curry Gap. Climbing much more steeply, it quickly ascends flowery meadows and enters the forest. After considerable huffing and puffing, it gains the ridge. Wandering possibilities galore are off-trail along the ridge, with some dry campsites with excellent views to the north. The trail stays below the ridgeline for a while, and then crosses it under Bald Eagle Mountain. This section of trail can have steep, hard snow late in season, but it is usually melted by August. (Bald Eagle can be scrambled off-trail on its east side.) The trail drops to a saddle between Bald Eagle and Long John Mountains. Here is an early-season camp (at 7.5 miles), with water from ponds. A better camp, well used, is below Long John Mountain at a spring (8.5 miles). (Long John can be scrambled on its south or east slopes.) Be prepared to see a lot of flowers in season!

The trail continues eastbound, climbing a ridge nearly to the top of June Mountain (5946 feet). Walk the short distance to the top to enjoy glorious views of the Blue Lakes, Johnson Mountain, Glacier Peak, and countless other peaks. The trail descends June Mountain to a junction at a saddle (11.2 miles). For better camps, continue to Blue Lake (12.7 miles), being careful to find the junction on Trail 652.1 (may be marked 652A), the Blue Lake High

Angel wing mushroom on the hike to Bald Eagle Mountain

Route. This trail is not built to the standards of the rest of the trail and has some considerably steep sections. But the scenery makes it well worth it.

After Blue Lake, the trail climbs to 6300 feet between two peaks, and then descends to a junction with the Bald Eagle Trail (13.8 miles) that you left soon after June Mountain. Continue straight on better tread to the meadows of Dishpan Gap (14.6 miles). Step for a moment on the Pacific Crest Trail, which winds its way from Mexico to Canada, then step back to find the trail down the Skykomish River. (This is a potentially confusing spot where several trails converge. The PCT heads north to White Pass, and south to Cady Pass and Stevens Pass.)

Skykomish River Trail 1051 heads in a generally western direction downhill, passing a few streams. There are good views of Skykomish Peak. The trail descends, passing through a flat meadow, and then into trees. Just before it crosses the Skykomish River (17.7 miles) is a good camp. The crossing will probably get your feet wet, unless you manage to cross a high log a bit upstream. Follow the trail downhill, staying straight at the junction with the Pass Creek Trail, to the end of FS Road 63. Then walk 1.5 miles on the road to the start of the loop.

40 ┊ CADY RIDGE LOOP

Round trip ■	**16 miles**
Loop direction ■	Clockwise
Hiking time ■	2 to 4 days
Starting elevation ■	3000 feet
High point ■	5600 feet
Elevation gain ■	2600 feet
Best hiking time ■	Mid-July through October
Map ■	Green Trails Benchmark Mountain, No. 144
Contact ■	Okanogan and Wenatchee National Forests, Lake Wenatchee Ranger District

There are three trails that depart the Little Wenatchee Ford Campground and intersect with the Pacific Crest Trail. Our recommendation for the most pleasing loop is to hike west up Cady Creek, north on the PCT, and east on the Cady Ridge Trail. Cady Creek has shorter and fewer stretches of heavy vegetation on the trail compared to the Little Wenatchee River Trail (Meander Meadows), and it lacks the considerable elevation gain of Cady Ridge. Hiking back on Cady Ridge allows for stunning views of Wenatchee Ridge/Poets Ridge and none of the relentless vegetation of Little Wenatchee River.

To get there, from Stevens Pass drive east on U.S. Highway 2 to the junction with State Route 207 (Lake Wenatchee Highway) and turn north (left) onto SR 207. At 4.3 miles from the US 2 junction, cross the Wenatchee River and stay left at a Y in the road. At 8.8 miles pass the Lake Wenatchee Ranger Station on the right, and at 10.7 miles, turn left as the White River Road goes right. At 16.8 miles continue straight following signs for FS Road 65 to the Little Wenatchee Ford Campground. On the left at 18.2 and 21 miles pass the Soda Springs and Wenatchee North Fork Creek Campgrounds, respectively. At 23.2 miles stay left at the Y, leaving asphalt, arriving at the trailhead at 26 miles from US 2, elevation 3000 feet.

From the trailhead, drop immediately to a bridge crossing the Little Wenatchee River. At 0.5 mile continue straight on Trail 1501, passing the junction with Cady Ridge Trail 1532. Hike the almost flat trail through virgin forest as it parallels Cady Creek, usually within earshot of the creek, but seldom within sight. At about 2.8 miles break out into a meadow with views west to the Pacific Crest. At 3.5 miles cross Cady Creek, 3400 feet, and find the first established campsites on the far side. From Cady Creek begin ascending the 900 feet to Cady Pass in a little more than 1.5 miles. At Cady Pass, 4300 feet and 5.2 miles from the trailhead, join the PCT. There are a number of possible campsites at Cady Pass, with water available a short 0.25 mile south on the PCT.

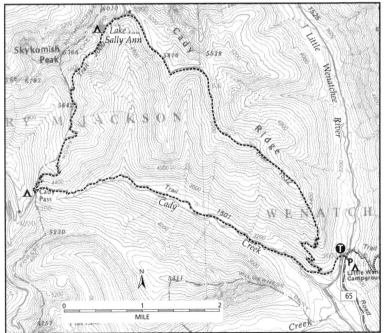

Ford at Cady Creek (Photo by Hally Swift)

From Cady Pass, switchback through forest and then meadows to grand views of the Cascade Mountains in all directions. Traverse the east slope of Skykomish Peak through lovely alpine meadows to Lake Sally Ann. Campsites are available at Lake Sally Ann and at the junction of the PCT and Cady Ridge Trail. The ideal trip would allow for an extra day or two of rambling up and down the PCT to explore lakes, peaks, and the numerous side trails. There are numerous campsites north of the PCT/Cady Ridge Trail, some dry, some near seasonal creeks.

For the return trip, pick up Trail 1532 at the junction of PCT/Cady Ridge Trail, elevation 5400 feet and 10 miles from the start of the trip. The trail first traverses the south side of Cady Ridge, walking through vertical meadows of corn lily, blueberries, and lupine. The trail switches back and forth from north to south, offering stunning views of the Pacific Crest including Glacier Peak, Skykomish Peak, and Wenatchee Ridge. In addition to zigzags from side to side, the trail also goes up and down with more up than you'd expect of a ridge walk. After approximately 3.5 miles the trail sticks to the south side of Cady Ridge and begins an earnest descent. After almost 1.5 miles of steep descent, hit the easy grade of eight switchbacks that meet up with Cady Creek Trail 1501. At the trail junction, elevation 3000 feet, turn left for the 0.5-mile return trip to the trailhead.

41 LITTLE WENATCHEE RIVER/ MEANDER MEADOWS

Round trip ■	18 miles
Loop direction ■	Counterclockwise
Hiking time ■	2 days
Starting elevation ■	3000 feet
High point ■	5800 feet
Elevation gain ■	2800 feet
Best hiking time ■	Mid-July through October
Map ■	Green Trails Benchmark Mountain, No. 144
Contact ■	Okanogan and Wenatchee National Forests, Lake Wenatchee Ranger District

Long valley-bottom hikes and an even longer ridge-top stroll await you here. This loop takes advantage of one of the most scenic stretches of the magnificent Pacific Crest Trail, providing wonderful views of Glacier Peak and all the fine summits of the Henry M. Jackson Wilderness.

To get there, from Stevens Pass drive east on U.S. Highway 2 to the junc-

The Little Wenatchee River holds native cutthroat as well as wily rainbow, and a few cut-bows.

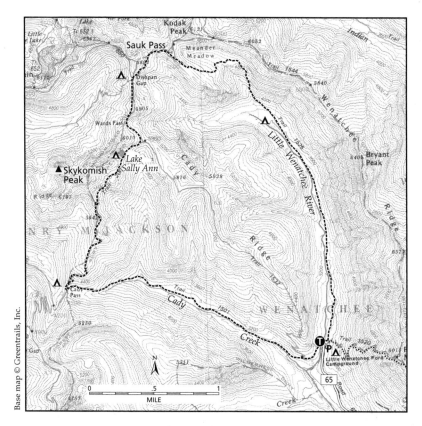

Base map © Greentrails, Inc.

tion with State Route 207 (Lake Wenatchee Highway) and turn north (left) onto SR 207. At 4.3 miles from the US 2 junction, cross the Wenatchee River and stay left at a Y in the road. At 8.8 miles pass the Lake Wenatchee Ranger Station on the right, and at 10.7 miles, turn left as the White River Road goes right. At 16.8 miles continue straight following signs for FS Road 65 to the Little Wenatchee Ford Campground. On the left at 18.2 and 21 miles pass the Soda Springs and Wenatchee North Fork Creek Campgrounds, respectively. At 23.2 miles stay left at the Y, leaving asphalt, arriving at the trailhead at 26 miles from US 2, elevation 3000 feet.

Several trails leave this trailhead, but for your purposes, you want the Little Wenatchee River Trail 1525. Follow this trail upstream, staying on the eastern side of the river for nearly 5 miles. The trail pierces lush forests and cuts through several open glades full of sunlight and bright flower blooms, often with the river tumbling along within earshot, if not always within view.

After 5 gentle miles, the trail turns away from the water and climbs steeply out of the valley and into the broad fields of Meander Meadow, first reached at about 6 miles. The grass-and-wildflower expanse serves as a natural pasture for resident deer but also for mountain goats as the meadows are set in a long, narrow cirque below Kodak Peak. At 7.1 miles, the trail intercepts the Pacific Crest Trail just south of Kodak Peak, at 5500 feet.

Turn left (south) on the PCT and hike on the rolling pass, neither gaining nor losing much elevation, to Sauk Pass and then Dishpan Gap, found at 7.8 miles. Great camping can be found at Dishpan Gap. Continue south from the Gap, staying roughly at the same elevation for most of the next 2 miles as you pass first Wards Pass (about 8.5 miles) and then Lake Sally Ann at 9.5 miles. Just before the lake, you'll see a side trail leading east along Cady Ridge. This is another option for the loop, saving you a couple miles in distance.

Staying on the PCT, though, you continue south around the flank of Skykomish Peak and at 13.5 miles, reach Cady Pass, 4300 feet. Turn left (east), and descend Cady Creek valley along a well-maintained trail, about 4.7 miles back to the trailhead, wrapping up an 18.2-mile trek.

42 ┊ INDIAN HEAD PEAK

Round trip ■	**26 miles**
Loop direction ■	Clockwise
Hiking time ■	3 days
Starting elevation ■	2300 feet
High point ■	5400 feet
Elevation gain ■	3100 feet
Best hiking time ■	July through mid-October
Maps ■	Green Trails Glacier Peak, No. 112, Holden, No. 113, Benchmark Mountain, No. 144, and Wenatchee Lake, No. 145
Contact ■	Okanogan and Wenatchee National Forests, Lake Wenatchee Ranger District

This long loop offers the best of both the east and west sides of the Cascades, including a trek along the crest of the mountain range. You'll find stupendous views from the Pacific Crest Trail, as well as from the summits of Kodak and Indian Head Peaks. To get those views, you'll pound up long, but scenic, valley-bottom trails, letting the massive old trees shade and cool you as you hike. Deer will walk near you, and birds will keep you company—first gentle little songbirds in the forests, and later soaring eagles and hawks on the highlands.

To get there, from Stevens Pass drive east 20 miles on U.S. Highway 2 to

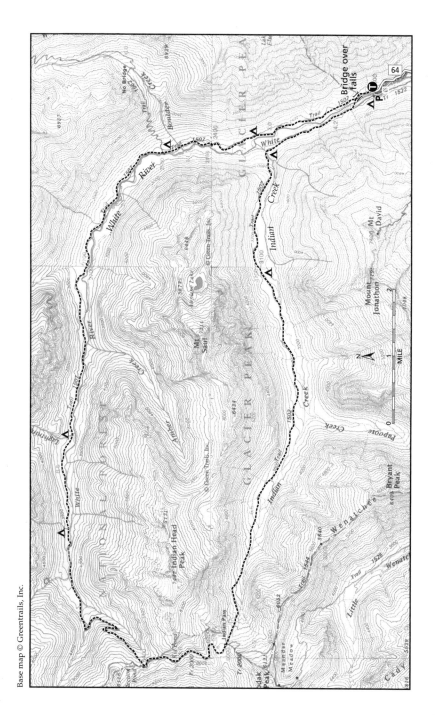

Coles Corner. Turn toward Lake Wenatchee on State Route 207. In 9 miles pass by the Lake Wenatchee Ranger Station. Turn right on the White River Road (FS 64) at 11 miles. The road changes to gravel after crossing the Napeequa River (17.5 miles). Continue to the end of the White River Road and the trailhead (21.5 miles).

Begin the trip by crossing the large bridge over the turbulent White River, near some small falls. The trail splits soon after the bridge. Continue left, upstream along the White River. The trail is within view of the glacial silt–filled, greenish river for some time. In about 2 flat miles, cross Indian Creek on a bridge and pass a camp (2400 feet, 2 miles). The trail climbs gradual switchbacks a short distance later, out of sight of Indian Creek. Then it flattens again as it heads west, and enters the first of many brushy sections. There are two camps (4 miles, 3200 feet) near creeks that drain into Indian Creek.

The flat valley has waist- to shoulder-high brush, interspersed with some forest areas, for several miles. There are some camps at 6.8 and 8.3 miles from the trailhead. The trail finally climbs switchbacks again. In the midst of these is an old shelter location (10 miles, 4800 feet) with a little water in late season. Just before Indian Pass, note an old sign on a tree prohibiting sheep grazing. Blueberries start here.

At Indian Pass (5000 feet, 10.7 miles) is the Pacific Crest Trail. Views

Indian Creek tributary in lush forest

expand of numerous play areas. One possibility is to hike southbound 1 mile to the flanks of Kodak Peak, then scramble up the path to the summit. Or turn right, heading northbound on the PCT. Scramble up the steep heather, pumice, and rock slopes to Indian Head Peak. Continue along the PCT to the White River Trail junction. There are more superb views farther north on the PCT, at White and Red Passes. But eventually, head down the White River Trail (campsite near the junction).

The trail descends through blueberry fields a few miles to the White River. There is a camp just before Foam Creek and the first crossing of White River. Another camp is lower on a more difficult crossing. This crossing may be difficult before mid-August. Now, enter the brushy White River valley for a long, gradual walk out. Camps are at Lightning Creek and the Boulder Creek Trail junction. Fifteen miles from the PCT is the end of the loop.

43 ┆ BASALT PEAK

Round trip ■	**10.2 miles**
Loop direction ■	Clockwise
Hiking time ■	2 days
Starting elevation ■	2500 feet
High point ■	5200 feet
Elevation gain ■	2700 feet
Best hiking time ■	Late June through October
Maps ■	Green Trails Wenatchee Lake, No. 145 and Plain, No. 146
Contact ■	Okanogan and Wenatchee National Forests, Lake Wenatchee Ranger District

Climb through cool forest full of wildlife. The trail loops through steeply climbing creek valleys and along smooth river-bottom meadows. You'll share the area with beasts large and small, from deer to deer mice. But you won't encounter many two-legged beasts since few people know of this scenic little sylvan route.

To get there, from Stevens Pass drive east on U.S. Highway 2 to Coles Corner and turn toward Lake Wenatchee. At 4.3 miles, after crossing the Wenatchee River turn right at the Y in the road, and in another 1.3 miles turn left at a road signed "Chiwawa Valley." Drive Chiwawa Valley Road (which becomes Chiwawa River Road and FS Road 6200 along the way) 14.6 miles to the Rock Creek Campground/Rock Creek trailhead (25 minutes). The last 5 miles are on a washboard gravel road.

Start the loop from the Rock Creek trailhead area by the Rock Creek Campground. If hiked in the autumn, you will find Rock Creek lined with yellow birch and gold-hued cottonwood trees. The 2.5 miles up the Rock Creek Trail passes through pretty, if fairly standard forest, staying well up from the creekside. The creek is a pretty, bouncing stream, and it's worth dropping off-trail for a rest break along its banks. The cold, clear water is a favorite hunting spot for American dippers, those spring-legged birds that bob and weave on rocks in the middle of tumbling rivers and streams before they lunge into the water to snatch aquatic insects from the river bottoms.

At a junction at 2.5 miles, turn right (east) and start a long steep climb up the Rock Creek Tie Trail. The 1.6-mile climb to the crest of Basalt Ridge gains a thigh-burning 1800 feet, and most of that comes in the first 1.2 miles! The long haul up this relentless trail is frequently broken with wildlife sightings—Douglas squirrels can often be seen tearing up cones for winter storage, while birds like the varied thrush hop and flit around the forest floor looking for bugs. Mule deer also make this forest home, and they can often be seen browsing through the rich ground cover between the trees.

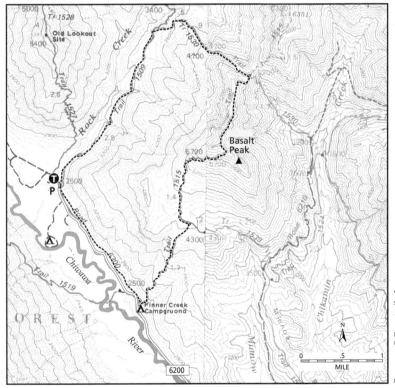

Base map © Greentrails, Inc.

Basalt Peak and the Chiwawa River valley, seen from Basalt Ridge

The junction with the Basalt Ridge Trail is reached at 4.1 miles. Turn right (south) and climb another 500 feet to Basalt Peak at 5.2 miles. From the west side of this mountain, just as the trails starts to descend, you'll be treated to views to the west and south that are awesome indeed.

From here, continue down the Basalt Peak Trail, and at 6.9 miles, find another trail junction, turn right and down, steeply now, another 1.7 miles to the Chiwawa River Road. As you near the road, you'll find the Finner Creek Campground at 8.5 miles. You could drop onto the road and hike the 1.7 miles back up the valley to the starting trailhead, but there is a well-maintained trail that parallels the road. This is the better option since it keeps you clear of the dust and traffic found on the road.

44 COUGAR MOUNTAIN

Round trip	11.2 miles
Loop direction	Counterclockwise
Hiking time	2 days
Starting elevation	4200 feet
High point	5900 feet
Elevation gain	1700 feet
Best hiking time	Late June through October
Map	Green Trails Plain, No. 146
Contact	Okanogan and Wenatchee National Forests, Lake Wenatchee Ranger District

Mad River Country offers some of the finest dry-side forest ecology in the state with a rich bounty of wildlife—four-legged beasts and winged

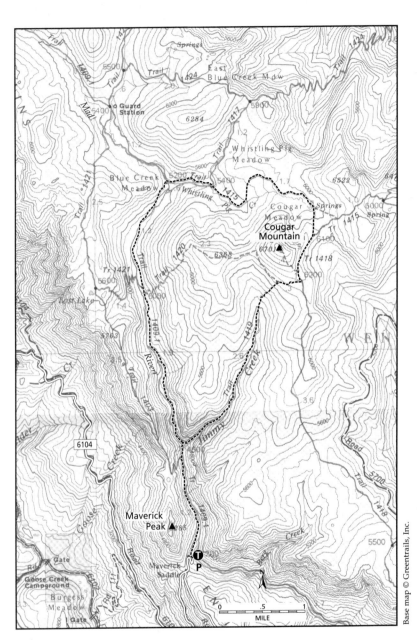

Base map © Greentrails, Inc.

avians—and an array of flora. You'll find fragrant forests of pine and fir and ridge-top meadows filled with lupine, balsamroot, and a slew of other wildflowers. Berries and mushrooms provide a natural bounty for food gatherers—just be aware that animals other than humans also are drawn to this bounty. Keep an eye out for black bears in this area since they thrive on the juicy fruits and rich green vegetation.

To get there, from Stevens Pass drive east on U.S. Highway 2 to Coles Corner and turn north onto State Route 207. Turn right onto Chiwawa Loop Road after crossing the river bridge 5.3 miles from US 2. Continue 5.4 miles on Chiwawa Loop Road and just after crossing a bridge and the Thousand Trails area, turn sharply left onto FS Road 6100. Drive 1.6 miles and turn right at Deep Creek Campground. At Morrow Meadow turn onto FS Road 6101 and continue 3.1 miles and turn left at Deer Camp Campground. Continue 3.1 miles and turn left at Deer Camp onto FS 6104. Continue 2.5 miles up a steep, rough route to Maverick Saddle, and drop down steeply to the left to the Mad River trailhead. (The drive to the trailhead at Maverick Saddle is worth the whole trip almost—amazing views to the west as you carefully drive up the last 2.5 miles! Just pray you don't meet someone head-on since backing up on this road would be a frightening experience.)

The trail begins through a beautiful, lichen-draped silver fir forest, following the beautiful Mad River upstream. The first bridge you cross (1.2 miles) is big enough to hold a locomotive—it was made to handle motorcycle traffic, as this nonwilderness trail is open to motorized use. Shortly past the mammoth bridge, turn right (east) and climb the Jimmy Creek Trail.

For the next 2.8 miles, you'll enjoy a slow elevation gain as you climb the gentle angle up the creek valley. The trail slices through a rich old forest

Close-up of snowfields on Glacier Peak, the dominant summit in the area

which contains, nestled like an oasis, a little valley covered with a lush meadow. The last mile of this climb changes tone and climbs steeply to the 6200-foot level on the flank of Cougar Mountain. Here, the trail cuts through wide, open meadows sprawling along the steep slopes of Cougar. These meadows boast a remarkable, rich crop of shooting-star blooms as well as a double-handful of other flower species.

At 4 miles, the trail intersects Cougar Ridge Trail 1418. Turn left (north) in just 0.1 mile, and come to a small side trail on the left. This boot-beaten track leads to the summit of Cougar Mountain in a short 0.5 mile, gaining just 500 feet to achieve the 6700-foot summit. This side trip is well worth the effort as you'll find stunning views in all directions from the lofty perch.

Back on the main trail, continue north and in another 0.5 mile, turn left again, this time on Whistling Pig Trail 1415. Descend through the picture-perfect fields of Cougar Meadow, skirt the edge of the vast, sprawling Whistling Pig Meadow, and drop into the valley-bottom pastures of Blue Creek Meadow at the junction with the Mad River Trail at 6.8 miles. Turn left onto the Mad River Trail and follow the river downstream, back to the trailhead at 11.2 miles.

45 | CATHEDRAL ROCK/DECEPTION PASS LOOP

Round trip ■	**14 miles**
Loop direction ■	Clockwise
Hiking time ■	7 hours, day hike or backpack
Starting elevation ■	3400 feet
High point ■	5600 feet
Elevation gain ■	2200 feet
Best hiking time ■	July through mid-October; wildflowers typically peak in late July
Map ■	Green Trails Stevens Pass, No. 176
Contact ■	Okanogan and Wenatchee National Forests, Cle Elum Ranger District

Warning: You may get a stiff neck from staring up at Cathedral Rock while trying not to trip over your feet during this spectacular walk along miles of the Pacific Crest Trail in the Cascades' Alpine Lakes section. But you should be willing to pay the price for so much beauty at so little cost. This hike can be done in a weekend at a modest pace, but if weather and schedule permit, linger and make side trips to various pristine alpine lakes.

To get there, from Seattle drive east on Interstate 90. Take Exit 84 off I-90, and follow State Route 903 through Roslyn (the set for TV's old sitcom *Northern Exposure*) into Wenatchee National Forest, passing Cle Elum Lake. Use Salmon la Sac Road to reach Salmon la Sac Campground, and then

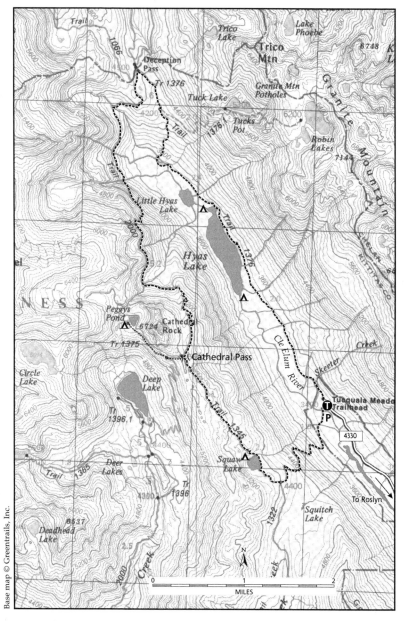

continue 12.6 miles on a good dirt road (FS Road 4330) to Tucquala Meadows trailhead in the Cle Elum River valley. Shortly before Tucquala Meadows you'll find unmarked car-camping sites left and right, but there is no camping at the meadows trailhead.

Cathedral Rock as seen from near Cathedral Pass

Cathedral Trail 1345 departs from the meadows, exacting its toll in a rapid ascent through switchbacks, rising from 3350 feet to 5500 feet just 4.5 miles later at Cathedral Pass. Take a long rest at lovely Squaw Lake, 2 miles in, 4841 feet. Plenty of water here all year, but overuse of the area has forced the forest service to move campsites away from the lake.

At Cathedral Pass, the Pacific Crest Trail enters from the south, in that direction a descent can be made to Deep Lake. Cathedral Rock (6724 feet, a tower shooting straight up) now looms just ahead, off the left side of the PCT heading north. The Rock and its many rockslides will be your constant companion from here on out. The ankles get a workout on some sections of scree.

After traversing alpine bogs where, under springtime snow cover the trail may be hard to locate, the PCT descends moderately but continues on the shoulder of Cathedral Rock for the next 4.5 miles. En route, two stream crossings may give you serious pause. Bone-chilling snowmelt, flushing fiercely down, can make these fords dangerous. One is shallow but wide, the next short but knee-deep. Your best bet is to confirm feasibility with the rangers before heading up, cross early in the morning, use walking sticks, keep dry clothing and boots protected, carry some rope, and unsnap your waist and chest straps on your backpack, and if in any doubt, reverse the course and enjoy hiking to alternate campsites.

En route now to Deception Pass, at the head of Cle Elum Valley, the rewards are constant. Marmots scamper across the rocks; a mountain goat may perch high above on a ledge of Cathedral Rock; alpine flowers—trillium, *Clintonia*, lupines, and more—grace the trailside; ravens, hawks, and the odd eagle ride the thermals up from the valley, especially in the morning sunshine. Deer roam here as do bear. Take precautions. Level campsites along this stretch of the PCT are primitive and few. It's a rocky world. Far down in the valley, Hyas Lake sparkles.

The gradual descent toward Deception Pass at 9 miles and 4475 feet brings you back into dense, cool, mossy and ever-so-quiet evergreen forest. The meeting with Marmot Lake Trail 1066 comes in a broad hollow where the PCT continues north but you turn south on Trail 1376, to drop steadily but easily to the level of Hyas Lake. You could also detour to Marmot Lake and back before heading for home (adding 7 miles to the round-trip distance). On Trail 1376, it's wide and smooth all the way to the Tucquala Meadows trailhead, under shady, towering pines and eventually, lower down, beneath hardwoods.

Paralleling the shoreline, look back across the marshy lake toward Cathedral Rock to admire your climbing efforts and to snap photos of the thin but intense waterfall plummeting off the steep side of the valley. You waded through that water. Odds are that when Tucquala Meadows reappears, you'll be sorry the trip is over.

46 ┊ SQUAW LAKE/TRAIL CREEK

Round trip ■	**21.5 miles**
Loop direction ■	Counterclockwise
Hiking time ■	2 to 3 days
Starting elevation ■	3400 feet
High point ■	5600 feet
Elevation gain ■	2200 feet
Best hiking time ■	July through mid-October
Maps ■	Green Trails Stevens Pass, No. 176 and Kachess Lake, No. 208
Contact ■	Okanogan and Wenatchee National Forests, Cle Elum Ranger Station

Broad, valley-bottom meadows, deep, cold lakes, and outrageous gorgeous views await you here. Of course, so too do mosquitoes, crowds of hikers, and long miles of forest hiking. But even those things can be appreciated—or last least minimized—by hiking this route in early autumn, when the bugs are dead, the hiking crowds have pretty much put away their packs, and the forests are alive with wildlife as the beasts race to put on weight for the long winter ahead.

To get there, from Seattle drive east on Interstate 90. Take Exit 84 off I-90, and follow State Route 903 through Roslyn (the set for TV's old sitcom *Northern Exposure*) into Wenatchee National Forest, passing Cle Elum Lake. Use Salmon la Sac Road to reach Salmon la Sac Campground, and then continue 12.6 miles on a good dirt road (FS Road 4330) to Tucquala Meadows trailhead in the Cle Elum River valley. Shortly before Tucquala Mead-

Base map © Greentrails, Inc.

ows you'll find unmarked car-camping sites left and right, but there is no camping at the meadows trailhead.

From the parking area, cross the Cle Elum River and start the modest climb up the west wall of the valley. You'll gain 1000 feet in the 1.8 miles to the junction with Trail Creek Trail. Stay right at the trail junction and continue up the ridge, pausing at the occasional opening in the trees to admire the view across the valley to the Wenatchee Mountains. Just 0.5 mile past the junction, you'll pass Squaw Lake. This gentle, shallow pond provides a perfect place to camp for families, but others should press on. From Squaw, the trail follows the ridge spine northwest for another 2.2 miles to intersect the Pacific Crest Trail at the foot of Cathedral Rock. Great views can be had

Squaw Lake en route to Cathedral Pass

all along this stretch of trail, and there are plenty of camping possibilities in the broad meadows and near the many small tarns that dot the ridgeline.

At the PCT junction, turn left (south) and in just 0.25 mile, cross over a sharp ridgeline and begin a long, steep descent to Deep Lake, at 7.6 miles. The trail winds down through forests and meadows before popping out into a meadow at the lake's outlet. You'll have to wade across Spinola Creek—the water is generally not more than shin deep—to find the great campsites along the south and west sides of the lake. Midway along the southwest side is best, as these provide good views up the side of Mount Daniel, which is lined with ribbons of waterfalls as the meltwater from the glaciers pours off the peak.

The PCT continues south from Deep Lake and slides down Spinola Creek valley through long expanses of meadow, to a trail junction at 11.1 miles. Stay left as the PCT goes right, and you'll be on the shores of Waptus Lake in just 1.5 miles. Campsites can be found all along the eastern shore of this 2-mile-long lake.

Hike south to the lake's outlet and continue down the Waptus River valley 1.5 miles to the mouth of Trail Creek valley and the junction with the Trail Creek Trail at 14.2 miles. Turn left up Trail Creek Trail and climb 2.5 steep miles to the 4300-foot intersection with the Lake Michael Trail. Bear left to stay in Trail Creek basin and in 3 miles you'll be back on the trail to Squaw Lake, at 19.7 miles. To close the loop, stroll down the 1.8 miles back to the trailhead.

47 TROUT LAKE

Round trip ■	**12.2 miles**
Loop direction ■	Clockwise
Hiking time ■	8 hours, day hike or backpack
Starting elevation ■	2800 feet
High point ■	5600 feet
Elevation gain ■	2800 feet
Best hiking time ■	July through mid-October
Map ■	Green Trails Chiwaukum Mountains, No. 177
Contact ■	Okanogan and Wenatchee National Forests, Leavenworth Ranger District

This aptly named lake should be of special interest to anglers, though anyone will appreciate the charm and beauty of the lake basin and the scenic forest ecology explored during the trek to the lake.

To get there, from U.S. Highway 2 in Leavenworth, from the north end of town, turn west onto Icicle Creek Road. Follow Icicle Creek Road about 17 miles from the highway. Just past Rock Island Campground, turn left into the Jack Creek trailhead.

The trail pushes gently up the pine-forested Jack Creek valley, crossing

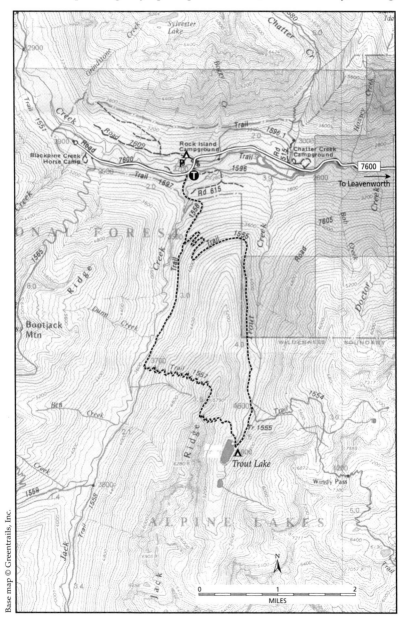

Jack Creek at 0.3 mile and entering the Alpine Lakes Wilderness just 0.1 mile farther on. The trail climbs the slope west of the creek and then traverses along the ridge wall until reaching a junction at 1.2 miles. This is the start of the loop, and by completing it clockwise, you'll enjoy a gentler climb. So turn left and enter a series of long, looping switchbacks which carry you up the snout of Jack Ridge and around to the Trout Creek valley. Once on the Trout Creek side of the ridge, the trail makes a straight shot south, slicing through bird-infested forests above the cascading waters of the creek.

The trail splits at 5.2 miles. Stay right this time to continue up Trout Creek. The climb is moderate from here, gaining just 300 feet in 0.5 mile to enter the Trout Lake basin at 5.7 miles. Stop, rest, set up camp, or just rig your fishing rod to try for some of the pan-sized trout in the lake. No matter what you do, take a moment or two to simply gaze at the beauty around you. The tall rocky top of Eightmile Mountain sits high above the lake, while the long line of Jack Ridge stretches to the southwest.

When its time to go, angle west from the lake's outlet as the trail climbs the slope to the crest of Jack Ridge. The trail climbs for 1.5 miles, but only gains about 800 feet, until you cross the spine of the ridge—amidst glori-

Western fence lizard along trail to Trout Lake

ous views—at 5600 feet, about 7.2 miles from the trailhead. Enjoy the views, then tighten your bootlaces and pack straps as preparation for the knee-jarring descent into Jack Creek valley.

Over the next 2 miles, you'll pound down 1900 feet through tight, twisting switchbacks, to return to the Jack Creek Trail. Turn right onto this path and enjoy the now gentle descent along the forested valley bottom. In 1.8 miles—11 miles from the trailhead—you'll pass the start of the loop route. The last 1.2 miles of trail back to the trailhead goes quickly as you wrap up the 12.2-mile loop.

48 ┊ THE CRADLE

Round trip	■	**21 miles**
Loop direction	■	Counterclockwise
Hiking time	■	2 to 3 days
Starting elevation	■	2900 feet
High point	■	6100 feet
Elevation gain	■	3200 feet
Best hiking time	■	July through mid-October
Maps	■	Green Trails Stevens Pass, No. 176 and Chiwaukum Mountains, No. 177
Contact	■	Okanogan and Wenatchee National Forests, Leavenworth Ranger District

The clear mountain air, strenuous climbing, and glorious scenery should have you sleeping like a baby when staying at Cradle Lake. But it's not the sleep you will come here for. It's the waking hours that make this trip a pleasure, especially if you like river valleys, old growth forests, and wildlife viewing opportunities. As a bonus, you'll find high alpine meadows, great mountain views, and peaceful alpine pools by which to camp.

To get there, from U.S. Highway 2 in Leavenworth, from the north end of town, turn west onto Icicle Creek Road. Follow Icicle Creek Road to its end, about 20 miles. At the road's end, find the trailhead near the Blackpine Creek Horse Camp.

Find Icicle Creek Trail 1551 at the end of road and start hiking upstream along the trail. After 1.5 miles of walking through pretty forests in the river valley, turn left onto French Creek Trail 1595. This long river valley curves around to the west and south. You'll find ancient ponderosa pine trees, intermingled with firs and larches, along this trail, with several broad meadows and forest clearings along the way. Look for deer as you quietly hike up the valley—black-tails are common in this basin and on the slopes about the creek. Also keep an eye open for smaller critters, from weasels and martens to raccoons and bobcats.

At 5.1 miles, you'll notice a side trail leading up and to the right. Ignore this path, but watch for the next junction, at 6.2 miles. Here, you have a

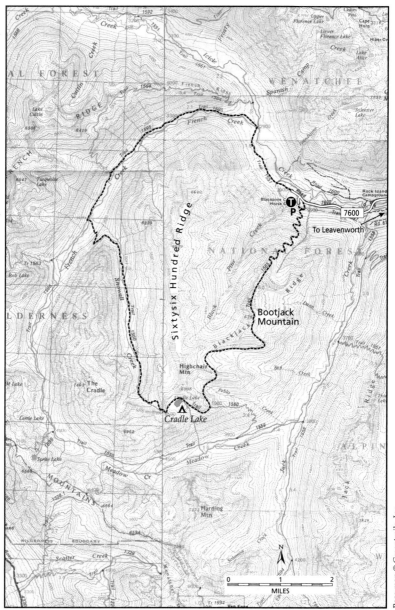

The new footbridge over French Creek

choice. The route straight ahead is easier going, but also longer and less scenic than the path to the left. Both loop around to the same place, but the best bet is to take the slightly shorter, steeper trail as the scenery is well worth the extra effort.

So turn left, cross French Creek, and climb steeply at times up the Snowall Creek valley. For 5.5 miles, the trail runs nearly straight up the valley, gaining more than 2700 feet. As you climb, take notice of the tall peak on your right (west). This is The Cradle (7467 feet). The view of The Cradle becomes increasingly clear and impressive as you climb the valley. At 11.7 miles, you cross the meadow-covered ridge above the headwaters of French Creek and traverse about 0.5 mile around into Cradle Lake basin. Excellent camps can be found around this alpine pool, with the best on the south side where you can peer up at Highchair Mountain.

From the lake, the trail descends about a mile to 5300 feet and another trail split. Turn sharply left to stay high and follow the contours of Black-jack Ridge north, rolling high along the eastern flank of Bootjack Mountain (6789 feet) at about 14 miles. From there, the trail drops to the north at an ever-steeper rate, until the last mile and a twisting mess of switchbacks lead back to the trailhead at 21 miles.

49 ICICLE RIDGE

Round trip ■	**19.6 miles**
Loop direction ■	Clockwise
Hiking time ■	2 to 3 days
Starting elevation ■	3000 feet
High point ■	6800 feet
Elevation gain ■	3800 feet
Best hiking time ■	July through mid-October
Map ■	Green Trails Chiwaukum Mountains, No. 177
Contact ■	Okanogan and Wentachee National Forests, Cle Elum Ranger District

This route explores country that's majestic and beautiful at all times, but to experience the true magic of this trail, hike it in autumn. The shimmering gold larches stand like living beacons along the route, while the crimson, amber, and bronze leaves of vine maples and slide alders color the slopes around you. Fiery red huckleberry bushes cover the forest floor, and amidst it all stand the dark, brooding green giants: Douglas fir, hemlock, cedar, and the orange-skinned ponderosa pine. This lasso-shaped loop necessitates a commute to the highlands that must be repeated, but is worth all the effort and then some.

To get there, from U.S. Highway 2 in Leavenworth, from the north end of town, turn west onto Icicle Creek Road. Follow Icicle Creek Road 15.8 miles from the highway. Turn right at the sign for the Chatter Creek Trail for 0.1 mile to the parking area. Just before this turnoff, near Chatter Creek Campground, are outhouses.

Begin hiking the Chatter Creek Trail 1580 along an old roadbed. After a short distance, the old road ends and the trail tilts uphill on a series of steep switchbacks. But the tread is kind to the feet and the climb (theoretically) doesn't last as long this way. Hikers starting in the afternoon can rest their weary bones at two campsites en route. The first is in about 2 miles near where the trail thankfully levels out for a short while. The second is 0.75 mile farther just before the forest gives way to splendid and expansive views of Icicle Ridge.

Enjoying the near continuous views for many miles, continue up and up to the shoulder of Grindstone Mountain (6800 feet). Although the scramble up Grindstone looks straightforward from this shoulder, the true summit is easier after descending over the other side for a short distance. Stop and soak in the terrain below. Behind and far below is the Chatter Creek drainage. Icicle Ridge is to your right. Ahead are peaks and valleys and meadow and tree heaven.

Losing 300 feet of precious elevation, follow the trail to a level rock-and-

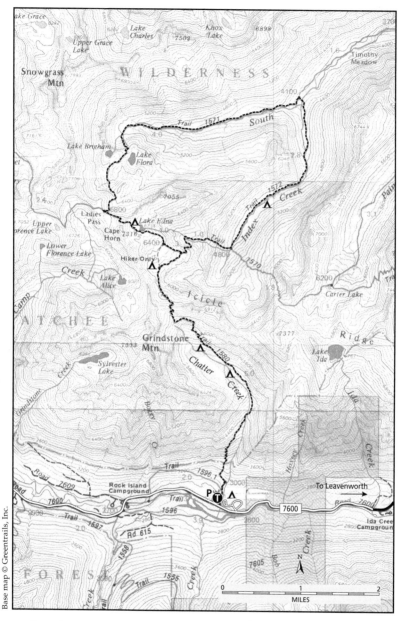

sand garden. The trail is a bit confusing through here, but follow cairns or footprints to glorious grassy meadowland. Here are camping possibilities at 5 miles. In the grass, the traffic isn't heavy enough to wear a solid path, so wander about looking for cairns and tread. Eventually the tread reappears shortly before the junction with the signed Icicle Ridge Trail 1570. Continue on the left branch to the barren Lake Edna at 5.8 miles. Camping is not allowed within 200 feet of Lake Edna, and besides, superior camps are just a few miles farther.

Continue up past Cape Horn, which can be scrambled on gravelly loose slopes, to Ladies Pass at 6.3 miles. Enjoy views of Mounts Rainier, Daniel, and Hinman. Here the paths diverge in more grass. Take Trail 1571 to the right, which descends down several generations of switchbacks to the forest.

Drop on switchbacks through the forest and brushy slopes to the bottom at 5300 feet. Towering cliffs rise above this mini–Napeequa Valley, carpeted with grass. The trail through the grass is confusing, but heading downstream along the river is the obvious direction. Keep poking about for the tread, which is faster and more pleasant than stomping through the meadow. The trail drops very gradually to a marked junction with Index Creek Trail 1572 at 10.8 miles and 4100 feet. Trust the sign, and continue through brush to more obvious tread in the trees.

Index Creek Trail is a lonely, rarely hiked path. It continues up through forest on a mostly gentle gradient for 2.8 miles. Halfway along is a lovely campsite at 12.2 miles, just before expansive meadows. Continue through the meadows to more forest trail to the junction with Icicle Ridge Trail 1570 at 13.6 miles. Turn right and go uphill. Be careful to stay on the path, because there are some spots where the trail can be lost in meadow. One mile after the junction is the end of the loop portion, and the 5-mile return to the trailhead via the high country with its expansive views.

50 ■ BULLS TOOTH

Round trip ■	**28.5 miles**
Loop direction ■	Counterclockwise
Hiking time ■	3 to 4 days
Starting elevation ■	2800 feet
High point ■	5600 feet
Elevation gain ■	2800 feet
Best hiking time ■	July through mid-October
Maps ■	Green Trails Wenatchee Lake, No. 145, Stevens Pass, No. 176, and Chiwaukum Mountains, No. 1757
Contact ■	Okanogan and Wenatchee National Forests, Leavenworth Ranger District

You never get to touch it, but Bulls Tooth is always there, sticking up from the center of this long, rambling route. The loop follows three creek valleys—Whitepine, Wildhorse, and Icicle—and crosses two low divides between them, in the heart of the Alpine Lakes Wilderness. You'll find great wildflower meadows, wonderful mountain-viewing opportunities, and a chance to meet and greet a variety of critters.

To get there, drive east from Stevens Pass on U.S. Highway 2, and turn

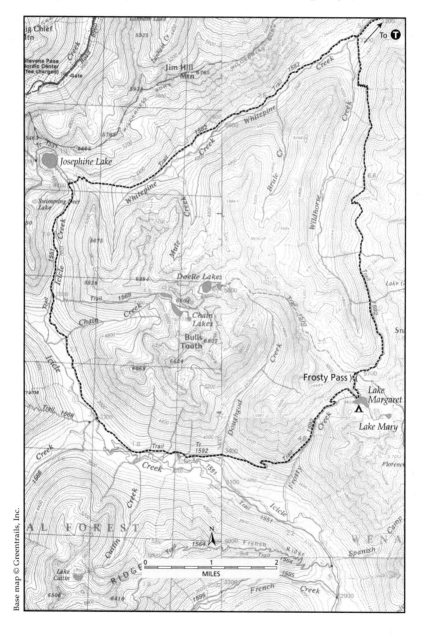

right (south) onto White Pine Creek Road (FS Road 6950). Drive past the campground to the road's end, about 4 miles.

The trail climbs 2.5 miles up the Whitepine Creek valley in the shadow of Arrowhead Mountain to the start of the loop. This initial stage of the trip gains just 400 feet, and you can move quickly through the cool forest of the valley bottom. At 2.5 miles, the trail splits. Go left (south) to do the loop counterclockwise for the best views. The trail climbs from the junction, sloping gradually up the wall of Wildhorse Creek valley, before encountering a short but rugged series of switchbacks at about 3.5 miles. Less than 0.5 mile of switchbacks lead back into a long, climbing ramble up the Wildhorse Creek basin. At about 5.5 miles, the trail pushes up into alpine meadows above 5000 feet and opens onto incredible views of Bulls Tooth (6807 feet) to the west and Snowgrass Mountain (7993 feet) to the southeast. You'll now hike south toward Snowgrass, still slowly gaining elevation until you reach a fork at Frosty Pass, on the flank of Snowgrass Mountain at 9.1 miles.

There is a four-way intersection at the pass. The right branch leads to what's essentially a dead end—a trail that hasn't been maintained for many years and is now nearly impassable. To the left is the Icicle Ridge Trail and potentially many more days of hiking. Straight ahead is our path. You could camp near the pass—you'll certainly have wonderful views if you do, but it will be a dry camp and likely very windy at dusk. A better bet is to push your tired legs a little farther and drop 0.5 mile down the other side of the pass to Lake Margaret at the head of Frosty Creek valley. There

Massive triple-trunk, old-growth cedar along the Whitepine Creek Trail

are wonderful camps available here and still nice views south into the Icicle Creek valley and beyond.

From Lake Margaret, the trail drops about 2 miles down Frosty Creek valley before rolling west in a long traverse to Doughgod Creek valley and then on across and down, eventually joining Icicle Creek Trail at 13.8 miles from the trailhead.

Turn right onto Icicle Creek Trail and trudge upstream along this stunning mountain creek for 6 miles. You'll find many clearings and sun-baked meadows along the river trail to break up the forest monotony, and in each of these, as well as in the forest between them, you have a fine chance of seeing some kind of wildlife.

At 19.8 miles turn right and climb a short 0.5 mile to a low saddle (4600 feet) separating Icicle Creek from Whitepine Creek. Once you're over the saddle, drop about a mile to the north bank of Whitepine Creek, which the trail now follows all the way back to the start of the loop at 26 miles. From there, you simply retrace your footsteps the last 2.5 miles to close out your tour.

51 ¦ WAPTUS LAKE

Round trip	■	**22.8 miles**
Loop direction	■	Clockwise
Hiking time	■	2 to 3 days
Starting elevation	■	2800 feet
High point	■	5500 feet
Elevation gain	■	2700 feet
Best hiking time	■	July through early autumn
Maps	■	Green Trails Snoqualmie Pass, No. 207, Kachess Lake, No. 208, and Stevens Pass, No. 176
Contact	■	Okanogan and Wenatchee National Forests, Cle Elum Ranger District

A modest hike up a spectacular river valley, a pretty little alpine lake, and a strenuous trek up and over and high, meadow-lined mountain ridge await you on this loop trip. More adventurous hikers can modify the route by adding excursions up to more remote and scenic lakes, down into deep river valleys, and/or around high, craggy peaks.

To get there, from Seattle drive east on Interstate 90 and take Exit 80 (signed "Roslyn/Salmon la Sac"), and head north on Salmon la Sac Road about 15 miles, passing through Roslyn and by Cle Elum Lake. Turn left (west) onto FS Road 46 and drive 5 miles to Cooper Lake. Turn right onto

Base map © Greentrails, Inc.

FS Road 4616, crossing the Cooper River, and continue 1 mile past the upper loops of the campground to the trailhead at the end of the road near the upper end of the lake.

Trail 1323 follows the broad Cooper River valley upstream for 4.4 miles to Pete Lake. The valley is blanketed with thick, old-growth forest and the occasional river meadow, but few views. Pete Lake, though, offers good views of Summit Chief Mountain to the west, and the surrounding ridges. The lake boasts good campsites, but because it is easily reached, the camps tend to fill up fast on hot summer weekends, and the rustic shelter near the lake seems to always have someone lingering in it.

The trail skirts the eastern and northern sides of the lake before heading up the Lemah Creek valley. The trail climbs steeply along the creek to a junction at 6 miles. Stay right on Trail 1323.2 which heads 0.75 mile up to Lemah Meadows on the Pacific Crest Trail (PCT) (the left fork slants south toward Spectacle Lake). There are camp possibilities in the meadows along the PCT; good water from Lemah Creek crosses the trail just south of where you join the PCT. From the meadows, you'll find wonderful view of Summit Chief Mountain.

Once on the PCT, head north as it continues up the north fork of Lemah Creek. After less than a mile of walking on the PCT the trail turns steep as it climbs a long series of switchbacks in the next 5 miles. Along the way, you'll find increasingly fine views as the forest gives way to broad, open meadows. In addition to Summit Chief Mountain, you can look north to the glacier-covered summit of Mount Daniel. As the trail crests

Deep Lake and Mount Daniel, a few miles from Waptus Lake on the PCT

the 5500-foot level on the ridge above Escondido Lake, the route levels out and traverses the meadows past a few small tarns—and a couple of nice campsites—before starting a slow descent toward Waptus Lake, seen to the north in the valley far below.

Before dropping too far, though, you'll leave the PCT. At the 5200-foot level—about 13 miles from the trailhead—look for a junction with a small trail leading off to the right. While the PCT continues north, Trail 1329.3 descends southeast to Waptus Pass, at the 16-mile mark. Note: You can add about 8 miles to your total loop distance by continuing to Waptus Lake, circling around its northern shore, then climbing to Waptus Pass on Trail 1329.

From Waptus Pass, turn right onto Trail 1329 and descend a steep series of switchbacks to the shores of Pete Lake. A quick left turn onto Trail 1323 returns you to your starting point.

52 WEST PEAK/THOMAS MOUNTAIN

Round trip ■	**12.8 miles**
Loop direction ■	Clockwise
Hiking time ■	8 hours
Starting elevation ■	2400 feet
High point ■	5400 feet
Elevation gain ■	3000 feet
Best hiking time ■	Early July through early autumn
Map ■	Green Trails Kachess Lake, No. 208
Contact ■	Okanogan and Wenatchee National Forests, Cle Elum Ranger District

Few unprotected areas surrounded by so much logging offer such a bounty of beauty. Sprawling alpine meadows filled with clouds of hummingbirds and herds of deer and elk await you. Great views of deep valley-bottom lakes and sky-scraped summits greet you. And solitude can be almost assured on this lonely, seemingly forgotten trail.

To get there, from Seattle drive east on Interstate 90 to Exit 70 at Easton. Turn left over the freeway, and left again onto the freeway side road. In about 0.5 mile turn right onto FS Road 4818. It becomes dirt and at 0.4 mile turn right under the power trestle (FS Road 203). After 0.6 mile of rough road there is a five-way intersection—take the most obvious left (about a 90-degree turn) and continue straight to the road's end at the trailhead area for the southern terminus of Trail 1315.

Even the most enthusiastic hiker will be slowed by the relentless climbing early in the hike. Indeed, just yards into the hike, the trail turns ruthless, pitching upward steeply as it gains more than 1700 feet in the first 1.8 miles. The route passes through vast fields of wildflowers, which typically

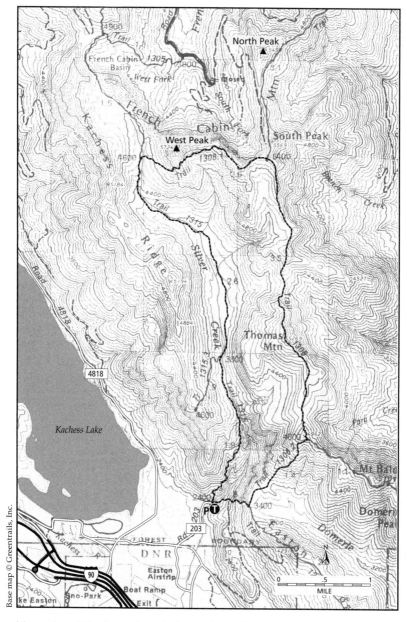

bloom from July through early September—by one count, more than forty-one different species filled the fields.

At 2 miles, a small way trail leads off to the left, climbing 1 mile to the summit of an unnamed peak to the west. The main trail continues north,

On the ridge, pass through fabulous meadows dotted with perfect alpine firs.

however, crossing the first of seven crossings of Silver Creek. The crossings, for the most part, lack foot logs and you might get wet feet as you rock-hop across the streams—a sturdy hiking staff, or better, a pair of trekking poles, is a great help.

After about 3.5 miles the trail begins to level off and you then spend the next 1.5 miles walking through incredible pristine meadows, which are a highlight of this trip. While the country around this trail sits well outside the protective embrace of the Alpine Lakes Wilderness Area, there is a wilderness feel to it. Few people use this trail, possibly because it is outside the wilderness, and as a result, deer and elk love the broad, foliage-rich meadows and can be frequently seen in the meadows, especially during morning and evening hours. Birds also love the area, and hummingbirds flock to the sweet blooms of the abundant wildflowers.

At the junction with the Silver Tie Trail, about 4.5 miles from the trailhead, turn right and climb through meadows along the south side of West Peak. The trail is faint and brush covered on its eastern end, but by sticking to the ridge crest at about 5200 feet, the trail is quickly found—just walk east and you'll run into South Peak Trail 1308, about 7 miles out.

Turn right (south) on the South Peak Trail and stroll south, enjoying the views down to Cle Elum Lake and up to the summit of Thomas Mountain. In 3.5 miles, turn right onto connector Trail 1308.2 and hike 2 miles southwest back to the trailhead.

53 THORP MOUNTAIN

Round trip	■	**8.5 miles**
Loop direction	■	Clockwise
Hiking time	■	8 hours
Starting elevation	■	3500 feet
High point	■	5854 feet
Elevation gain	■	2300 feet
Best hiking time	■	June through early autumn
Map	■	Green Trails Kachess Lake, No. 208
Contact	■	Okanogan and Wenatchee National Forests, Cle Elum Ranger District

It's a short hike, but one to tax the strength of even the toughest hiker. The strenuous climb earns you great rewards. The top of Thorp Mountain sports a rustic old fire lookout cabin, and anywhere these watch stations were constructed you'll find outstanding views in every direction. Thorp is no different—from the heather-carpeted top of the peak you can scan the horizon, picking out peaks and valleys throughout the Alpine Lakes Wilderness, but also down into the South Cascades (Mount Rainier can be seen on clear days). The ridges rolling away from the mountain sport colorful wildflower meadows, and the blue pool of Kachess Lake sparkles in the deep valley at the foot of the mountain.

To get there, from Seattle drive east on Interstate 90, take Exit 80 (signed "Roslyn/Salmon la Sac"), and head north on Salmon la Sac Road about 15 miles, passing through Roslyn and by Cle Elum Lake. Just past the upper end of the lake, turn left onto French Cabin Creek Road (FS Road 4308). Drive 3.25 miles up FS Road 4308 to FS Road 4312 on the right. Go right and drive 1.5 miles to another road junction, with FS Road 4312-121. This road is typically gated, so park here (do not block the gate), and walk around the gate and 0.25 mile to a bridge over Thorp Creek. Cross the creek and turn left. The true trail starts 0.25 mile up this road on the left.

The trail climbs steadily but modestly as it parallels the tumbling Thorp Creek. Keep your eyes wide open and you might be lucky and spot a lot of wildlife along the lower trail, especially as the path leaves the stands of forest and pops briefly into old, overgrown clear-cuts. These transition zones are popular places for deer to hang out, since they provide good cover (the forest) as well as close proximity to good browse (the clear-cuts).

About 1.5 miles from the gate, the trail starts to climb more steeply, angling upward away from the creek. As the trail gains elevation, the forest thins more and more, providing more sun breaks and viewpoints. At nearly 3 miles, a small side trail drops 0.5 mile to Thorp Lake. If time permits, this makes a nice side trip on the return. But on the way up, bypass this trail and continue climbing as the trail sweeps upward around the headwall of the Thorp Creek valley.

At 3 miles, another junction is reached, this time with the Kachess Ridge Trail. Stay left as it angles west around the flank of Thorp Mountain and in

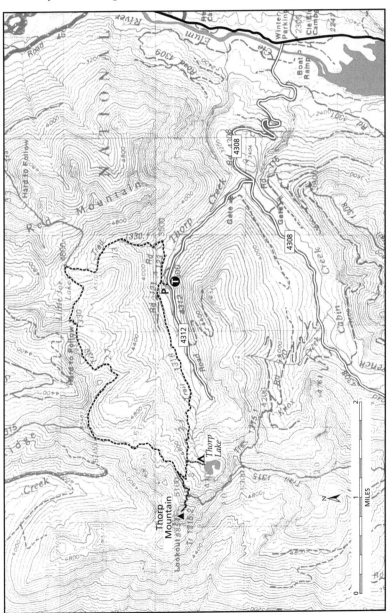

Base map © Greentrails, Inc.

Thorp Mountain Lookout, one of only three staffed lookouts in Wenatchee National Forest

less than 0.25 mile, go left to climb the steep scramble trail to the top of the mountain and its awesome views.

To complete the loop, drop back down the Kachess Ridge Trail and follow it northeast along No Name Ridge for 1.5 miles. At that point, about 4.5 miles from the trailhead, turn right onto a faint trail heading west and follow it to Little Joe Lake, at 7 miles. This trail can be brushy and hard to follow at times. At Little Joe Lake, turn right and descend 1.5 miles along the trail back to the trailhead.

54 POLALLIE RIDGE

Round trip ■	**19.4 miles**
Loop direction ■	Counterclockwise
Hiking time ■	2 days
Starting elevation ■	2400 feet
High point ■	5428 feet
Elevation gain ■	3000 feet
Best hiking time ■	June through early autumn
Map ■	Green Trails Kachess Lake, No. 208
Contact ■	Okanogan and Wenatchee National Forests, Cle Elum Ranger District

Early summer and late autumn are the prime times here, though the trail is open all summer and wildflowers color the ridge through much of July and August. But those wildflowers are there for a reason—to partake of the bounty of sunlight. The sun beats down on Polallie Ridge with unrelenting heat during the dog days of summer, and the lack of water along the high route makes for a long, dry day on the trail. Visitors who hit the trail during the mellow temperatures of June or September will still find wildflowers and won't be blinded by endless rivers of sweat in their eyes. And you do want to be able to see, for the ridge provides grand views, sweeping in an array of peaks, ridges, and valleys that form the eastern face of the Cascade Range.

To get there, from Seattle drive east on Interstate 90, take Exit 80 (signed "Roslyn/Salmon la Sac"), and head north on the Salmon la Sac Road about 15 miles, passing through Roslyn and by Cle Elum Lake to Salmon la Sac. At the Y in the road near the Salmon la Sac Campground, take the left branch toward Salmon la Sac Campground. Cross the Cle Elum River bridge and turn right away from the campground to the trailhead parking in another 0.5 mile.

This loop is best done counterclockwise so you only have easy downhill and flat hiking to do the last 7 miles. The trail begins with a long climb up the eastern side of Polallie Ridge, ascending through open, sun-baked switchbacks weaving through rock gardens. In 3 miles, the trail finally

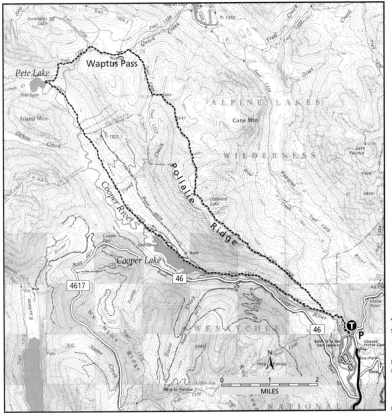

Base map © Greentrails, Inc.

Mount Hinman from Polallie Ridge

tapers to a more moderate pitch around 5000 feet elevation. But the respite from the climbing is short lived. A few hundred yards of easy ridge-top hiking is followed by a roll down to 4800 feet, and then a climb up to 5300 feet. Soon, it's down to 4900 feet, then up to 5200, down to 4700, up to 5500. And on and on.

The effect is like a roller coaster ride, except in the end, the ups are always a bit longer and steeper than the downs, so after 8 miles, you have a net gain of more than 3000 feet, but when you add in all the gains and losses, you have a total gain of more than 4500 feet! The saving grace is you have stellar views all along the way, with a jewel of a lake— Diamond Lake—nestled in a broad meadow about 4 miles up the trail.

At 8 miles, the trail intersects the Waptus Pass Trail at 4200 feet. Turn left, cross through the pass and descend 1.5 miles through meadow-covered slopes speckled with clusters of rock gardens. Great views of the Cooper River valley are had from this section of trail. At 9.5 miles, the trail drops into forest and, in another mile, reaches Pete Lake. Turn left at the lake and head downstream along the Cooper River Trail, reaching Cooper Lake trailhead in 5.4 miles (16 miles from the trailhead). From here, cross the parking lot and locate Cooper River Trail 1311 and head down the river, descending 3.4 miles to the starting point.

55 KACHESS LAKE NATURE LOOP

Round trip ■	**1 mile**
Loop direction ■	Clockwise
Hiking time ■	1 hour
Starting elevation ■	2250 feet
High point ■	2300 feet
Elevation gain ■	50 feet
Best hiking time ■	Year-round
Map ■	Green Trails Kachess Lake, No. 208
Contact ■	Okanogan and Wenatchee National Forests, Cle Elum Ranger District

This trail proves that not all hikes have to be epic adventures to be enjoyable. Though short, this loop provides a great learning adventure for folks of all ages, though pre-teen kids will especially love it as it explores the watery worlds of the lakes and creeks, as well as dives deep into century-old forests.

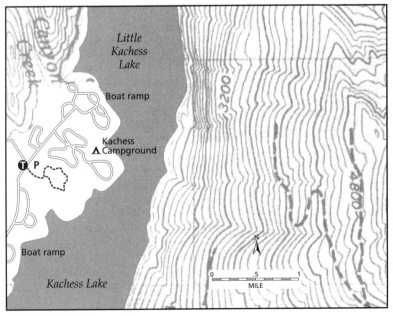

Pete Lake, near Kachess, in the Alpine Lakes Wilderness

To get there, from Seattle drive east on Interstate 90, take Exit 62, and drive north on Kachess Lake Road for 5 miles to a three-way intersection. Take a right and enter the Kachess Campground. Just past the fee (camping fee only) booth at the entrance, turn left and drive about 0.5 mile to the parking area for Little Kachess Trail 1312.

The hard-packed trail is open with access for all users, including folks in wheelchairs, making it perfect for anyone. Toddlers can bobble along, as can anyone who wants a nature adventure but can't walk far. The grade is gentle and the trail is well maintained.

The trail loops over the pretty little Box Canyon Creek—stop on the bridge and peer down, trying to spot the small trout that dart through the clear waters in pursuit of aquatic insects. Once over the creek, the trail climbs gently to a bench above the lake that provides views down on the creek and along the lakeshore.

The return portion of the loop rolls by a slab of moss-covered rock as big as a parking lot—note the many tall trees growing from this seemingly solid surface. Kids will marvel at the works of seeds and roots in forcing the rock open to allow the tree to grow.

56 PARIS CREEK

Round trip	■	**10 miles**
Loop direction	■	Counterclockwise
Hiking time	■	7 hours
Starting elevation	■	2400 feet
High point	■	4700 feet
Elevation gain	■	2300 feet
Best hiking time	■	Mid-June through early autumn
Map	■	Green Trails Kachess Lake, No. 208
Contact	■	Okanogan and Wenatchee National Forests, Cle Elum Ranger District

You can expect little company on this trek. Few hikers know of or use the trails here possibly because they are open to motorcycles, but savvy walkers realize most motorized trails are only occasionally visited by motorcycles. The trail climbs to stunning views and passes through prime habitat for deer—look for them along the edges of clearings and meadows. As you hike watch the sky, and you'll likely see a veritable air force of raptors—red-tailed hawks, Cooper's hawks, turkey buzzards, and even bald eagles frequently can be seen overhead.

To get there, from Seattle drive east on Interstate 90, take Exit 80 (signed "Roslyn/Salmon la Sac"), and head north on the Salmon la Sac Road about 15 miles, passing through Roslyn and by Cle Elum Lake to Salmon la Sac. Turn right into the Jolly Mountain trailhead/Cayuse Horse Camp parking area.

The Jolly Mountain Trail is open to all types of users, including motorcycles, but few users of any type—except horses—travel this trail, so don't expect to see hikers, let alone motorcycles, but don't be surprised if you do, either.

From the trailhead, climb steeply up the slope above Salmon la Sac Creek. This is an old trail, built before switchbacks were popular, so the trail climbs ruthlessly upward, without benefit of thigh-saving twists and turns. In the first 3.2 miles, you'll gain 2300 feet in elevation. Halfway up this section the trail slices through a clear-cut only a couple of years old, yet despite its relatively fresh cutting, the forest is already showing signs of rebirth. Fireweed and huckleberries fill the sun-brushed spaces between the stumps, and deer frequently browse through this rich foliage. The cut also provides stunning views across the valley toward Kachess Ridge.

At 3.2 miles, stay left at the trail junction found at 4700 feet. Another 0.5 mile of steep climb leads you to 5200 feet, followed by a 1500-foot dive in 1.5 miles to the Paris Creek Trail 5.2 miles from the trailhead. You won't find any bridges over Paris Creek and the trail crosses it three times. In the spring, when the creek is running full, a sensible alternative to wading

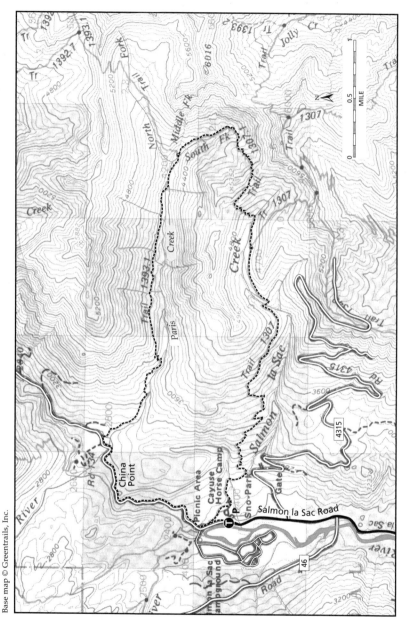

Base map © Greentrails, Inc.

through the torrent is to simply bushwhack down its shoreline the short
distance to pick up the trail at the next crossing. This is really only a spring
concern, however, as once the worst of the snowmelt has occurred (by mid-
July) the creek is reduced to a trickle.

Swift Paris Creek passing through a lovely hanging valley

At about 6.5 miles, the trail pops out into an old clear-cut and climbs onto an old logging road for a short distance. Turn left onto the roadbed and in less than 0.5 mile, look for a signpost marking the return to trail tread. The trail drops off the left side of the road and heads down the Paris Creek valley. There seems to be a huge population of grouse here as every visit to the area has flushed countless birds out of the trees on the last couple miles of trail.

The trail ends at 8.4 miles at the Paris Creek trailhead on Salmon la Sac Road. Hop onto the road and hike 1.6 miles back down to the Jolly Mountain trailhead where you parked.

57 MIDDLE FORK TEANAWAY/ELBOW PEAK

Round trip	**23 miles**
Loop direction	Counterclockwise
Hiking time	2 to 3 days
Starting elevation	2700 feet
High point	6443 feet
Elevation gain	3000 feet
Best hiking time	Mid-June through early autumn
Maps	Green Trails Kachess Lake, No. 208 and Mount Stuart, No. 209
Contact	Okanogan and Wenatchee National Forests, Cle Elum Ranger District

Teanaway country is home to an assortment of birds and animals, as well as some truly magnificent wild country. It's not protected as wilderness, so you might hear or see motorcycles along the trails, but the grandeur of the country is worth that risk—fortunately, when you encounter motorcycles they disappear quickly from sight, even if the exhaust fumes and ringing in your ears lingers for a time.

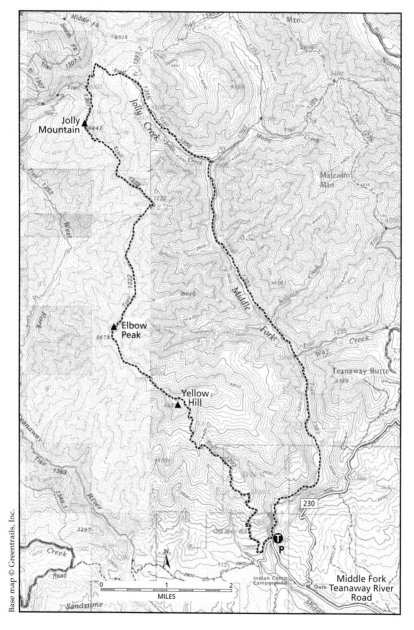

This route covers a lot of stunning country, providing oodles of opportunities to see wildlife, bird life, and plant life.

To get there, from Cle Elum drive north on State Route 970, cross the Teanaway River bridge, and in another mile, turn left onto Teanaway River Road. At the Teanaway Campground, turn left onto the Middle Fork Teanaway River Road and drive about 4.5 miles to Indian Camp

Balsamroot (Balsamorhiza sagittata) *along the trail to Yellow Hill*

Campground, and continue 0.5 mile farther to the trailhead on the right, found near a sharp left turn in the road.

Middle Fork Teanaway Trail 1393 climbs gradually along the pretty river for 7 miles, gaining just 800 feet in that distance. That makes the hiking easy and fast, if you can keep from stopping to gawk at the pretty forest and river scenery. Mule deer are abundant and can frequently be seen browsing in the forest and crossing the trail to get to the river. At 7 miles, turn left at a fork and climb west along the Jolly Creek Trail. In 2.5 miles, the trail climbs through the meadows at the head of the creek valley, and at 11 miles from the trailhead, the path intersects the Jolly Mountain Trail at 6000 feet.

Turn left and climb 400 feet in the next mile to the summit of Jolly Mountain (6443 feet) with its great 360-degree views of the sprawling Teanaway country.

Continue south from Jolly Mountain, following the ridgeline 4.5 miles to the top of Elbow Peak (5673 feet). Elbow provides views nearly as nice as those found on Jolly, so take your time before moving on. From the top of Elbow Peak (16.5 miles from the trailhead) drop south again, still following the high ridgeline as it now turns somewhat east and leads in 2 miles to the top of Yellow Hill (5527 feet). There are more picture-perfect views here, followed by a 2.7-mile descent to an old spur road largely reclaimed by the forest, leaving just a faint trail. Follow this old roadbed 1.5 miles out to the Middle Fork Teanaway River Road, then turn left and hike 0.25 mile up the road back to the original starting point and your waiting vehicle, for a loop of 23 miles.

58 MALCOLM MOUNTAIN

Round trip ■	**10.4 miles**
Loop direction ■	Clockwise
Hiking time ■	8 hours, day hike or backpack
Starting elevation ■	3100 feet
High point ■	5400 feet
Elevation gain ■	2900 feet
Best hiking time ■	Late June through October
Map ■	Green Trails Mount Stuart, No. 209
Contact ■	Okanogan and Wenatchee National Forests, Cle Elum Ranger District

Views of the entire North Fork Teanaway River valley await you from the top of Medra Pass along this route. Then there's Mount Stuart: the massive monolithic rock towers over the northern horizon. Overhead, Cooper's hawks commonly soar, and underfoot, carpets of wildflowers surround the trail. This is truly a glorious wilderness trail, even if it's not officially recognized as wilderness.

To get there, from Seattle drive east on Interstate 90, take Exit 85,

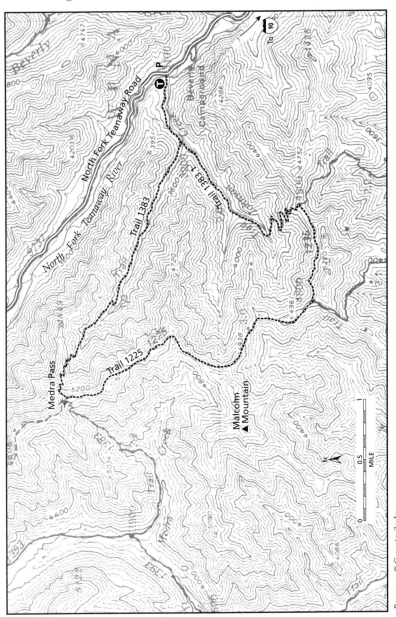

and drive approximately 6 miles on State Route 970. Turn left (west) onto Teanaway River Road. At 13 miles the pavement ends; veer right onto FS Road 9737. Continue 4 miles and just after passing the Beverly Campground in 0.3 mile look closely on the left side of the roadway at a slight curve in the road and find an unmarked trailhead for Johnson Creek. Parking is best in the small primitive camp area across the road from the trailhead, as the pullout along the roadway can only handle one or two cars. No privy, but Pines and Beverly Campgrounds are stocked with outhouses.

We highly recommend hiking the loop clockwise. This lets you make all the crossings of Johnson Creek in the morning (when the water is lower) and gets you up the steepest climb along the route before the temperatures get too hot.

This route is exceptional. The first 0.7 mile of the trail is constantly in earshot and mostly in sight of beautiful Johnson Creek on a mostly flat trail that moves you quickly to the first trail junction. Take the left fork to climb Jungle Creek Trail 1383.1;

The area around Malcolm Mountain is well signed. Photo by Kathy Kelleher)

about four steps from the junction is the first of about seven creek crossings in the next 1.5 miles. All are manageable without getting too wet, but a couple of the crossings are a bit difficult early in the year when the snowmelt raises the water levels.

The trail leaves the creek at 2.3 miles from the trailhead and begins to climb steeply to the ridge about 800 feet above. As the trail nears a junction at 2.7 miles, the views open up to the north across the Teanaway River valley. At the trail junction turn right and hike a mile west along the ridge top, following Way Creek Trail 1235 through rocky meadows and clearings. Bitterroot blooms in many protected pockets in the sandy rock gardens. At the next trail junction, at 3.7 miles, turn right onto Koppen Mountain Trail 1225. Stroll 3 miles north, following the faint trail along the rocky ridgeline. The actual trail seems to come and go in the sparsely covered meadow-topped ridge, but cairns fill some of the gaps, and even without markers, the route is easy to follow—just stay atop the ridge crest as you cross the flanks of Malcolm Mountain (4938 feet) and then keep climbing to a junction with the Medra Pass Trail at the pass (5400 feet). Enjoy incredible views from the pass, then turn right and descend Trail 1383 back to the trailhead, completing a 10.4-mile loop.

59 ┆ DeRoux Creek

Round trip ■	**12.3 miles**
Loop direction ■	Counterclockwise
Hiking time ■	7 hours
Starting elevation ■	3800 feet
High point ■	5900 feet
Elevation gain ■	2100 feet
Best hiking time ■	July through mid-October; wildflowers typically peak in late July
Maps ■	Green Trails Mount Stuart, No. 209 and Kachess Lake, No. 208
Contact ■	Okanogan and Wenatchee National Forests, Cle Elum Ranger District

While standing along the shores of Gallagher Head Lake, our volunteer watched a small band of mule deer browse through the meadows, providing a picturesque foreground to match the panoramic background, which was dominated by Hawkins Mountain and the Esmeralda Peaks. The vast meadows around the lake are awash in color much of the summer as scores of wildflower species push up into bloom at various times and seasons.

To get there, from Seattle drive east on Interstate 90 to East Cle Elum Exit 85. Exit the freeway here and, after crossing over the freeway overpass, turn right (northbound) on State Route 970. Continue approximately 6 miles and turn left onto Teanaway River Road. At 13 miles the pavement ends at a Y, veer right onto FS Road 9737, and continue 8 miles. Turn left at the signed road to DeRoux Creek trailhead, found 0.4 mile down the road at the campground.

This hike should definitely be done counterclockwise for best viewing of the beautiful scenes along DeRoux Creek in the upper meadows, as well as for clear lighting of the mountains surrounding Gallagher Head Lake.

A new bridge provides access across the North Fork Teanaway River 0.5 mile into the hike, but even before the bridge was built, the creek was easy to ford. For 1.6 miles, hike upward somewhat as the trail meanders through open forest generously sprinkled with broad clearings and wildflower meadows. The trail stays near DeRoux Creek along this stretch, and indeed crosses the creek a little over a mile in—this crossing lacks a bridge

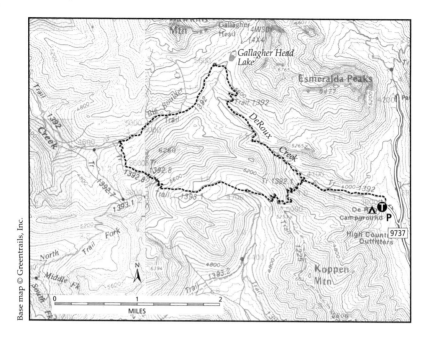

Base map © Greentrails, Inc.

and can be a tricky ford in early spring when the meltwater swells the stream to a roaring torrent.

At the 1.6-mile mark, the trail splits. On the left is the steep trail you'll descend to close the loop. For now, bear right and continue climbing, more steeply now, through the broad meadows of upper DeRoux Creek basin. Toward the head of the basin, the trail turns sharply upward. Fortunately, rocky outcroppings blanketed with dozens of wildflower species—every color imaginable, it seems—keep your heart light as you gain more than 1000 feet in slightly over a mile to reach another trail junction at 5600 feet, 4.1 miles from the start.

The right fork of this trail junction leads to Gallagher Head Lake in just a few hundred yards. This lake is a beautiful jewel well worth visiting. There is a faint jeep track leading to the lake from the north, so expect to see some ORV damage along the shoreline, however.

After a visit to Gallagher Head Lake, return to the trail junction and follow the left fork to the south, finding grand views of the Cle Elum Range and beyond, Mount Stuart. In 2 miles, the trail drops more than 1000 feet along Boulder Creek to another junction. Turn left onto Trail 1392.8 and regain the 1000 feet you lost as you puff up a mile of trail to yet another junction, this time meeting Paris Creek Trail 1393.1, at 7.1 miles

Turn left and descend steeply once more for 1.6 miles, then turn left again and climb more than 500 feet in the next mile to cross a small pass (5000 feet) on the north shoulder of Koppen Mountain. Drop another mile down a steep

Gallagher Head Lake and Hawkins Mountain

series of switchbacks to close the loop at 10.7 miles. Turn right on the DeRoux Creek Trail and follow it 1.6 miles back to the trailhead at 12.3 miles.

60 KOPPEN MOUNTAIN

Round trip ■	**14 miles**
Loop direction ■	Clockwise
Hiking time ■	8 hours, day hike or backpack
Starting elevation ■	3760 feet
High point ■	6031 feet
Elevation gain ■	2300 feet
Best hiking time ■	July through mid-October
Map ■	Green Trails Mount Stuart, No. 209
Contact ■	Okanogan and Wenatchee National Forests, Cle Elum Ranger District

Koppen Mountain offers incredible views of the Stuart Range and the jagged peaks of the Teanaway country. These views are found on many of the trails in this area, but what those other routes don't have is the quiet and solitude found at Koppen. Enjoy this largely forgotten trail, and you'll be able to soak in those views without having to share.

To get there, from Seattle drive east on Interstate 90 to East Cle Elum Exit 85. Exit the freeway and, after crossing the freeway overpass, turn right (northbound) on State Route 970. Follow this for approximately 6 miles to Teanaway River Road (on your left, after crossing the Teanaway River) and turn left. Follow it 13 miles to Twenty-nine Pines Campground. It will have become North Fork Teanaway River Road (FS Road 9737) by then. The

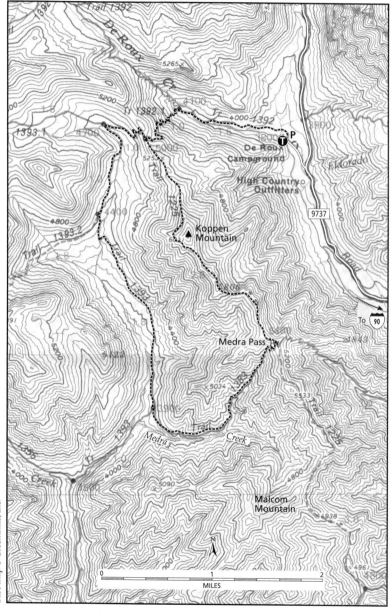

Koppen Ridge (Photo by Jim Cavin)

pavement ends at Twenty-nine Pines Campground. Pass Beverly Campground in 4 miles, and continue to abandoned DeRoux Campground and the trailhead. There is a pit toilet at the trailhead.

Start on Boulder–DeRoux Trail 1392. Cross the North Fork Teanaway River and travel northwest on flat terrain through forest about 1.5 miles to DeRoux Spur Trail 1392.1. Ascend switchbacks about a mile to a pass (elevation 5040 feet). This is where the loop is closed on the return trip. There are views of Mount Stuart, but better ones are on the return loop. There is also a hunters' camp here, but no water.

Descend through meadow. On the descent we saw a kestrel. After about a mile, back in the trees, come to the intersection with Middle Fork Teanaway Trail 1393. Follow it south. The trail stays out of sight of the stream most of the time. After the first crossing of the Middle Fork Teanaway, it's a pretty mellow, gradual downhill grade. There's abandoned junk/artifacts, perhaps of the old Skookum Mine, alongside the trail. At an unmarked intersection, stay left. Just after recrossing the Middle Fork, a trail, looking suspiciously of motorcycle origin, goes left, stay right. And there is one more unmarked intersection, stay left. Finally almost 3 miles after starting on the Middle Fork Teanaway Trail and about 3 hours from the trailhead, you're at the signed intersection with Johnson-Medra Trail 1383.

Follow the Johnson-Medra Trail up, it quickly climbs above Medra Creek and proceeds up the ridge by following the drainage. There are numerous instances of crossing side drainages and then climbing steeply up out of them. The trail becomes indistinct in several places; just keep going up, perhaps following the motorcycle tracks. The ridge top is at 5400 feet, 2.25 miles and 1.5 hours from the last junction.

Turn north on the abandoned Koppen Mountain Trail 1225. You'll be treated to outstanding views of Stuart, and turning the other way, of Rainier and Adams. Follow the trail; if you lose it, it never goes far from the top of the ridge. Ascending Point 5806, a trail branches left and soon starts descending: wrong way. The trail goes directly over the top of Koppen—you have to work at avoiding the summit. Next, head steeply downhill for 0.5 hour to the 5040-foot pass, turn east, and retrace your steps to the trailhead. Or go for another lap.

The wildlife highlight of the trip was seeing two wild turkeys between Beverly Campground and Twenty-nine Pines the way home.

61 STAFFORD TO STANDUP CREEK

Round trip ■	**13.2 miles**
Loop direction ■	Counterclockwise
Hiking time ■	8 hours
Starting elevation ■	3100 feet
High point ■	5800 feet
Elevation gain ■	2700 feet
Best hiking time ■	July through mid-October
Map ■	Green Trails Mount Stuart, No. 209
Contact ■	Okanogan and Wenatchee National Forests, Cle Elum Ranger District

This route covers some of the best of the Teanaway country, offering high ridge-top views, cool valley-bottom strolls, and acres of wildflowers all along the way.

To get there, from Seattle drive east on Interstate 90 to East Cle Elum Exit 85. Exit the freeway and, after crossing the freeway overpass, turn right (northbound) on State Route 970. Follow this for approximately 6 miles to Teanaway River Road (on your left, after crossing the Teanaway River) and turn left. Follow it 13 miles to Twenty-nine Pines Campground and continue north another 1.5 miles before bearing right onto Stafford Creek Road (FS Road 9703). Continue about 4 miles to the Stafford Creek trailhead.

Stafford Creek Trail climbs alongside the stream, passing through pretty, fragrant pine forest. The trail sticks to the east side of the creek, where trail crews have restored or replaced several flood-damaged sections of the trail. The trail climbs moderately for 4 miles, and then gets steeper as it pushes up the headwall of the creek valley. Here, for more than a mile, you'll trudge upward. The tiresome climb is made tolerable, and indeed, enjoyable, by the vast expanse of wildflowers spread before you and around you. The whole upper basin is blanketed in wildflower meadows.

At about 5 miles, the Stafford Creek Trail ends at junction with the Standup Creek Trail. Turn left and hike west straight toward Earl Peak, a towering knob of rock due west of the trail junction, and only about 1.5 miles off.

Standup Creek Trail climbs from the Stafford Creek basin for 2 miles, pushing right up onto the flank of Earl Peak and to the headwaters of Standup Creek, at 7 miles. Here, the trail splits. To the right is more climbing through broad meadows to cross a shoulder of Earl and enter the Bean Creek basin. That trail can be faint and hard to follow, however. Instead, turn left and descend through more flowers and rock gardens into Standup Creek

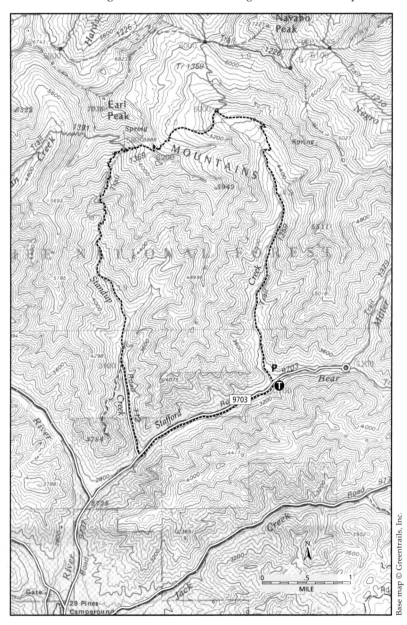

Base map © Greentrails, Inc.

Earl Peak seen from Navaho Pass area above Stafford Creek

basin. For the next mile, you'll stroll past so many flowers you'll feel like you're in a painting—or a perfume factory. Watch for hummingbirds here as the energetic little things swarm the flower fields in great numbers.

The trail descends into forest and at 11 miles, ends at a trailhead. Walk about 0.75 mile down the road to find Stafford Creek Road. Turn left onto the road and hike another 1.5 miles back to your starting point at the Stafford Creek trailhead.

62 EARL AND IRON PEAKS

Round trip	■	**14.4 miles**
Loop direction	■	Clockwise
Hiking time	■	10 hours
Starting elevation	■	3600 feet
High point	■	6400 feet
Elevation gain	■	2400 feet
Best hiking time	■	July through mid-October
Map	■	Green Trails Mount Stuart, No. 209
Contact	■	Okanogan and Wenatchee National Forests, Cle Elum Ranger District
Note	■	Portions of this trail may be brush-covered and hard to follow at times. Map-and-compass navigation skills are essential.

Scrambling along open ridge tops draped in grass and wildflowers, hikers here can easily lose the trail as it fades under the rich plant life and disappears between jumbles of rock. Further complicating things, the glorious views from the ridge prevent hikers from devoting their full attention to the trail—there's just too much beauty and natural splendor to enjoy. Great meadows stretch out all around, and on every horizon stand

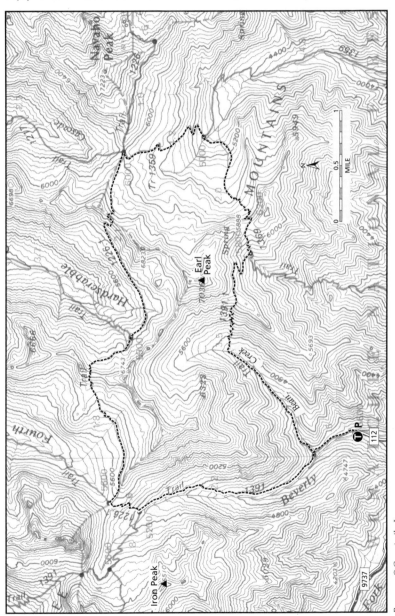

Mount Stuart and surrounding Teanaway country, from the route near Iron Peak

picture-perfect mountain ranges, with the hulking presence of Mount Stuart to the north dominating all other views. Enjoy these sights, but make sure you give plenty of attention to the route, too, and don't be afraid to turn back and hike out the way you came if you lose the loop.

To get there, from Seattle drive east on Interstate 90 to East Cle Elum Exit 85. Exit the freeway and, after crossing the freeway overpass, turn right (northbound) on State Route 970. Follow this for approximately 6 miles to Teanaway River Road (on your left, after crossing the Teanaway River) and turn left. Follow it 13 miles to Twenty-nine Pines Campground. Continue north about 4 miles before turning right (east) onto FS Road 9737-112, signed as "Beverly Creek." Drive 1.4 miles to the end of this road to find the trailhead.

The trail angles northeast along Beverly Creek for 0.5 mile before the path diverges. Go left to stay alongside Beverly Creek and in the next 2.2 miles climb the steep, narrow valley of this creek to a junction with small trail on the right. Leave the creekside here and climb steeply to the right (north) to reach a pass separating Beverly Creek basin from Fourth Creek basin.

This pass, 3.3 miles from the start, sits on the spine of the Wenatchee Mountains, below the craggy rock summit of Iron Peak. One look at the reddish hue of the mountain explains the name—the iron-rich rocks have oxidized (rusted) to a russet orange.

From the pass, turn right and follow a long traverse to the east, loop around the head of the basin of Fourth Creek, climbing slowly to a high pass between Fourth Creek and Hardscrabble Creek valleys. The trail then drops to a junction with the Hardscrabble Creek Trail at 5.1 miles. The trail to the left descends Hardscrabble Creek, and while it can be narrow and brushy, it is generally easy to see. Straight ahead, though, our path plays hide-and-seek in the broad fields of rocks and wildflowers. The trail can be hard to follow here, but by maintaining an easterly heading and staying at the 5900-foot elevation contour, scramblers can work their way across the 2-mile stretch of trail between Hardscrabble and the Cascade Creek Trail. Enjoy the views down into Ingalls Creek valley and across that valley to Mount Stuart and the jagged line of the Stuart Range.

Once you reach the junction with the Cascade Creek Trail, about 7.2 miles from the trailhead, turn right and hike south, descending into the Stafford Creek valley. After about a mile, you'll encounter Standup Creek Trail. Turn right once more and follow this path up and over the ridge between Stafford and Standup Creeks, and cross the pass on the flank of Earl Peak. At 10.5 miles, the trail splits. The main, easily followed trail drops along Standup Creek, but the faint, hard-to-follow path we want cuts west along the flank of Earl Peak and drops steeply into the Bean Creek basin. It's about 1.8 miles from the junction of Standup Creek Trail to the bank of Bean Creek, and then another 1.6 miles down the valley to Beverly Creek. Turn left on Beverly Creek Trail and follow it 0.5 mile downstream, and back to your car at the end of a 14.4-mile trek.

63 ELDORADO TO INGALLS CREEK

Round trip ■	**16.5 miles**
Loop direction ■	Clockwise
Hiking time ■	8 hours, day hike or backpack
Starting elevation ■	3900 feet
High point ■	5600 feet
Elevation gain ■	2100 feet (accomplished twice)
Best hiking time ■	July through mid-October
Map ■	Green Trails Mount Stuart, No. 209
Contact ■	Okanogan and Wenatchee National Forests, Cle Elum Ranger District

If you are looking for a workout with some great views along the way, this is the route for you. Three of the four trails that comprise this loop run steeply up or down and the fourth trail, while providing a bit of a respite from the vertical, is the shortest of the sections. But the workout is worth it, especially if you like wild country full of wildflowers and wildlife. Deer, elk, mountain goats, marmots, pikas, black bears, porcupines, bobcats, and coyotes all live here, as to do a host of other bird and animal species. Then there are the flowers. Vast meadows of lupine, shooting star, columbine, phlox, paint-brush, daisies, buckwheat, and flowers too numerous to mention sprawl over the ridge tops. Topping it all off, you can expect to encounter few other folks here as not many hikers extend themselves along these trails, though horse riders love the rugged, remote route.

To get there, from Seattle drive east on Interstate 90 to East Cle Elum Exit

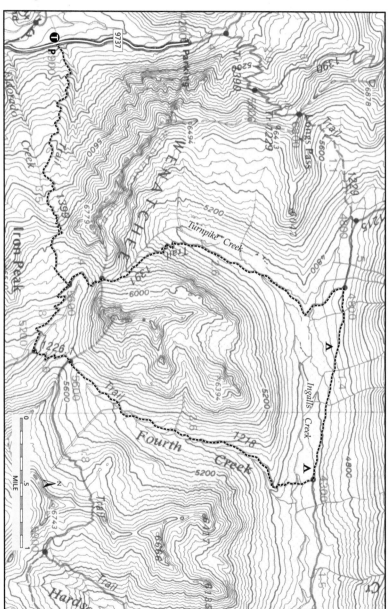

Base map © Greentrails, Inc.

85. Exit the freeway and, after crossing the freeway overpass, turn right (north-bound) on State Route 970. Follow this for approximately 6 miles to Teanaway River Road (on your left, immediately after crossing the Teanaway River) and turn left. Follow it 13 miles to Twenty-nine Pines Campground. Continue north along FS Road 9737 another 9 miles or so to the Eldorado trailhead, found about 0.5 mile past the High Country Outfitters Horse Camp.

From the trailhead, climb the steep, switchbacking Eldorado Creek Trail for 3.5 miles as it slices upward toward the rocky crest of Iron Peak. You'll gain more than 1700 feet as you slog up through open pine forests into increasingly broad meadows, and finally onto the rocky slopes of Iron Peak. Here, the meadows are more like rock fields interspersed with heathers, grasses, and clumps of flowers.

The trail intercepts the Turnpike Creek Trail at 3.5 miles. Turn left and traverse 0.4 mile north across a saddle on the ridge of the Wenatchee Mountains before dropping down along Turnpike Creek as it slopes northward into the Ingalls Creek basin. As you descend, Mount Stuart stands immediately in front of you—be careful not to let the view capture too much of your attention or you'll stumble on the rough trail. At 6.3 miles—now back in

Mount Stuart from the Turnpike Creek Trail

forest—cross Ingalls Creek and find the Ingalls Creek Trail at 6.5 miles. Turn right and follow the trail downstream for 1.5 miles. There are fine campsites along this stretch of trail.

At the 8-mile mark, look for a trail on the right. Turn here, cross Ingalls Creek once more, and start climbing the Fourth Creek Trail. You'll gain just 1300 feet in 3.6 miles as you ascend this valley. About halfway up, the trees thin and views open, providing looks south up onto Earl Peak and the Wenatchee Mountains ridgeline. Behind you to the north stands the majestic Mount Stuart and the Stuart Range.

At 11.6 miles, the trail passes a small side trail on the left. This is the Hardscrabble Creek Trail. Ignore it and continue straight ahead, dropping 400 feet in the next 0.5 mile to the Beverly Creek Trail. Turn right, regain that 400 feet as you climb the northeast flank of Iron Peak to find the Eldorado Creek Trail again at 13 miles. Turn left and descend the 3.5 miles back to the trailhead.

64 : MILLER PEAK

Round trip ■	**11 miles (11.8 miles with side trip to the summit)**
Loop direction ■	Counterclockwise
Hiking time ■	7 hours
Starting elevation ■	3200 feet
High point ■	6400 feet
Elevation gain ■	3200 feet
Best hiking time ■	Early July through mid-October
Maps ■	Green Trails Mount Stuart, No. 209 and Liberty, No. 210
Contact ■	Okanogan and Wenatchee National Forests, Cle Elum Ranger District

Teanaway Ridge is an open, sun-baked expanse that provides incredible views and wonderful wildflower experiences. That exposure to the sun, combined with the reflective nature of the light-colored soil and rocks, can create a hot trek for unsuspecting hikers. Our researcher recommends hiking the route counterclockwise primarily because it puts the sun behind you while hiking the open country along Teanaway Ridge and up the barren slopes leading to Miller Peak. This proved valuable even in mid-June when temperatures were only in the 70s. Be sure you carry and use sunscreen, as well as water, on this route.

To get there, from Seattle drive east on Interstate 90 to East Cle Elum Exit 85 and go north on State Route 970 for approximately 6 miles. Turn left onto Teanaway River Road and follow it 13 miles to Twenty-nine Pines Campground, where the pavement ends. Veer right and continue about 1.5 miles before veering right again onto Stafford Creek Road (FS Road 9703). Drive 4.5 miles to road's end at the trailhead area.

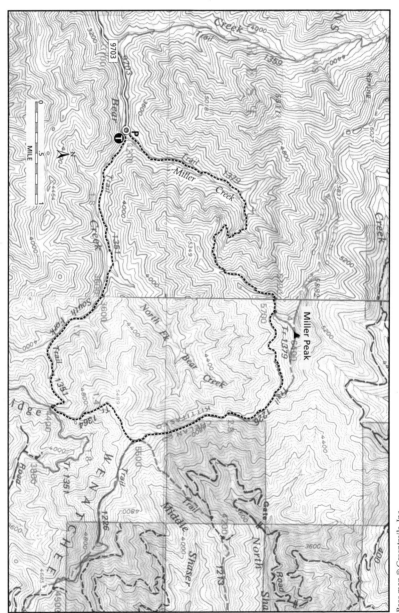

Base map © Greentrails, Inc.

The Stuart Range from the Teanaway Ridge Trail

Leave the trailhead at the end of the Stafford Creek Road and begin climbing the Bear Creek Trail. The trail follows this lovely little creek for much of the first 3 miles, and pierces a remarkably peaceful forest of pine and fir. This dry forest is open and airy, hosting an array of forest wildflowers including trilliums, glacier lilies, vanilla leaf, paintbrush, and phlox.

As the trail nears the upper creek basin at 2.5 miles, the route steepens and the next 0.7 mile or so entails a strenuous climb to the crest of Teanaway Ridge at 4400 feet. Turn left onto the Ridge Trail and you'll soon find that this trail follows a remarkably narrow, but incredibly scenic ridge crest north. Fantastic views in all directions are enjoyed from this lofty path, and the views just get better the farther you hike, with more and varied wildflowers growing underfoot. For 4.2 miles, the trail hugs the ridge crest, rolls north and west through meadows and periodic stands of forest, to reach the flank of Miller Peak and a side trail to the summit at 7.4 miles. The 0.4-mile side trail to the 6400-foot summit of Miller is worth the time and effort as the views are better than any you've enjoyed so far. To the west is the Teanaway Range and north of that, the mighty Stuart Range, dominated by the hulk of Mount Stuart. Around your feet on the slopes of Miller, locoweed and bitterroot grow through the rough scree, and pikas cheep and chirp all around you.

Back on the main trail below the summit, continue west, descending Miller Creek valley to return to the trailhead in 3.6 miles, for a total loop of 11 miles (11.8 miles if you went to Miller Peak's summit).

65 SILVER PEAK

Round trip ■	**8 miles (10 miles with side trip to summit)**
Loop direction ■	Clockwise
Hiking time ■	6 hours
Starting elevation ■	3000 feet
High point ■	4500 feet (5605 with side trip to summit)
Elevation gain ■	1500 (2600) feet
Best hiking time ■	July through mid-October; wildflowers typically peak in late July
Map ■	Green Trails Snoqualmie Pass, No. 207
Contact ■	Okanogan and Wenatchee National Forests, Cle Elum Ranger District

The summit of Silver Peak provides a unique and beautiful view of the Snoqualmie Pass Peaks. Hikers frequently find themselves perched here, above the clouds, looking down on a sea of white with mighty islands of rock projecting up through the clouds. But even if the summit of Silver Peak isn't reached, hikers will find that this loop offers wonderful forest and meadow scenery throughout its length.

To get there, from Seattle drive east on Interstate 90 to Exit 54 at Hyak. Turn right, and just as you enter the ski area parking lot go left on a road, which then curves to the right, passes some houses, and then passes the right side of a water treatment plant. Just past here the road becomes FS Road 9070 and at 3.4 miles from I-90 is the trailhead.

This is an excellent loop route for many reasons. For the Puget Sound population it's easy to get to since it is right off of Snoqualmie Pass. It is packed with a visual bonanza of beauty, from wildflowers to massive views. Finally, it offers a side-trail chance for adventure in the "not so easy" bagging of an impressive mountain: Silver Peak!

From the Cold Creek trailhead, hike up the valley to Twin Lakes, a pair of pools surrounded by dark, thick forests. The lakes have an air of mystery to them, especially when visited in the early-morning hours when there is a fog rising from the water.

At the lakes, at 0.8 mile, turn left and climb a steep, boggy slope straight up the side of Tinkham Peak. The first 0.5 mile of this climb pushes through a tangle of nettles and devil's club—you'll want to stay on the trail here—before climbing into drier forests. At 2.5 miles, the trail intercepts the Pacific Crest Trail. Turn east on the PCT and skirt around the flank of Tinkham Peak, and across the ridge to Silver Peak. This section of the PCT, while lacking in panoramic views, is gorgeous as it passes through numerous areas of small ponds/bogs, full of wildflowers. Huge areas of skunk cabbage can be seen along the trail and Solomon seal grows thick as a carpet.

About a mile along the PCT, begin looking for the side trail to the Silver

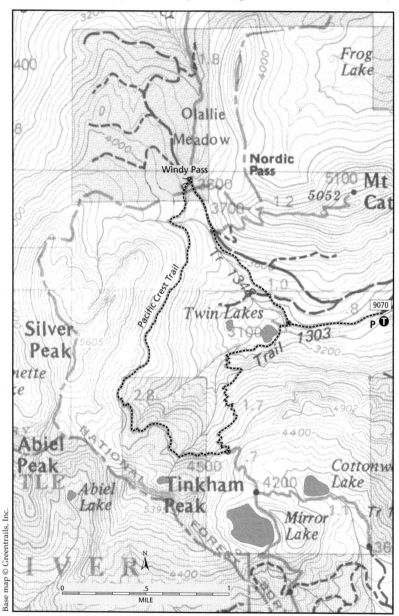

Annette Lake from the summit of Silver Peak

Peak summit, on the left just past a set of small ponds. The route is marked with a small rock cairn but at times the cairn gets knocked down.

The climb up to the saddle between Silver and Tinkham Peaks is steep and muddy in places, with beargrass pushing up all around you. Once at the saddle turn right and follow the easily recognizable trail that will take you to Silver Peak. Some beautiful tarns offer stunning photography whether they are reflecting the summit of Silver Peak or surrounded by beargrass in bloom. The last 0.25 mile to the summit isn't for beginners. It's all rock, and the last 350 feet of elevation is really a scramble of sorts requiring hand-use numerous times. If the climb is more than you want, don't push it—the views from the flank of the peak are impressive enough.

Back on the PCT, continue north along the trail to Windy Pass at 5.3 miles (not counting the Silver Peak side trip). The last 0.25 mile of this stretch crosses an old clear-cut—a veritable huckleberry bonanza—then drops onto a gravel road. The PCT continues north on the other side of the road, but for our loop, turn right and hike a few hundred yards down the road to find Mount Catherine Trail 1348 on the right.

This 1.5-mile stretch of trail descends through pleasant forest, rather overgrown in places. You then intersect the Cold Creek Trail just before it reaches Twin Lakes. The last mile back to the trailhead completes your 8-mile loop.

66 : SNOQUERA FALLS

Round trip	■	**6 miles**
Loop direction	■	Counterclockwise
Hiking time	■	3 hours
Starting elevation	■	2300 feet
High point	■	2800 feet
Elevation gain	■	500 feet
Best hiking time	■	March through November
Map	■	Green Trails Greenwater, No. 238
Contact	■	Mt. Baker–Snoqualmie National Forest, Snoqualmie Ranger District, Enumclaw Office

This lush, moss-laden forest is reminiscent of the rain forests of the Olympic Peninsula, and for good reason. The western foothills of the Cascades can get twice as much annual rainfall as the Puget Sound area, making the low forests of these regions wet, mossy, and rich in plant (and animal) life. In short, a rain forest. The trail here is short, but scenic, perfect for late-season hikes when the days are short and hiking time is at a premium.

To get there, from Enumclaw drive east on State Route 410 (Chinook Pass Highway) through the town of Greenwater. Continue past the Dalles

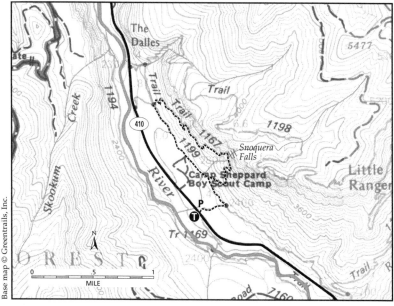

Calypso orchids (Calypso bulbosa) *bloom each May along Snoquera Falls Trail*

Campground, and find a small parking area on the left (north) side of the highway, just a few yards south of the Camp Sheppard Boy Scout Camp.

The trail angles into the forest on the northwest side of the highway, climbing gradually through the lush old cedar and hemlock forest. The route winds through sweeping carpets of moss—spotted with splashes of yellow and white (skunk cabbage and trillium) in the spring, and garlands of red and umber (Oregon-grape leaves and drying ferns) in the fall. The trail steepens after the first 0.5 mile, as it slants up the lower slope of Little Ranger Peak.

Big-leaf maples and a few scrub oaks now fill the spaces between the hemlocks and Douglas firs. In 1.2 miles, the trail drops into a little rocky basin, filled with maples, and crosses a small stream below the fantail waterfall on Snoquera Creek. This pretty waterfall can be roaring in the spring as the winter's snowpack melts, but it can turn off, leaving just a trickle, later in the fall. For the full experience, plan to visit at least twice to see the difference in water levels and how it affects the whole basin.

From the waterfall basin, the trail continues north, rolling along the base of a steep, rocky slope for 1.5 miles before descending a few short switchbacks to a junction with the lower valley trail. Turn left and follow this trail south 1.3 miles, passing the Boy Scout Camp, before turning to your starting point.

After your hike, if you have an extra hour, cross the highway and find a trail leading into the woods. Hike south 0.5 mile on this trail to a long, steel-cabled suspension bridge over the White River. This bouncy bridge provides access to the Skookum Flats Trail on the far side of the river. Enjoy the views of the river, and then return to your car.

67 ARCH ROCK

Round trip ■	**20 miles**
Loop direction ■	Clockwise
Hiking time ■	2 days
Starting elevation ■	4950
High point ■	5900 feet
Elevation gain ■	2400 feet
Best hiking time ■	Mid-June through early October
Map ■	Green Trails Lester, No. 239
Contact ■	Mt. Baker–Snoqualmie National Forest, Snoqualmie Ranger District, Enumclaw Office

This could be the loneliest loop in the South Cascades. Few hikers venture out along this trail, and fewer still complete the long loop past Echo Lake along the Pacific Crest Trail. The trail lacks the countless panoramic vistas that mark so much of the high wilderness trails of the state, but this remote portion of the Norse Peak Wilderness offers its own measure of wild beauty. The trail sticks to deeply forested ridges, passes a few craggy rock outposts with fabulous views, and dips into a cool river valley where it passes a wonderfully clear, cool lake with many fine campsites and good fishing opportunities.

The trail begins humbly, with the trailhead perched on the upper edge of a clear-cut, and the first 0.5 mile of trail cuts through a thin, second growth forest still marred by slash piles of rotting trees. But while much of the Greenwater River valley has been razed by logging companies, this long loop rambles through some of the last remnants of ancient Douglas-fir for-

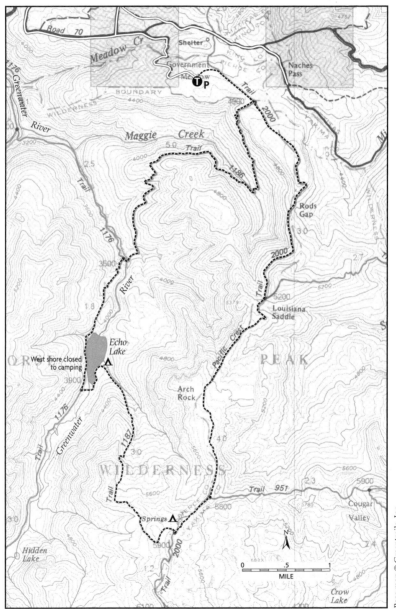

Curious chipmunk along the PCT

ests that blanketed the entire central Cascades not too many years ago.

To get there, from Enumclaw drive east on State Route 410 to the small town of Greenwater. About 1 mile east of the Greenwater Fire Station (on the east end of the community) turn left (north) onto Greenwater River Road (FS Road 70). Drive about 15 miles to the trailhead at the road's end in an old clear-cut. Note that the last mile of road is dusty, rough, and at times, deeply rutted. Use care when traveling it, especially in passenger cars and other low-clearance vehicles.

The trail leaves the clear-cut at the trailhead on an old logging road that leads into the trees. In 0.5 mile, the broad connector trail ends at a junction with the PCT. Turning left on the PCT leads you to Government Meadow in about 0.5 mile—these broad, marshy meadows are a haven for deer and elk, and are worth a visit if you have the time and inclination to go look for critters. The loop route, though, begins by turning right (south) on the PCT. The trail is fairly flat for the next few miles as it weaves through the thick, old forests. About a mile from the trailhead, a secondary trail leads off to the right. This is the other end of your loop route— stay left on the PCT, knowing you'll be returning via that side trail.

In about 3 miles, you'll find your first chance at a view. Just before the trail starts to descend into a few switchbacks down to Rods Gap you'll find a small clearing on the left side of the trail. Looking south and east, you'll enjoy the view of rolling hills and gray-green forests spread out before you, but beware the dangers of looking northeast where you'll see huge scars on the land beyond the wilderness boundary.

Rods Gap is a small, forested saddle on the ridge separating the Greenwater River valley from the Naches River valley. From the gap, the trail turns upward and climbs for the next 5 miles. Just a mile past Rods Gap, you'll cross Louisiana Saddle near a junction with Trail 945A on the left. Continue upward on the PCT and you'll encounter a few clearings along the ridge where views of the nearby peaks present themselves. To the southeast you'll see the rocky top of Raven Roost while directly ahead is the prominent peak of Arch Rock.

The trail passes Arch Rock at 7 miles, and for the next mile, the trail stays on the open flank of the peak before reentering forests near another trail junction (Trail 951) on the left. Stay right on the PCT and in 0.7 mile veer right on Echo Lake Trail 1187. You can find campsites in the next 0.5 mile as the trail crosses a couple of small spring-fed creeks before dropping 2000 feet in 3 miles to reach the shores of Echo Lake.

This pretty forest lake offers excellent camping along its southern and eastern shores—the west shore is closed to camping—with many sites offering great views of the spires of Castle and Mutton Mountains to the southwest.

The Echo Lake Trail ends at junction with Greenwater Trail 1176 on the south shore of the lake. Turn right (north) onto this trail and drop down to the Greenwater River valley for nearly 2 miles, before turning right onto Trail 1186 and climbing back to the PCT at a gradual rate of 1400 feet in 5 miles. Back on the PCT, turn northwest, and in 0.5 mile, bear left onto the connector trail back to the trailhead.

68 RAVEN ROOST

Round trip ■	**15 miles**
Loop direction ■	Clockwise
Hiking time ■	8 hours, day hike or backpack
Starting elevation ■	6000 feet
High point ■	6000 feet
Elevation gain ■	1700 feet
Best hiking time ■	Late July through September; with peak wildflowers in late August
Map ■	Green Trails Lester, No. 239
Contact ■	Okanogan and Wenatchee National Forests, Naches Ranger District

Get to Raven Roost early in the morning in mid- to late September and you can hear nature's greatest symphony—the raucous bugling of bull elk during the autumn rut, when the big males are competing for the attentions of the elk cows. But if you miss the rut, don't worry, there are plenty of other great features to enjoy here, including other wildlife encounters. Great numbers of spruce grouse and ruffed grouse live in the forested areas that the trails pass through. Raptors of many species use the thermals near Raven Roost for putting on an air show in late afternoon. And deer commonly browse along the forest fringe in groups of two or more.

To get there, from Enumclaw drive east on State Route 410. After crossing Chinook Pass continue east another 22.6 miles (3.6 miles past Bumping Lake Road) and turn left (north) onto Little Naches River Road. Drive 2.7 miles on Little Naches River Road and turn left over a bridge signed "Raven Roost 14." While not 14 miles to the trailhead (it is 13), continue on the main road, which quickly turns to gravel (in less than a mile). Finally, at 13 miles from the Little Naches Road, is a junction near the top. Go left for the last 0.2 rough miles to road's end, and the trailhead with a view! Allow 25 to 30 minutes driving time from Little Naches River Road. There are no toilet facilities, so stop back at Sand Creek trailhead or farther back at the campgrounds that you've passed in the lower Little Naches River valley.

The trailhead provides great views in its own right, but don't waste too much time admiring Mount Rainier and the other Cascades peaks from the parking lot, instead, start the hike up the 2.2 miles to Cougar Valley. If you're here in the fall, chances are you'll hear elk bugling all along this

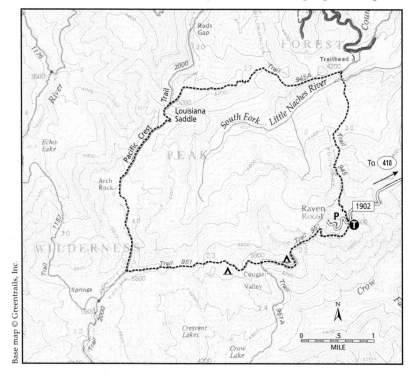

Base map © Greentrails, Inc.

The PCT passes through high alpine meadows near Arch Rock, west of Raven Roost.

stretch. The trail here follows an old roadbed to Cougar Valley, which is surrounded by the Norse Peak Wilderness. The views through this stretch are the grandest of the entire hike, with Raven Roost standing above you. The route also provides a unique perspective on the long ramparts of Fifes Ridge to the east.

Near the trail junction that heads down through Cougar Valley, two campsites nestled above lovely meadows are available for overnight hikers, and for those who really want to soak in the elk experience—the elk turn up the bugling another notch after dark.

Upon entering the wilderness in Cougar Valley, the most difficult portion of the hike is encountered as you climb 2.3 miles to reach the Pacific Crest Trail (PCT) at 5.5 miles. This stretch is through lovely forest with some remarkable rocky outcrops to explore. As it crosses the ridge, the trail continues up, and then up some more with nary a switchback in sight.

Once you reach the PCT, the hardest work is done and you can enjoy the 4-mile stroll north along the trail, ending at Louisiana Saddle at 9.5 miles. Turn right at the saddle and after dropping 1000 feet in 2.5 miles to the junction with Trail 945, you'll have a final 1800-foot climb back to Raven Roost in the last 3 miles, for a loop trip of 15 miles.

69 ┊ SAND CREEK

Round trip ▪ **5 miles**
Loop direction ▪ Clockwise
Hiking time ▪ 3 hours
Starting elevation ▪ 3600 feet
High point ▪ 4100 feet
Elevation gain ▪ 500 feet
Best hiking time ▪ June through November
Maps ▪ Green Trails Lester, No. 239 and Easton, No. 240
Contact ▪ Okanogan and Wenatchee National Forests, Naches Ranger District

This is a fun short loop to enjoy in the springtime. It melts out early compared to many regions due to its elevation and the warm east-slope conditions. Plus, by coming before Memorial Day you are unlikely to see much

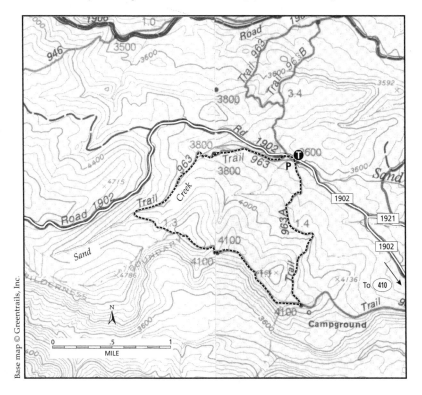

Base map © Greentrails, Inc.

Elk tracks in the Sand Creek Trail

of the summer motorbike crew that uses this trail. However it isn't one of the mainline trails in the Naches Ranger District by any means and thus makes for a great weekday hike all summer as well!

To get there, from Chinook Pass drive east on State Route 410 and continue 3.6 miles east of Bumping Lake Road before turning left (north) onto Little Naches River Road. Drive 2.7 miles on Little Naches River Road and turn left over the bridge signed "Raven Roost 14." Sand Creek trailhead is on the left 6.2 miles from Little Naches River Road. Toilet facilities are located at the trailhead.

I started hiking down Lower Sand Creek Trail 963A to connect to Sand Creek Trail 963. This clockwise direction had no real advantages over the other way, so feel free to enjoy it either direction. The 1.4 miles to Sand Creek Trail 963 went quickly as the trail is very flat for much of its length.

The trail does gain a quick 300 feet in elevation at about 1 mile and here, a postage stamp–sized meadow to the side of the trail beckons. This little glade is filled with wildflowers worthy of any postcard. Take some pictures and return to the trail.

Upon reaching the Sand Creek Trail, head west. But as soon as you start up this trail, stop. If you feel up for some exploration, leave the trail by veering to the right and strolling north through open forests and meadows to a small knob about 150 feet above the trail. This vantage point offers tremendous views southwest to the rarely seen north face of Fifes Ridge and Fifes Peak.

Back on the trail, continue west along Sand Creek Trail, as it rambles along at a gentle, easy pace through cool, dense forest. This entire stretch of trail follows the Norse Peak Wilderness boundary, so you are as good as being in the wilderness area itself. At about 3 miles, the trail banks north, following a curve of the wilderness boundary, and then at 3.8 miles, hooks back eastward and in just over a mile, returns to the trailhead.

70 LODGEPOLE CREEK

Round trip ■	**11.5 miles**
Loop direction ■	Counterclockwise
Hiking time ■	6 hours
Starting elevation ■	2800 feet
High point ■	4200 feet
Elevation gain ■	1400 feet
Best hiking time ■	June through November
Maps ■	Green Trails Easton, No. 240 and Cle Elum, No. 241
Contact ■	Okanogan and Wenatchee National Forests, Naches Ranger District

Too often hikers forget the wild, remote country south of Interstate 90 in the Cle Elum area—perhaps because it's unprotected forestland, open for motorized recreation. But that's no excuse to miss out on the rugged beauty

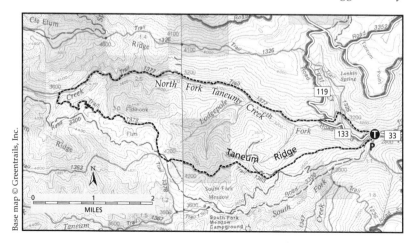

Base map © Greentrails, Inc.

of this region. Majestic pine forests fill the valleys of the Taneum basin, and vast herds of Rocky Mountain elk—wapiti—roam far and wide through the region. This trail explores some of that picturesque country, taking you into the heart of the wapiti rangelands.

To get there, from Seattle drive east on Interstate 90 to Exit 93 (signed "Taneum Creek") and turn north, crossing the freeway, and then take an immediate right onto Upper Peoh Road. Continue 3.4 miles from the exit to a stop sign. Turn right onto North Taneum Creek Road and in 9 miles, pass the Quartz Mountain/Buck Creek junction just past the Ice Water Creek Campground. Another 2.6 miles takes you to end of pavement and a junction in the road. At the Y on the right side of the road is another signed access to the North Fork Taneum Creek Trail 1377. Parking can be found at the Taneum Ridge trailhead just across the bridge over Taneum Creek to your left. This is where you will come back down Taneum Ridge later.

The first mile of this route is entirely in forest and can be hiked quickly to get to the crossing of FS Road 133. Here the trail drops 200 to 300 feet— about the same amount of elevation that was gained in the first mile. The net elevation gain along this long trail is modest, but don't let the fact that only 1400 feet separates the low country from the highest ridges lure you into thinking it's a fast or easy hike. Taneum Ridge is all ups and downs, making the total gross elevation gain closer to 3000 feet.

At about 2 miles from the start the trail levels off and the next 3 miles pass quickly as the trail climbs just 500 feet. Meadows begin to dot the forested landscape about 3 miles from the trailhead. Sure, there are motor-bike tracks in the trail, and it's overly muddy and eroded in places (especially in flat areas where the water just sits there). But this is a very special area that needs appreciation since it is so rich with wildlife.

The trail splits at 5.5 miles, at a junction with Fishhook Flats Trail. Turn left and hike south toward the flats. The next 3 miles cover the most spectacular section of the loop. The first mile after the trail junction climbs steeply to Taneum Ridge. The next 2 miles are particularly beautiful, passing mostly through open meadow known as Fishhook Flats. This region gets fairly heavy hunting pressure in the fall but is largely ignored by the masses the rest of the year (the deer and elk seem to know this as they congregate here in the spring and summer, but make themselves scarce come September).

At 8.5 miles, the trail intercepts FS Road 3300 and just a few dozen yards east, find the trail back onto Taneum Ridge. From here, it's a relatively easy and highly enjoyable 3-mile hike back across Taneum Ridge to the starting point. A lot of ups and downs, and while the ridge is mostly forested (don't expect wide-open views at this low elevation) there are a handful of really pretty areas with great views of Cle Elum Ridge and the Stuart Range. The last mile was a fast downhill back to the trailhead.

Opposite: *North Fork Taneum Creek*

71 ┆ NISQUALLY DELTA DIKE HIKE

Round trip ■	1- or 5-mile loops
Loop direction ■	Clockwise
Hiking time ■	1 to 5 hours
Starting elevation ■	50 feet
High point ■	50 feet
Elevation gain ■	0 feet
Best hiking time ■	Year-round, though half the 5-mile loop is closed November through January
Map ■	USGS Nisqually Delta
Contact ■	Nisqually National Wildlife Refuge

It's all about the birds. Whether you bring the kids and enjoy a simple stroll along the 1-mile loop, or gear up for a leg-stretching jaunt around the 5-mile loop, it will be the birds that capture your attention and imagination. The Nisqually National Wildlife Refuge plays host to a huge array of waterfowl—both migratory and resident. There are ducks and geese, of course, but also swans and cranes. A huge blue heron rookery resides on the slope at the south side of the refuge and bald eagles gather here in great number, too. What's more, you can enjoy all these birds—and far more besides—from a flat, well-maintained trail. Indeed, according to some birdwatchers here, there are more than a hundred resident species, and half as many more migratory species. A total of more than 20,000 individual birds migrate through the refuge each year.

To get there, from Interstate 5 between Tacoma and Olympia, take Exit 114 (Nisqually), turn west, and go under the freeway. Follow the signs to the refuge.

From the parking lot near the new visitors center, hike south along what appears to be an old road—and that's just what it is. The road/trail runs straight south through an intersection (turn right at the intersection for the shorter 1-mile loop to the old barns and back) to the dike separating the marshy delta lands from the Nisqually River. This dike, and others around the property, were built by turn-of-the-twentieth-century farmers who planted the rich delta with crops (hay is still raised on portions of the property to help fund the refuge).

At the river dike, turn north and follow it in a broad loop north along the river, then east along the tidal lands facing Puget Sound. Take note of the different species on either side of the dike—some prefer the calm, fresh water of the marshes in the delta, others favor the rolling tidal waters of the sound.

At about 3 miles, the trail turns back south and follows another dike

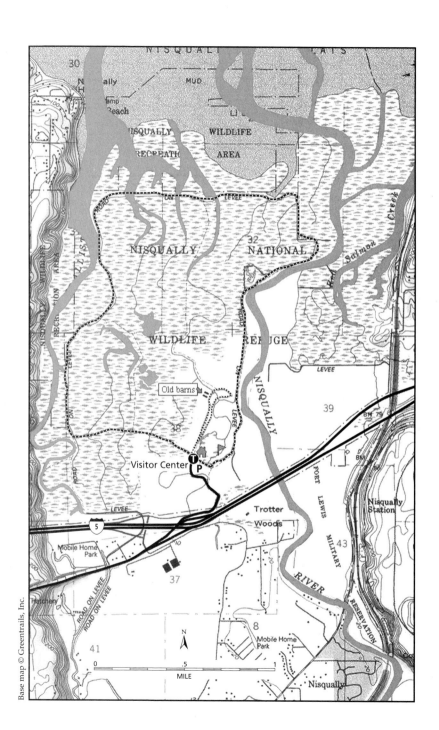

More than 20,000 birds migrate through the refuge each year.

along McAllister Creek back to the trailhead. This leg of the trip passes under several stands of alder trees. An array of songbirds nest here, so keep your eyes and your ears on the alert.

72 PARADISE/GLACIER VISTA

Round trip	■	**3 miles**
Loop direction	■	Clockwise
Hiking time	■	2 hours
Starting elevation	■	5400 feet
High point	■	6300 feet
Elevation gain	■	900 feet
Best hiking time	■	July through October; but can be snowshoed the rest of the year!
Map	■	Green Trails Paradise, No. 270S
Contact	■	Mount Rainier National Park

Sure, it's only 3 miles in length, but this loop packs in more scenic charm and outright mind-blowing beauty than many routes ten times its length. After all, this area is called Paradise for a reason—the expansive wildflower meadows leading up to stunning views of majestic Mount Rainier create a paradise on Earth.

To get there, from Ashford drive east on State Route 706 through the Nisqually Entrance of Mount Rainier National Park and continue on this road to the Paradise Lodge parking lot.

There is no wrong way to do this hike. Hike it in either direction. Use it as a "filler hike" when you only have part of the afternoon to get out for a hike. Or simply use it as a way to show off the glory of The Mountain to visiting company—especially if that company isn't used to long hikes at high elevation. It is perfect for children as well—keep in mind, however, that even though relatively short, this trail does boast a steep 900-foot elevation gain!

For optimal views, head up the Alta Vista Trail first. Even though the trail is hard surfaced, keep an eye out for wildlife—the critters here have become somewhat accustomed to people and it's not unusual to see deer, or even red foxes, in the meadows just a short distance from the parking lot. The trail climbs steeply to a junction with the Skyline Trail—take your time here since this is the most strenuous part of the journey.

From here, then trail moves beyond the endless fields of green grasses and colorful wildflowers and into a high alpine meadow environment, where clumps of heather, mounds of rock, and tuffs of grass vie for space, creating a rock garden feel to the landscape. Here, too, the marmots frolic

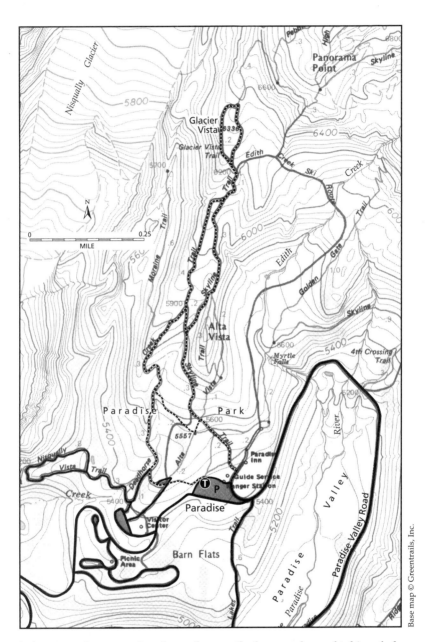

Base map © Greentrails, Inc.

in large numbers, sunning themselves on the large rocks, and taking shelter in dens under those same rocks.

You'll leave the Skyline Trail and turn-off onto the Glacier Vista Trail with impressive views of The Mountain straight ahead of you. The Glacier

Deer in Paradise meadows

Vista Trail leads you down the edge of the meadows, with views down into the steep canyon holding Nisqually Glacier. Stop and listen for several minutes and you'll likely hear rocks falls from the walls above the ice—the mountain is ever eroding.

The trail then loops back through the Paradise meadows to the parking area.

73 PANORAMA POINT

Round trip ■	**5 miles**
Loop direction ■	Clockwise
Hiking time ■	4 hours
Starting elevation ■	5400 feet
High point ■	7000 feet
Elevation gain ■	1600 feet
Best hiking time ■	July through October; but can be snowshoed the rest of the year!
Map ■	Green Trails Paradise, No. 270S
Contact ■	Mount Rainier National Park

Hiking to Panorama Point gives nonclimbers the barest taste of mountain climbing, since the trail leads you high above the meadows of the subalpine and alpine meadows into the alpine zone where rock and ice dominate. Indeed, Panorama Point boasts an old rock shelter built decades ago to provide shelter for climbing parties as they worked their way up the mountain. Today, only a few low walls remain from that old rock shelter. But it's not just human history and climbing experiences you'll find here. Glorious views await you. You can of course stare up at the looming Mount

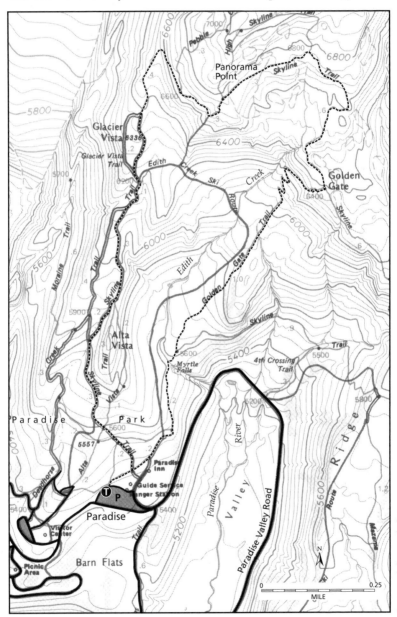

Base map © Greentrails, Inc.

Mount Rainier from Panorama Point

Rainier, but you can also look southward to the abbreviated crown of Mount St. Helens and the dome-like summit of Mount Adams. You can see the jagged line of the Goat Rocks peaks, and closer in, the ragged edge of the Tatoosh Range, dominated by The Castle and Pinnacle Peak.

To get there, from Ashford drive east on State Route 706 through the Nisqually Entrance of Mount Rainier National Park and continue on this road to the Paradise Lodge parking lot.

Set out from Paradise by crossing in front of the Paradise Lodge and dropping into the Edith Creek Basin on the Golden Gate Trail. The basin holds an array of wildflowers, as well as the pretty little Myrtle Falls, about 0.5 mile from the parking lot. Birds gather in large numbers in the small subalpine firs that dot the area, and the clumps of trees near the falls are especially popular with the avians as a place to take shelter between runs out into the meadows to gather berries, seeds, and insects.

From the falls the trail climbs steeply in the next mile to intersect the Skyline Trail at Golden Gate. As you climb, remember to stop often to turn around and enjoy the view behind you—Mount Adams and Mount St. Helens slowly appear beyond the jagged line of the Tatoosh Range to the south.

Turn left onto the Skyline Trail and continue upward, now crossing open fields of rock and ice—the rock is largely glacial moraine (rock pushed up by slowly moving glaciers) and the ice is the lingering patches of snow that generally never fully melt. Indeed, one broad permanent snowfield covers the trail for several hundred yards most years, requiring extra care and caution when crossing.

Panorama Point is reached at 2.5 miles. This knob of rock sticks out above the Paradise Valley like a guard tower. Enjoy stunning views from here—on clear summer days, not only are Mount Adams and Mount St. Helens visible, but also Mount Hood and even Mount Jefferson far to the south in Oregon.

From the point, follow the trail west as it loops along the rocky ridgeline, slowly descending toward Glacier Vista and down into the heather and wildflower meadows below Alta Vista. As you descend the steep slopes below Panorama, take a moment to admire the rock work along the trail. Many people worked long hours to build dry-fitted rock walls to retain the loose scree and talus of this slope and make the trail safe.

The trail ends at 5 miles back at the parking lot of Paradise Lodge.

74 WONDERLAND TRAIL

Round trip ■	**95 miles**
Loop direction ■	Clockwise
Hiking time ■	7 to 14 days
Starting elevation ■	2800 feet
High point ■	6800 feet
Elevation gain ■	Endless ups and down result in a cumulative gain of more than 20,000 feet
Best hiking time ■	Late July through early October
Maps ■	Green Trails Mount Rainier West, No. 269 and Mount Rainier East, No. 270
Contact ■	Mount Rainier National Park

This is the granddaddy of loops in Washington. The trail encircles Mount Rainier, rolling up and down the ridges that project from the mountain like spokes on a wheel. The trail runs through forests that stood before Columbus sailed, and over ice fields that hold snow that fell when the trees were saplings. Deep river valleys are explored, and glaciers are skirted. Alpine meadows of unmatched beauty are crossed, and thundering waterfalls are found. This is a magical trail that explores all that Mount Rainier National Park has to offer.

To get there, from Ashford drive east on State Route 706 through the Nisqually Entrance of Mount Rainier National Park and continue to Longmire. Hikers can access the trail at several locations, but we offer the route description from Longmire.

Pick up your backcountry camping permits at the Longmire Ranger Station and then head north. In the 33-odd miles from Longmire to the

Mowich Lake area, you'll find yourself moving up and down over tall, steep ridges in a never-ending rhythm of thigh-burning ascents and knee-crunching descents. From Longmire, traverse through the upper Kautz Creek valley and then climb steeply to Devils Dream Camp at 5.1 miles. This makes a good destination for the first day if you get a late start.

From Devils Dream Camp, the Wonderland continues north, rolling across the wide meadows and grass fields of Indian Henrys Hunting Ground, below the cone-like peaks of Iron Mountain, Copper Mountain, and Pyramid Peak. At the north end of the meadows, the trail drops to the Tahoma Creek valley, and crosses a deep, narrow gorge of that river on a bouncy old suspension bridge. This is one of the highlights of the trip—take your time crossing, and peer down into the chasm below to see the remnants of a massive mudflow that rushed through here a few decades before.

From Tahoma Creek, the trail climbs to the northeast into the alpine zone, and then runs along the edge of the Tahoma Glacier before dropping to cross the Puyallup River near its headwaters. A long, steep climb follows as you gain more than 2000 feet in the next 2 miles to get to St. Andrews Lake and the adjacent parkland meadows. The camp at Klapatche Park, just 0.5 mile farther, proves a good stopping point as it offers lakeside campsites with views of The Mountain. You'll have hiked 15 miles to get to Klapatche.

The trail now drops steeply to the North Fork Puyallup River and then traverses a long slope on the north side of that valley, cutting through an

Hiker crossing rough-sawn walkway in Spray Park

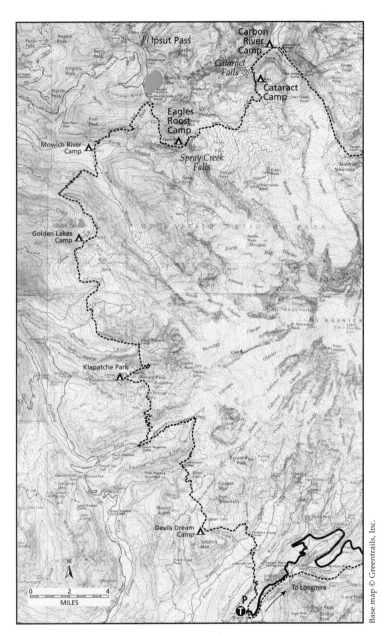

old forest fire burn site now awash in huckleberries. It is a steady climb from here to Golden Lakes Camp at 22.4 miles. Another long, steep descent gets you to Mowich River Camp at about 29 miles. Just past the river, the trail climbs the flank of Paul Peak and makes a steady turn to the east.

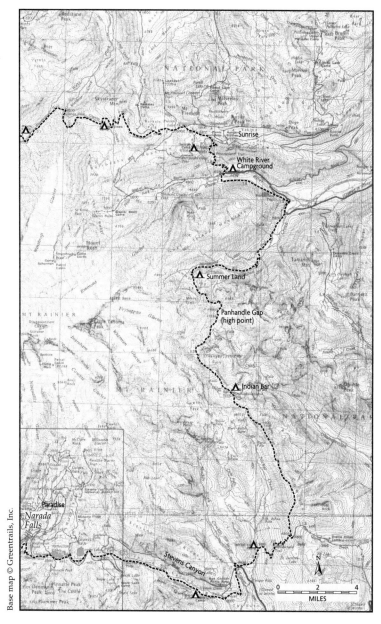

Base map © Greentrails, Inc.

You're now leaving the western side of the mountain and beginning your traverse around to the north side.

At 33 miles the Wonderland Trail passes within 0.5 mile of Mowich Lake for those who want to get off the trail at this point, or who want to join it here. (From Mowich, hikers could descend northward along Ipsut Creek to the Carbon River, and then climb the Carbon River valley. But the far more scenic—and generally accepted—route of the Wonderland hiker is to climb to Spray Park.) From Mowich, the trail climbs southward toward the mountain, hugging the top of Eagle Cliff and passing the glorious Spray Creek Falls. The trail turns east and runs up a steep series of switchbacks to enter the vast meadows of Spray Park. You'll climb through grass fields, heather meadows, and acres upon acres of wildflowers dotted with tiny blue alpine tarns before pushing up into the rock and ice zone to a high point of 6400 feet. At that point the trail begins to drop and you'll roll east, down through Seattle Park—another wonderland of meadows—to reach the Carbon River Camp at the west end of the suspension bridge over that river, about 8 miles from Mowich and 41 miles from the trailhead.

Cross the Carbon River on the bouncy suspension bridge and start a long, steady climb along the steep valley wall above the Carbon Glacier. For the next 3.6 miles, you'll gain 2500 feet to reach Mystic Lake at 44 miles. This cold lake is surrounded by meadows and forest, and marks the start of a long series of meadows and parklands along the north side of the park.

Descend from Mystic Lake into the Winthrop Creek basin, crossing the creek near the end of Winthrop Glacier, and then climb steeply to Berkeley Park. From there, it's an easy ramble through open parklands to Sunrise, about 53 miles from Longmire.

Grab a burger and soda at the visitors center café at Sunrise and then continue your trek. Drop from Sunrise to the White River Campground, and then head east along the White River on a new stretch of trail (built by Washington Trails Association volunteers) paralleling the road, to the Frying Pan Creek valley. Turn south and climb this valley to reach Summer Land at 62 miles.

Summer Land offers great campsites on the edge of a sprawling meadow in a cool basin, with views of Mount Rainier and Goat Island Mountain. About 1.4 miles south of Summer Land, the Wonderland Trail crosses its highest point at Panhandle Gap, 6800 feet. Keep a sharp eye out as you move through this area as there is a large herd of resident mountain goats living around the gap and they can usually be seen between Summer Land and the gap.

The trail drops from Panhandle into the upper fields of Ohanapecosh Park, then down into the deep flower-filled basin of Indian Bar. From there, the trail climbs to the crest of Cowlitz Divide and rolls south along that ridge crest to Box Canyon at 83 miles, on the Stevens Canyon Highway.

Cross the highway, and find the trail on the south side as it turns west and enters Stevens Canyon, rolling upward along the southern wall of that canyon until it finally crests out near Reflection Lakes. The trail then drops past Narada Falls and follows the Paradise River down to the Nisqually, and the Nisqually out to Longmire, to close this long, rambling loop at 95 miles.

75 SPRAY AND SEATTLE PARKS

Round trip	■	**15 miles**
Loop direction	■	Counterclockwise
Hiking time	■	2 to 5 days
Starting elevation	■	4930 feet
High point	■	6400 feet
Elevation gain	■	1500 feet
Best hiking time	■	Late July through early October
Map	■	Green Trails Mount Rainier West, No. 269
Contact	■	Mount Rainier National Park

There is a fine line between mere fog and a cloudy whiteout, and a huge difference between the rampant alpine meadow colors of late spring and the brown tones of the off-season in the same place. Widely regarded as one of Mount Rainier's premier hikes, this loop is attractive throughout the hiking season, but it can be dangerous in dubious weather, and the payoff during spring bloom for alpine flowers is far disproportionate to the effort required. Plan accordingly.

To get there, from State Route 410 in Buckley drive southeast on SR 165, staying right at the junction with SR 162 near Burnett and continuing east through Wilkeson. Note: Backpackers planning to camp in the park's backcountry should stop at the Red Caboose in Wilkeson to pick up their backcountry camping permits. Continue driving east on SR 165 (Mowich Lake Road). You'll cross the stunning single-lane Fairfax Bridge over the Carbon River and reach a Y junction. Veer right as the road climbs around an old clear-cut and leaves the river valley. Continue following this road as it climbs into the park and eventually ends at a trailhead parking area at Mowich Lake. Although outhouses are provided, potable water is not. Use the lake as your source, but purify.

For a shorter loop when a car shuttle is possible, arrange to drop a vehicle at the park's Ipsut Creek Campground (found by staying left at the Y junction). It will generally take at least 2 hours to make the second-car drop, however.

From the parking area at Mowich Lake, you have a decision to make. In addition to the loop through Spray Park, the lakeside trail at Mowich is delightful, especially for birders. This short trail, about a mile, can be enjoyed in under an hour.

The Wonderland Trail exits from the campground but after only 0.2 mile splits off onto Spray Park Trail, which is level and deeply shaded under towering evergreens for the first hour as you circle Hessong Rock. Eagles Roost Camp, right, at 2.2 miles, is the first official campsite but for a 2-day circuit you'll want to press onward. A detour, however, again right, to

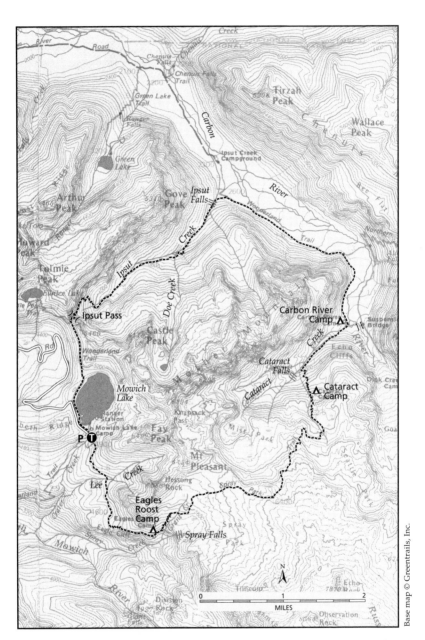

Base map © Greentrails, Inc.

Spray Falls is a must. The side trail gets you to water's edge in 0.3 mile for a partial view up to the left, but to see the entire falls, scramble carefully upstream a few hundred feet. Wide and misty, the falls lives up to its name.

Mount Rainier reflected in one of many Spray Park tarns

A rapid climb (600 feet in 0.5 mile) on a well-maintained, switchback trail follows the falls, opening onto Spray Park, a vast alpine meadow where thousands of shrubby and ground-hugging plants bloom from late June into July, depending on snow cover. Alpine plants are well adapted to their harsh environment, but they are not adapted to being stepped on. Stay on the trail. Rock outcroppings at several points in the "park" make good picnic tables. Backpackers should not be surprised to see numerous groups of day hikers passing through, including botany classes—notebooks and hand lenses at the ready. Amused marmots scamper across the rocks, observing the observers. Clear-day views of glaciers above Echo Rock and Observation Rock are dramatic. Nearing the high point of this hike, about 4.2 miles from the start (at 6400 feet on a ridge, often snow covered, dividing Spray and Seattle Parks), lucky hikers may glimpse the far North Cascades over the lower shoulders of Mount Rainier.

Or you may be fogged in. Upper Spray Park is high enough to put you in the clouds. Map, compass, concentration, and voice communication between hikers may all be necessary to navigate the snowfields between the two parklike alpine meadows. Not every set of footprints leads in the right direction. Use caution. The descent to Cataract Camp takes a good hour or more, through winding and wet trail where shale and moss vie for groundcover control. Although Cataract Camp stands about midway through this loop hike at approximately 6.9 miles, it tends to be dank and offers no views. Running water is abundant, and a primitive latrine is helpful, but if time allows, forge ahead downhill.

Easily negotiated switchbacks end where Cataract Falls spills out of the woods at your left. A long straight section descends slowly to Carbon River Camp, a lovely site by a dramatically rushing glacial stream (at about 8.5 miles). The riverbed is surprisingly wide, an indication of the power of snowmelt run-off from the Carbon Glacier, not too far upstream. Spray Park Trail ends here; turn left to join the Wonderland Trail, heading north and downstream. A suspension bridge crosses the Carbon River upstream from the junction with the Spray Park Trail, taking the Wonderland Trail the other way.

For the next hour, to the Ipsut Creek Trail, the hike is an easy ramble on a cliff-side trail above the Carbon River. Watch for raptors and other birds riding the thermals rising up from the riverbed. At 0.9 mile from the trail junction, a ford across the Carbon River leads to the Northern Loop Trail. Ignore this and stay on the left bank for another 1.6 miles, then turn left onto the Ipsut Creek Trail. Or end the hike by taking a right to Ipsut Creek Campground where your shuttle car awaits. Ipsut Creek Trail passes the detour to Ipsut Falls just 0.2 mile from the turn, then climbs steadily for 3.5 miles through dense forest in an ever-narrowing valley. Carry plenty of water here. There is tough work ahead and the streams uphill may be dry. At the head of the valley a set of arduous switchbacks claws its way up to 5100 feet. In late spring or early summer the trail here may be overgrown with rampant greenery and entangling flowers, but you're not likely to be an inquisitive botanist now. If the wind is hiding on the other side of Ipsut Pass, abundant mosquitoes may inspire you to climb faster. Once on top, however, the view back down the valley you have just climbed is superb.

Resting at Ipsut Pass at 15.4 miles, you can contemplate the option of doing the entire hike in reverse. It is just a mile from here down to Mowich Lake and your car on a highway-wide, pine needle–covered trail, climaxing on the shores of the lake. Had you hiked in a clockwise direction, Carbon River Camp could again have been your overnight destination. And if you had 2 nights to spend on the loop, Eagles Roost Camp below Spray Park would serve well for the second night. Coming out on the third morning would take only minutes.

Hike on weekdays here to see Spray and Seattle Parks in relative solitude, or embrace the fact that you and many other hikers share the same passions for great mountain vistas and astonishing botanical colors right at your feet.

76 ▐ NORTHERN LOOP

Round trip ■	**34 miles**
Loop direction ■	Clockwise
Hiking time ■	3 to 5 days
Starting elevation ■	6400 feet
High point ■	2600 feet
Elevation gain ■	3800 feet
Best hiking time ■	Late July through early October
Maps ■	Green Trails Mount Rainier West, No. 269 and Mount Rainier East, No. 270
Contact ■	Mount Rainier National Park

Consider this the mini–Wonderland Trail—it doesn't encircle the mountain, but it does explore some of the most spectacular country in the park, and because it's not as well known as the Wonderland, it gets far fewer visitors. The loop explores high ridges, deep valleys, and broad meadows, and provides remarkable views of Mount Rainier along the way.

To get there, from State Route 410 in Buckley drive southeast on SR 165,

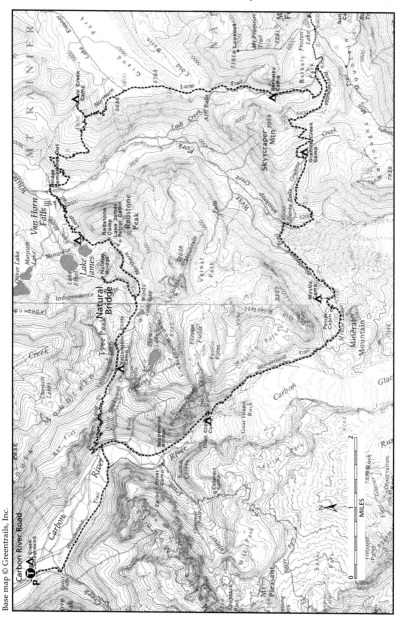

staying right at the junction with SR 162 near Burnett and continuing east through Wilkeson. Note: Backpackers planning to camp in the park's backcountry should stop at the Red Caboose in Wilkeson to pick up their backcountry camping permits. Continue driving east on SR 165 (Mowich Lake Road). You'll cross the stunning single-lane Fairfax Bridge over the Carbon River and reach a Y junction. Stay left and follow the Carbon River into the park and to the road's end at Ipsut Creek Campground.

Hike up the Carbon River Trail from the east end of the campground, and in just 2 miles, look for a side trail to the left. This is the official start of the loop, but because there is no true bridge across the river here—just a series of long, foot logs that have a tendency to wash out in the spring—hikers might have to push on to the Carbon River Suspension Bridge at 3 miles to cross the river, then backtrack down the opposite shore to the start of the loop route.

Assuming you can cross the river at the lower point, however, find the trail on the northeastern shore, and start a long, steep climb through a seemingly endless series of switchbacks. This punishing climb will tax even the strongest hiker as it gains a whopping 3000 feet in just over 3 miles. The good news is the climb is through heavy, cool forest most of the way, and as you near the top, the forest opens on broad meadows and wind-swept ridges. At about 5 miles (based on the lower river crossing) you'll reach Yellowstone Cliffs. The cliffs form a tall wall of yellow-tinted rocks towering over a long, sloping meadowland. Deer and mountain goats share this area, with the goats preferring the rocks and the meadows on top, and the deer favoring the meadows abutting the forests below the cliffs. A fine campsite is nestled in the trees near Spukwush Creek, with good views of the cliffs and the meadows.

Continuing on past the cliffs, the trail keeps climbing, now in the broad meadows, for another 1.5 miles to the U-shaped basin of Windy Gap at 6.5 miles. Plant life is sparser here, with just a bit of heather and grasses pushing up through the rocks and around the edges of the many little tarns that dot the gap. There is a perpetual breeze blowing through the gap (hence the name)

Mystic Lake shrouded in fog

but not much of a view. If you have the time, and inclination, an off-trail scramble is worthwhile here. Climb the rocky slope on the south side of the gap to attain the ridge crest above. Here, you can peer down to the west on the sapphire-blue waters of Crescent Lake and south to the emerald-green plain of the Elysian Fields. Towering above the fields is mighty Mount Rainier.

Back on the trail at the gap, hike to the eastern edge of the gap and find a side trail on the left (north). This path traverses the slope for a mile to a viewing point above the Natural Bridge—an arch of rock that stretches across a deep valley. The bridge is set at an odd angle, so it's not easily viewed, but the trail is easy and the bridge is impressive enough to warrant the side trip.

To continue the loop, however, keep hiking east from the gap and descend 2 miles to fine forest camps at Lake James. Still descending, the trail rolls on past the lake to a crossing of the White River near Van Horn Falls—a pretty little waterfall—at 10.6 miles. Now the trail climbs again, grinding upward at a steep, ruthless rate. But the exertion is worth it as the trail eventually levels off in the enormous expanse of Grand Park. Hundreds, if not thousands, of acres of meadowland sprawl across this table-like plateau. You might want to set aside some time to explore the park, as our trail merely skirts the western edge of the meadows before it climbs the long valley of Lodi Creek to Berkeley Park.

At Berkeley Park, the Northern Loop Trail intersects the Wonderland Trail, about 19.6 miles from the start. Turn right (west) onto the Wonderland and follow it down into the Winthrop Creek basin, and back up to Mystic Lake at 26.4 miles. Then drop down for the long, slow 4.6-mile descent along the Carbon Glacier to the Carbon River Suspension Bridge. Cross the bridge and hike the final 3 miles out to the trailhead.

11 BURROUGHS MOUNTAIN

Round trip ■	**12 miles**
Loop direction ■	Counterclockwise
Hiking time ■	7 to 8 hours
Starting elevation ■	4300 feet
High point ■	7400 feet
Elevation gain ■	3100 feet
Best hiking time ■	Late July through early October
Map ■	Green Trails Mount Rainier East, No. 270
Contact ■	Mount Rainier National Park

Sitting atop Second Burroughs Mountain at 7400 feet, our researcher found his lunch interrupted by the remarkable sight of a golden eagle soaring in the strong thermal lift coming off the open rock slopes. The massive raptor glided along the ridgeline, cruising less than 50 feet from the hikers atop the peak. These great hunters soar over the area frequently, taking advantage of the local thermals and—more importantly to them—the large population of marmots.

Of course, this route offers more than just wonderful wildlife viewing. The loop over Burroughs Mountain provides hikers outstanding views of the northeast face of Mount Rainier. Little Tahoma can be see flanking Rainier, and the tower-topped peak of Mount Fremont stands to the north. All in all, the views and the local wildlife make this loop an unbeatable day-hike option for hikers young and old.

To get there, from Enumclaw drive east on State Route 410 (Chinook Pass Highway) past the park archway at the junction with Crystal Mountain Boulevard. About 4.5 miles farther along SR 410, turn right onto the Road to Sunrise (signed as Sunrise/White River Campground). Follow this road through the park entrance fee station, and 5.4 miles after leaving SR 410, turn left to follow signs to the White River Campground. Continue another 1.3 miles and park at the large visitor parking lot in the campground. The Wonderland Trail leg of this loop begins near the back of Campground Loop C.

The loop can be started at Sunrise, but we recommend the White River trailhead because it allows you to complete the bulk of elevation gain early rather than late. Starting here also gives you the benefit of hiking toward Mount Rainier the entire trek up high atop Burroughs Mountain!

From the campground, head north up the Wonderland Trail for 2.6 miles

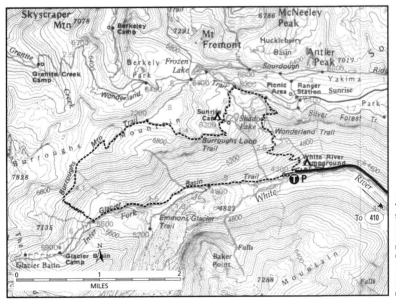

Glacier Basin and Mount Rainier from Burroughs Mountain

to reach Sunrise. This portion of the route is mostly standard forest hiking, though there is one notable scenic item along the way—a lovely little water-fall about halfway to Sunrise. The rest of the hike up is confined to trees with only a few fleeting views over the White River valley. As you near the top of the hill, you'll hit a trail junction. Turn left toward Sunrise Camp to avoid having to hike into the asphalted Sunrise parking lot and visitors center. At the camp at 3.5 miles—this was once a drive-up car-camping campground, but is now a walk-in tent camp—stay left and skirt around the south side of Burroughs Mountain. The trail traverses along the flank of the mountain for a short distance, then turns steeply upward and climbs to the 7200-foot sum-mit of First Burroughs. The trail then follows the ridgeline across to Second Burroughs before it angles southwest and descends around the side of Third Burroughs. Before starting this descent, stop at Second Burroughs and enjoy the view. It is worth your time to relax here a long time to not only enjoy the views, but hopefully to be lucky enough to see some avalanche and rockslide activity on the Willis Wall or the other glaciers that are so close to you. The sound of one of these events will stick in your memory forever.

From here it is a very leisurely stroll back home. The 1800-foot decent to the Glacier Basin Trail is very steep dropping off Third Burroughs Moun-tain. The shade of some trees below 6000 feet is a welcomed blessing from the midsummer sun. The Glacier Basin Trail provides a fast hike out the last 2.5 miles on good trail.

78 SUNRISE MEADOWS/FROZEN LAKE

Round trip	■	5 miles
Loop direction	■	Counterclockwise
Hiking time	■	3 hours
Starting elevation	■	6400 feet
High point	■	6800 feet
Elevation gain	■	400 feet
Best hiking time	■	Late July through early October
Map	■	Green Trails Mount Rainier East, No. 270
Contact	■	Mount Rainier National Park

This is the perfect outing for families or for anyone wanting an easy day in the glorious wildflower fields of the Sunrise area. Indeed, if you have out-of-town guests you want to impress, this gentle mountain stroll will have them thinking you live in a heaven on Earth. This little loop explores wonderful alpine meadows and provides glorious view of Mount Rainier, with very little elevation gain.

To get there, from Enumclaw drive east on State Route 410 (Chinook Pass Highway) past the park archway at the junction with Crystal Mountain Boulevard. About 4.5 miles farther along SR 410, turn right onto the Road to Sunrise (signed as Sunrise/White River Campground). Follow this

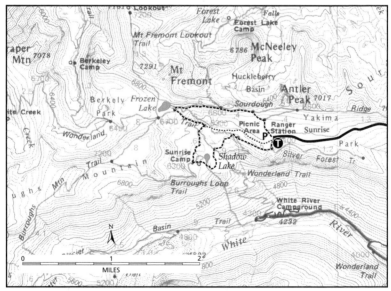

Mount Rainier from near Sunrise

road through the park entrance fee station and, 5.4 miles from the junction with SR 410, turn right onto Sunrise Road and continue to its end at the Sunrise Visitors Center.

At the trailhead near the restrooms on the north side of the parking lot, head up the slanting trail to the top of Sourdough Ridge. The hard-packed trail climbs 400 feet in about 0.5 mile, then follows the crest of Sourdough Ridge to the west. Before moving on, though, stop to catch your breath and enjoy the views. From the ridge, you can look south to Mount Rainier and beyond. Little Tahoma Peak stands to the southeast of the mountain, and the deep green valleys of the William O. Douglas Wilderness push away to the east. To the north is the stunningly pretty valley of Huckleberry Creek, and the long line of the Sourdough Mountains stretch away to the northeast.

Looking toward Mount Rainier, study the triangular bulge on its northern side—this is Steamboat Prow (so named because it resembles the prow of a ship). A small climbers' camp, Camp Schurman, sits at the end of this formation, and frequently in the summer you can see climbers (binoculars are a must) strung out on the glaciers above this camp, as they go for the summit.

Continuing on your loop, push west along the crest of Sourdough Ridge, crossing a long, steep, rocky slope. The trail here was painstakingly constructed—crews meticulously built dry-fitted rock walls to hold the talus slope in place to keep hikers safe. At about 1.6 miles, you'll find yourself near a small snowfield topped by, of all things, a fence. This fence rings Frozen Lake, since the lake is the sole water source for the Sunrise Visitors Center and staff quarters. The lake is so named because even in the heart of summer there is a permanent snowfield pushing down into the frigid waters.

From the lake, turn left and follow the trail to the southeast, looping down into the grassy meadows below Sourdough Ridge, and rolling back toward Sunrise Camp. Drop into Sunrise Camp for a taste of history and to see how nature can reclaim its own. This camp was once a popular car-camping site, but the road was pulled back and the campsite reverted to a hike-in, tent camping facility, about 3.6 miles from the start of the hike.

From here, pass Shadow Lake to climb through broad wildflower fields back to the Sunrise Visitors Center at 5 miles.

79 ▌ EAST SIDE LOOP

Round trip ■	**35 miles**
Loop direction ■	Counterclockwise
Hiking time ■	3 to 5 days
Starting elevation ■	3700 feet
High point ■	6800 feet
Elevation gain ■	3100 feet
Best hiking time ■	Late July through early October
Map ■	Green Trails Mount Rainier East, No. 270
Contact ■	Mount Rainier National Park

The Wonderland Trail wraps all the way around Mount Rainier, but the section rolling down the eastern flank of the peak may be the most con-

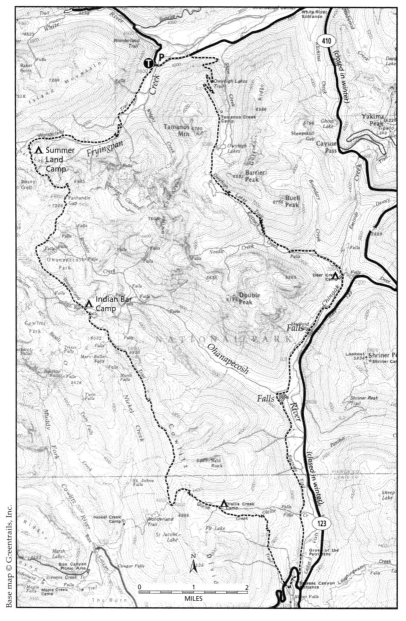

Base map © Greentrails, Inc.

tinuously scenic leg of the entire trail. This loop lets you enjoy that stretch, from White River to the Cowlitz Divide, without having to do all 95 miles of the Wonderland. You'll experience the mountain goat haven of Summer

Pink monkey flowers (Mimulus lewisii) *line this Summer Land creek.*

Land, the fantastic views from Panhandle Gap—the highest point on the Wonderland—and the glorious meadow of Ohanapecosh Park and Indian Bar. What's more, you'll also explore the deep, cathedral forests of the Ohanapecosh River valley, and the pretty basin of Owyhigh Lakes.

To get there, from Enumclaw drive east on State Route 410 (Chinook Pass Highway) past the park archway at the junction with Crystal Mountain Boulevard. About 4.5 miles farther along SR 410, turn right onto the Road to Sunrise (signed as Sunrise/White River Campground). Follow this road through the park entrance fee station and continue about 3.5 miles to the Wonderland trailhead at the base of Fryingpan Creek valley. The trailhead parking area is found just past the highway bridge over Fryingpan Creek.

Start the loop by heading south along the Wonderland Trail, climbing through the cool forest of the lower Fryingpan Creek valley for 2 miles, before the forest begins to open onto periodic glades and clearings. At about 3 miles, the valley narrows and you enter a series of avalanche run-out chutes. These are filled with vine maples and assorted wildflowers, but more importantly, these sun-filled slopes are largely covered in huckleberry.

The trail crosses the churning waters of the creek at about 3.4 miles, and then climbs steeply for the next 0.8 mile to Summer Land Camp, set amidst the broad green meadows of Summer Land. A huge colony of marmots reside on the large hill across the trail from the group camp, and a pretty stream tumbles down the slope behind the camp. Enjoy views east to Tamanos Mountain and west to Mount Rainier.

From Summer Land, the trail climbs through rocky moraine fields—prime mountain goat habitat—to Panhandle Gap at 5.6 miles, and then descends on a long traverse into the upper fields of Ohanapecosh Park. Likely, you'll have to cross a few permanent snowfields here, so don't let the stunning views down into the park distract you or you might lose your footing. Better to stop and gawk at the scenery than to try to walk on the snow while gawking.

The trail continues south 3 miles from Panhandle Gap to Indian Bar, and the last mile of this involves a steep descent through flower-swaddled switchbacks into the circular basin of Indian Bar at 8.6 miles. The most scenic camp in the park is set on the eastern end of the Indian Bar. Wildflowers stretch right up onto the tent pads, and if you set your tent facing west, the views from your door will include the sprawling fields of flowers through the Indian Bar basin and the Ohanapecosh River as it sweeps through the center of it. Above the basin stands the mighty Ohanapecosh Glacier.

Leaving the Indian Bar Camp (reluctantly), continue south, climbing steeply for 1.5 miles before starting downward at a gentle angle along the crest of the Cowlitz Divide. About 4.7 miles south of Indian Bar (13.3 miles from the start), you'll find the trail splits. The Wonderland Trail continues to the right, dropping southwest to Nickel Creek and Box Canyon. We want to go left, however, and descend eastward into the Olallie Creek valley. This trail rolls down into deep, shadowy forest and, 1.5 miles from the fork, passes Olallie Creek Camp, where the pitch steepens and you descend more rapidly for the next mile before traversing south to the Ohanapecosh River valley. You'll cross the Stevens Canyon Highway at 17.4 miles, and just 0.1 mile farther on, join the Eastside Trail on the west bank of the Ohanapecosh River. Turn left (north) and in about 0.3 mile, recross the Stevens Canyon Highway and continue north along the river. At 18.2 miles, pass the Grove of the Patriarchs and keep moving north, as the trail climbs onto the hillside above the river to explore some lush old growth forest stands.

At about 22 miles, you'll follow the Ohanapecosh, as it swings westward, and then cross the river just above a beautiful waterfall. From here, you continue north, now following the Chinook River—a tributary of the Ohanapecosh. A couple miles north of Ohanapecosh Falls, you'll see Stafford Falls, and at 25 miles, find Deer Creek Camp at the point where Deer Creek empties into Chinook Creek from the east, while Kotsuck Creek pours in from the west. Just as there are multiple streams merging here, so too are there multiple trails.

To complete the loop, leave the Eastside Trail and turn left (west) onto the Owyhigh Lakes Trail and climb 4.7 miles along Kotsuck Creek to Owyhigh

Lakes basin, nestled in the low valley between Tamanos Mountain and Barrier Peak. Now, it's just 3.8 miles north along this trail to the White River Road. Turn left on the shoulder of that road and walk a short mile to the Fryingpan Creek trailhead and your waiting car.

80 ┊ NACHES PEAK

Round trip	■	3 miles
Loop direction	■	Clockwise
Hiking time	■	1.5 to 2 hours
Starting elevation	■	4500 feet
High point	■	5800 feet
Elevation gain	■	1300 feet
Best hiking time	■	Late July through early October
Maps	■	Green Trails Mount Rainier East, No. 270 and Bumping Lake, No. 271
Contact	■	Okanogan and Wenatchee National Forests, Naches Ranger District

Easy access, wildflowers, big views, easy hiking, lakes—this trail has it all. For these reasons the Naches Peak loop trail is immensely popular with old and young hikers alike.

To get there, from Enumclaw drive east on State Route 410 to Mount Rainier National Park. From the wooden arch stretched across the highway that marks the park entrance (found at the base of Crystal Mountain Boulevard), drive another 13 miles east on SR 410 to Chinook Pass. Park in

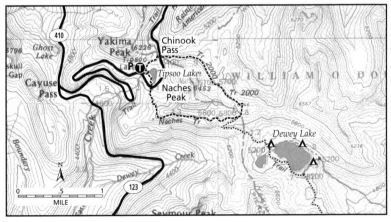

Base map © Greentrails, Inc.

Spectacular flower shows line the Naches Peak loop.

the lot on your left just past the footbridge marking Chinook Pass. Follow the trail on the west side of the highway to the footbridge and cross it to join the Pacific Crest Trail on the south side of the highway.

Meander upward through wildflower meadows for 0.6 mile to the boundary of the William O. Douglas Wilderness. As you stroll up the trail, enjoy masses of western anemone, beargrass, lupine, paintbrush, and more. Just 0.25 mile past the wilderness boundary, stop to admire—and maybe wet your toes in—a nameless tarn set like a jewel among the green fields of the meadow.

At 1.2 miles, stop for a rest or a leisurely lunch at the wide bench overlooking Dewey Lake. You'll find the trail splits here. Our loop route goes right. For a longer hike, however, continue to your left down the Pacific Crest Trail to reach Dewey Lake in a 1.2 miles, gradually at first, then losing 650 feet in the last mile. At Dewey Lake, bear left. Campsites are located on the north side of the lake.

Whether or not you take the Dewey Lake side trip, complete your loop by going right at the junction and hike west around the southern flank of Naches Peak. You'll soon see Mount Rainier thrusting skyward before you, while more meadows open up at your feet. In 1.7 miles, you'll have looped back around the south and west side of Naches and be back at the highway, opposite Tipsoo Lake. Cross to the north side of the highway and follow the access trails near the lake back to your car.

81 PICKHANDLE GAP

Round trip	■	**7.7 miles**
Loop direction	■	Clockwise
Hiking time	■	4 hours
Starting elevation	■	4800 feet
High point	■	6360 feet
Elevation gain	■	1560 feet
Best hiking time	■	Late July through early October
Map	■	Green Trails Bumping Lake, No. 271
Contact	■	Okanogan and Wenatchee National Forests, Naches Ranger District

Hikers find early rewards along this loop. A short 2 miles up the trail, stunning views of Washington's South Cascades dominate the scenery. The hillside meadows full of wildflowers and the forests teeming with wildlife are splendid and offer wonderful close-up viewing pleasures, but few sights can match the dominance of Mount Rainier. Here, the mighty peak can be seen looming over Crystal Mountain Ski Area with Rainier's younger sister, Mount Adams, gracing the southeastern horizon. As the trail rolls along the ridgeline, and to the Blue Bell Pass junction with the Pacific Crest Trail to Bear Gap at 4.3 miles, hikers are blessed with views of those towering volcanoes as well as the lesser peaks of the Norse Peak and William O. Douglas Wilderness Areas.

To get there, from Enumclaw drive south on State Route 410 to Crystal Mountain Boulevard. Turn left onto Crystal Mountain Boulevard (FS Road 7190) and follow the road toward the Crystal Mountain Ski Area. Approximately 5 miles from SR 410, turn left onto FS Road 410 at the Sand Flat Horse Camp turnout. After 0.2 mile, pass the trailhead for Norse Peak Trail 1191. The single-lane gravel road gradually climbs to a switchback 2.2 miles from FS Road 7190. Park your vehicle safely on the side of the road at this switchback and find the trailhead for Bullion Basin Trail 1156 on the uphill side of the road switchback.

The trail begins at an access road switchback that continues on to the upper lodge at Crystal Mountain. The two trails for this loop hike begin about 50 feet apart at the switchback turn while the road continues up, switchbacks again, and crosses a ski run to reach the top of the easternmost ski lift. Parking is somewhat limited at the switchback. Pull off to the side of the road and park carefully to avoid blocking the road.

For the best perspective on views from the loop, begin hiking up Bullion Basin Trail 1156 from the uphill side of the switchback. A short hike uphill reaches the upper road, crosses it, finds the trail again, and crosses a creek on a wide horse-duty bridge. The wide, dusty tread has two main switchbacks at the start, gaining 400 feet of elevation in a little more than

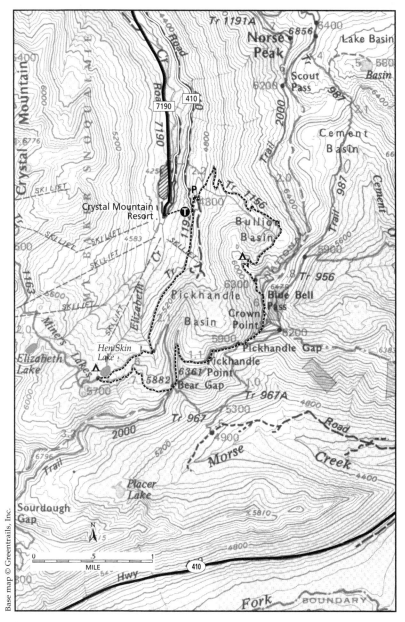

0.5 mile. Grassy, wildflower slopes are passed as the trail pulls away from the creek until the rushing waters can no longer be heard.

After about one hour, the trail flattens and turns south, entering Bullion Basin where a large horse camp is found with hitching posts. What little water is available here comes from the marshy source of the creek. At the camp, an unmaintained, unofficial trail breaks off from the main trail and climbs steeply up through the basin, joining the Pacific Crest Trail on the ridge. Continuing from the horse camp, the main trail gains elevation to reach a scenic, rocky outcropping. Mount Rainier looms over the Crystal Mountain Ski Area, with Mount Adams clearly visible to the south. Shortly after the viewpoint, the trail meets the PCT at a highpoint of 6300 feet near Blue Bell Pass.

After hiking south on the PCT for 0.6 mile, the trail turns east and leads to a junction with the Cement Basin Trail (Trail 987) at Crown Point in another 0.1 mile. Views are found looking east from the junction at the Norse Peak Wilderness up the Union Creek watershed. Continuing on the ridge for another 20 minutes takes you to Pickhandle Gap and a possible extension to the loop on Trail 967. Staying on the PCT maintains ridge-top views and avoids a 600-foot elevation drop.

At Bear Gap excellent views are offered with a decision at a five-way junction. For the loop, follow Trail 1163 to Hen Skin Lake or a steeper, shorter route signed for Pickhandle Basin. Either route soon enters mature timber. The Hen Skin Lake route descends to the small lake and several comfortable camps. The junction at Hen Skin Lake goes to the right, passing the shore of the lake and joining some unmarked mountain biking trails within the Crystal Mountain Ski Area.

Male elk near Pickhandle Gap

Another 0.5 mile from Hen Skin Lake, the short cut from Bear Gap is joined near a small stream. From there, the trail descends for 2.1 miles, passing under the easternmost ski lift after emerging from the trees. The end of the route offers an up-close perspective of the ski area. Early in summer, brush may be tall in the ski runs. Closer to fall, all of the brush will have been cleared. Begin a short road walk at the far edge of the ski run to return to your vehicle at the road switchback.

82 CRAG MOUNTAIN

Round trip ■	**20.2 miles**
Loop direction ■	Clockwise
Hiking time ■	2 to 3 days
Starting elevation ■	3600 feet
High point ■	5600 feet
Elevation gain ■	2000 feet
Best hiking time ■	July through late autumn
Map ■	Green Trails Bumping Lake, No. 271
Contact ■	Okanogan and Wenatchee National Forests, Naches Ranger District

Head up this trail anytime in September, pitch camp, and along about twilight, listen closely. A large herd of Rocky Mountain elk—known as wapiti to the Plains Indians—has established itself in the Bumping River valley; and during their annual mating season, known as the rut, the males issue long bugling calls, challenging each other for the rights to reproduce. Autumn isn't the only time to visit, of course. This route can be enjoyed all summer, and though you may not hear the elk, you might very well see them as they browse through the rich forage of the forest and meadows along the river. The trail climbs along upper reaches south of Crag Mountain and sweeps down a long, scenic stretch of the Pacific Crest Trail and down through the lush meadows and quiet forest lakes of the upper American Ridge area.

To get there, drive east on State Route 410 from Chinook Pass for 19 miles and turn right (south) onto Bumping River Road. Drive 12 miles to the end of the paved road (at the entrance of the Bumping Lake Campground on the right). Continue south along the road, which becomes FS Road 18 near the end of the pavement. At 13.5 miles, the road forks. Stay right (still on FS Road 18) and continue to the road's end and trailhead—about 4 miles farther along the rough, dirt track.

Start out with a 0.7 mile hike along a level track to the edge of Bumping River, then—after stripping off your boots and socks—ford the river. Early in the year, when the snowpack is at full melt stage, the river can be

Base map © Greentrails, Inc.

deep and difficult to wade, but by midsummer (most years) the water drops to no more than knee deep and the broad ford keeps the water flowing gently.

From the river ford, the trail climbs gently for 0.5 mile to a trail junction. Stay left here and follow the Bumping River Trail upvalley to its headwaters in Fish Lake, about 7 miles from the trailhead. The trail parallels the river along its length, and at about 3 miles, you'll cross Red Rock Creek. There are decent forest camps here, on the banks of the creek. This is a good place for a rest stop if nothing more.

The Bumping River Trail actually ends at a junction with the PCT about 0.3 mile before reaching Fish Lake. Here, the southbound section of the PCT takes off to the left while the northbound PCT pushes up the Bumping River the last 0.3 mile to Fish Lake. At the lake, the PCT turns right and climbs in long, looping switchbacks up the southwest flank of Crag Mountain, and curves west around the Crag Lake basin to reach another trail junction at 9.9 miles.

Stay right to continue north on the PCT and in just over a mile, you'll pass the small pools of Two Lakes on your right. There are campsites here and views east to Crag Mountain. Push on north and in another 2.5 miles, you'll find the start of the American Ridge Trail, about 13.5 miles from the trailhead. Turn

Vanilla leaf (Achlys triphylla) *sprinkled with dew*

right onto the American Ridge Trail in the heart of a vast huckleberry field and descend gradually for about a mile to the shores of American Lake. Great camps can be found here as the lake is a picturesque pond backed by a pair of rocky spires on the ridge separating American Lake from the Cougar Lakes basin.

From American Lake, you'll roll down through grassy meadows—still rich in huckleberries. One mile east of American Lake, turn right onto Swamp Lake Trail 970 and follow this past the forest lake that gives its name to the trail. Return to the junction with the Bumping River Trail at 19.5 miles. Cross the river and follow the connector trail the last 0.7 mile to the trailhead.

83 AMERICAN RIDGE

Round trip ■	**26.7 miles**
Loop direction ■	Counterclockwise
Hiking time ■	2 to 3 days
Starting elevation ■	5400 feet
High point ■	5800 feet
Elevation gain ■	2200 feet
Best hiking time ■	July through early October
Maps ■	Green Trails Mount Rainier East, No. 270 and Bumping Lake, No. 271
Contact ■	Okanogan and Wenatchee National Forests, Naches Ranger District

Hikers with allergies to horsehair might want to think twice before tackling this trail. The American Ridge Trail is a popular riding route for equestrians, but that's no reason for hikers to avoid the route. Indeed, there are ample opportunities for hikers to find solitude and quiet along this rambling ridgeline. More, there's plenty of scenery and stunning alpine views to enjoy for one and all. Hike the route in late August, and you'll also find nature's greatest bounty: sweet, ripe huckleberries, aka purple treasure! The trail rolls gently along the spine of the ridge, cutting through huge expanses of huckleberry meadows—excellent places to savor the essence of pine forest, just be aware that berry hungry bears also like to gobble the juicy fruit.

To get there, from Enumclaw drive east on State Route 410 to Mount Rainier National Park. From the wooden arch stretched across the highway that marks the park entrance (found at the base of Crystal Mountain Boulevard), drive another 13 miles east on SR 410 to Chinook Pass. Park in the lot on your left just past the footbridge marking Chinook Pass. Follow the trail on the west side of the highway to the footbridge and cross it to join the Pacific Crest Trail on the south side of the highway.

From the trailhead, climb the grassy hillside on the south side of the highway and follow it as it climbs southeast for 0.5 mile. This small connector trail slices through a few small stands of trees but generally rolls through broad meadows of alpine wildflowers. To the west, Mount Rainier fills the horizon. The trail climbs gradually for the first 0.5 mile then levels out until reaching a trail junction at 1.5 miles. This is where you meet the true PCT. Turn right (south) and descend 650 feet in the next 1.2 miles, passing through old, sun-dappled pine and fir forest, to reach a small forest clearing on the northwest shore of Dewey Lake.

From the southeast end of Dewey Lake, the trail rolls gently south. Hikers can eat their fill of huckleberries before hiking on to Anderson Lake at 5

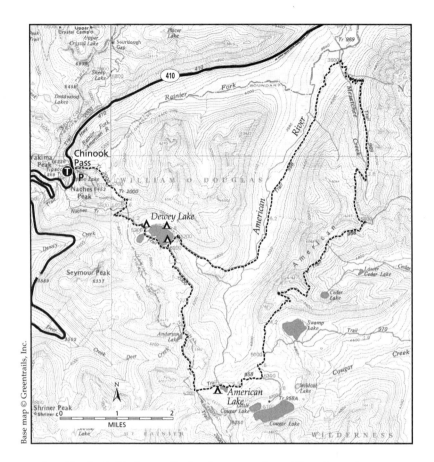

Base map © Greentrails, Inc.

miles. The trail climbs gently for the next mile, rolling along the western flank of a small unnamed peak before reaching the junction with the American Ridge Trail at 6 miles. For a good campsite, hike east about a mile on the American Ridge Trail to American Lake, where you'll enjoy more huckleberry fields and scenery that includes a rocky pinnacle to the south and the deep valley of the American River to the north.

Continue northeast from American Lake, sticking to the meadow-covered ridge for 5.2 miles to a 5800-foot knob on the crest of American Ridge. Here, you'll find a junction with the Mesatchee Creek Trail at 12.7 miles from the start. Turn left and descend Mesatchee Creek Trail, dropping through forest and sparse meadows for nearly 4 miles to a junction with the American River Trail.

Turn left onto the American River Trail and begin the long, slow ascent back to Dewey Lake, following the river to its source. You have about 5 miles of forested trail until you cross the creek at 4000 feet near the

Hiker fording Bumping River on the Swamp Lake Trail (Hike 82)

headwater basin and begin a steep, grueling climb, gaining 1200 feet in the next 1.2 miles to the shores of Dewey Lake (22.7 miles from the start). This will put you on the southeastern edge of the lake. It's a long 1-mile walk to loop back around the lake and get to the western edge on the PCT below Naches Peak. From here, its 3 miles back to the trailhead to close out the hike.

84 KETTLE LAKE

Round trip ■	**15.5 miles**
Loop direction ■	Counterclockwise
Hiking time ■	10 hours, long day hike or backpack
Starting elevation ■	3500 feet
High point ■	6000 feet
Elevation gain ■	2500 feet
Best hiking time ■	Late June through early October
Map ■	Green Trails Bumping Lake, No. 271
Contact ■	Okanogan and Wenatchee National Forests, Naches Ranger District

Choose this trail for a refreshing midsummer hike. Long climbs along forested valleys lead to high meadows atop a spectacular ridge, graced with stunning views of the eastern William O. Douglas Wilderness, including the tall summit of Goat Peak at the end of American Ridge. Best of all, the walk along American Ridge provides unmatched views north to the large rock walls and spires of Fifes Ridge.

To get there, drive east on State Route 410 (Chinook Pass Highway) over Chinook Pass and continue another 12 miles east to Pleasant Valley Campground. Turn right and drive the access road, crossing the American River and passing the campground. About 0.25 mile past the campground, at the end of the road, find the trailhead.

The cool forests of the Kettle Creek valley shelter you from the blazing sun for the first 5.9 miles as the trail follows the creek to its headwaters at Kettle Lake on the spring of American Ridge. This stretch of forest is filled with woodland wildflowers, including beargrass, vanilla leaf, trillium, and Indian pipe. There's also a plethora of huckleberries growing in the thinnest sections of forest where the sun can filter through and ripen the purple fruit.

The lake at the head of Kettle Creek valley offers great campsites, or at least a fine place for lunch. Turn left on the American Ridge Trail and climb 400 feet in the next mile to a high knob with stunning views. To the north stands the line of Fifes Ridge, punctuated on its western end by the craggy dual summits of Fifes Peaks.

From this point, continue east, descending gently, then climbing, then descending again, along the rolling line of American Ridge. At 11.5 miles, at a small saddle at the end of one of the gentle descents, find a trail leading off the left (north) away from the ridge crest. This is the Pleasant Valley

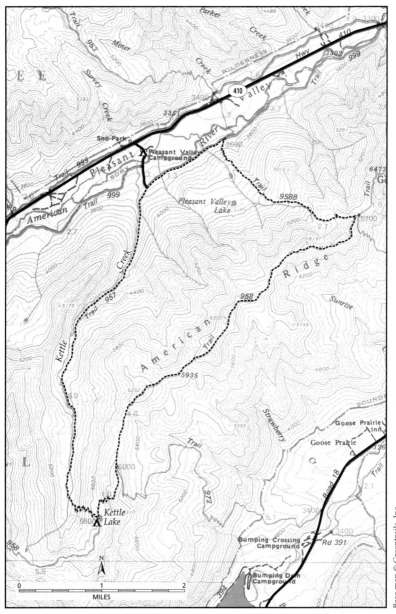

Grand views westward toward Fifes Ridge and Rainier from American Ridge

Trail and it drops more than 2000 feet in 2.7 miles back to the banks of the American River. Turn left when you reach a trail alongside the river and hike west 1.3 miles back to the trailhead.

85 · BLANKENSHIP MEADOWS RAMBLE

Round trip ■	9 miles
Loop direction ■	Counterclockwise
Hiking time ■	7 hours, day hike or backpack
Starting elevation ■	4800 feet
High point ■	5400 feet
Elevation gain ■	600 feet
Best hiking time ■	Late June through November
Maps ■	Green Trails Bumping Lake, No. 271 and White Pass, No. 303
Contact ■	Okanogan and Wenatchee National Forests, Naches Ranger District

The William O. Douglas Wilderness is a haven for dog hiking, but it is best visited late in the summer and fall. The endless ponds, puddles, and lakes offer the reason why: bugs. This route crosses through Mosquito Valley, after all—you don't want to visit the area too early in the year when the bugs are at full strength. Wait until a few cold nights have knocked down the population before you attempt this route.

Once the biters are thinned out, though, the sprawling meadows and pot-holes offer unmatched opportunities for wilderness rambles, letting you explore on and off trail in an infinite array of loops. This route offers a good introduction to the varied wonders of the William O. Douglas Wilderness. It rolls around the octopus-shaped basin of the dual pools of Twin Sisters Lakes. It leads under the shadow of the cratered volcanic summit of Tumac Mountain. It ambles through the sprawling fields of Blankenship Meadows, around the Blankenship Lakes, and across the heart of broad Mosquito Valley. It leads through the home ranges of elk, mule deer, and black bear. You'll find yourself crossed by the shadows of raptors aloft, and you'll be entertained by the antics of fearless camp robber jays and flying squirrels.

To get there, drive east from Chinook Pass for 19 miles and turn right (south) onto Bumping River Road. Drive 12 miles to the end of the paved road (at the entrance of the Bumping Lake Campground on the right). Continue south along the road, which becomes FS Road 18 near the end of the pavement. At 13.5 miles, the road forks. Veer left onto FS Road 395 and drive to the road's end, some 7 miles farther up the valley. The trailhead is found at the lower end of the Deep Creek Campground loop.

The trail climbs modestly from the trailhead, following around the snout of a low ridge to reach the broad basin of Twin Sisters Lakes in about 1.5 miles. The forest along this early section of trail holds a good population of squirrels—you might catch a glimpse of them leaping from tree to tree. Also listen for the head-banging hammering of woodpeckers as they search for insects in the many dead snags standing in this old forest.

Twin Sisters Lakes provides many great campsites, and the sisters, though easily reached, are incredibly beautiful alpine lakes. But the easy hike in often means the lakes are crowded with noisy campers. Move on

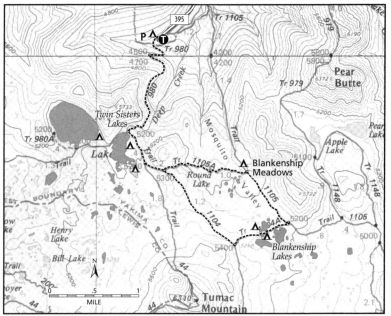

Base map © Greentrails, Inc.

Low water level at Blankenship Lakes reveals the lakebed's volcanic rock.

after a rest along the picturesque shores—enjoy a view over the Little Twin Sister to Tumac Mountain. Follow the trail as it leads south toward Tumac. About 0.4 mile after reaching the shores of the lake, the trail splits. To the right is a track that leads to the summit of Tumac Mountain. Stay left and skirt southeast around the flank of the cinder cone. In another 0.25 mile, reach another junction. This is the start of a loop. Stay right to complete the loop in a counterclockwise direction.

Hike nearly a mile south along this trail as it rolls gradually upward through thin forest and scattered clearings before reaching long, broad meadows. About 3.5 miles from the trailhead, you'll find yet another trail junction (trails crisscross the William O. Douglas Wilderness like strands of a spider web—the loop-hiking alternatives are seemingly endless). At this junction, turn left and amble east through the cluster of Blankenship Lakes. Find a campsite near these lakes, or continue on into the Blankenship Meadows. To find the meadows, continue on the trail, past the lakes, and turn left at yet another junction. This leads along the eastern fringe of a meadow that stretches thousands of acres west and north, broken only by occasional narrow bands of forest. For assured solitude, head off into the meadows and find a campsite along the forest fringe deep in the meadow. Countless small ponds dot the area.

To close the loop, continue along the Blankenship Meadows leg of the loop and, about a mile past the last junction near the Blankenship Lakes, reach another junction. Turn left once more to hike a mile west, closing the loop at the junction just south of Twin Sisters Lakes. Hike north to those lakes and on out to the trailhead.

86 CRAMER MOUNTAIN

Round trip ■	**15.8 miles**
Loop direction ■	Clockwise
Hiking time ■	10 hours, long day hike or backpack
Starting elevation ■	4200 feet
High point ■	5900 feet
Elevation gain ■	1700 feet
Best hiking time ■	Late June through November
Map ■	Green Trails White Pass, No. 303
Contact ■	Okanogan and Wenatchee National Forests, Naches Ranger District

If Minnesota is the land of Ten Thousand Lakes, the William O. Douglas Wilderness is a distant cousin of that lake-rich land. The "William O." boasts scores of lakes and hundreds of small ponds and tarns, and this loop takes advantage of many of those. You'll find all the great scenery that follows lakes, from rich foliage, great numbers of birds, and tons of small mammals. There are also a few big critters wandering the area, too, from massive mule deer to proud Rocky Mountain elk.

To get there, from Packwood drive east on U.S. Highway 12 to White Pass. At the east end of the long parking strip on the north side of the highway, find the faint, unsigned, dirt road leading north to White Pass Campground on the north shore of Leech Lake. The Pacific Crest Trail north trailhead is located just before the start of the campground loop.

Start north on the PCT and in just over 2 miles, amble through the broad meadows east of Deer Lake. From Deer Lake hike north, and you'll find Sand Lake in less than a mile. As you near Sand Lake, broad meadows open all around you. Strolling into the Sand Lake basin, take note of the masses of wildflowers on the shoreline—lupines dominate, but there's a wealth of paintbrush, columbine, and assorted lilies, too. Also, check the bogs on the north end of the lake for a massive bog filled to overflowing with bog orchids.

Continuing north from Sand Lake, you'll find endless meadows and stands of silver fir forests before you reach Buesch Lake at 6.6 miles. As the PCT curves east around the north shore of Buesch Lake, find a trail junction. Turn right and hike down to the shore of Dumbbell Lake, in the shadow of Cramer Mountain.

Cramer Mountain sits across the lake from the trail, and many of the

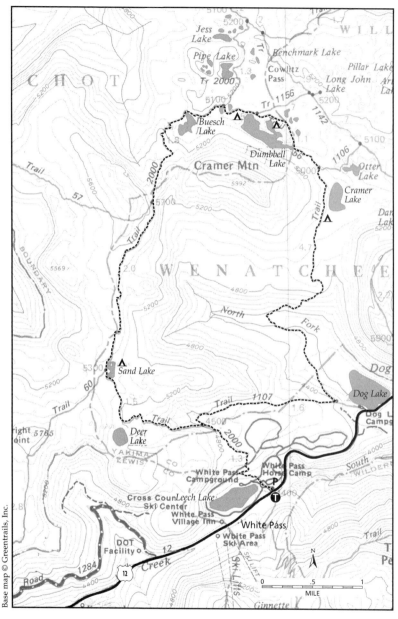

camps along the north side of the lake provide bountiful views of this big cone-shaped peak. The trail curves south around the shores of Dumbbell and rolls straight south past Cramer Lake, along the flank of Spiral Butte, to Dog Lake at 12.9 miles. A nearly flat Dark Meadow Trail 1107 leads 1.6

Hiker on the PCT at Sand Lake

miles west from Dog Lake to the junction with the trail leading 1.3 miles back to the trailhead at White Pass, completing the 15.8-mile loop.

87 SNOWGRASS FLATS/GOAT LAKE BASIN

Round trip ■	**13.5 miles**
Loop direction ■	Counterclockwise
Hiking time ■	8 hours, day hike or backpack
Starting elevation ■	4620 feet
High point ■	6600 feet
Elevation gain ■	2000 feet
Best hiking time ■	Late July through September; with peak wildflowers in late August
Maps ■	Green Trails Packwood, No. 302, White Pass, No. 303, Blue Lake, No. 334, and Walupt Lake, No. 335
Contact ■	Gifford Pinchot National Forest, Cowlitz Valley Ranger District

Natural inclination usually leads us to hike in a clockwise loop, but fighting that urge and hiking this route counterclockwise leads to greater rewards. Hitting the trail as early as possible means hiking through the forests of the lower trail while the light of the day builds, and by the time you reach the broad flower-filled meadows of Snowgrass Flats, the glorious morning sun will wash those fields of color in a warm golden light. If the sun is hiding in the clouds, never fear—there's plenty more to see and enjoy along the loop. Powerful mountains scratch the sky above you, an array of wildlife thrive in the wilderness around you, and the very air of this high basin is a tonic to cure what ails you.

To get there, from Randle drive east on U.S. Highway 12 past Randle. About 2 miles before entering Packwood, turn south onto FS Road 21 and continue 13.1 miles on gravel road to a well-signed junction with FS Road 2152. Turn left and continue 3.2 miles to the Snowgrass Flats trailhead (approximately 40 minutes from US 12), just past the turnoff to the Chambers Lake Campground. Toilet facilities are available at the adjacent Chambers Lake Campground.

The trail quickly dips into the Goat Rocks Wilderness and the first mile rolls through lovely forest with very little elevation gain, allowing ample

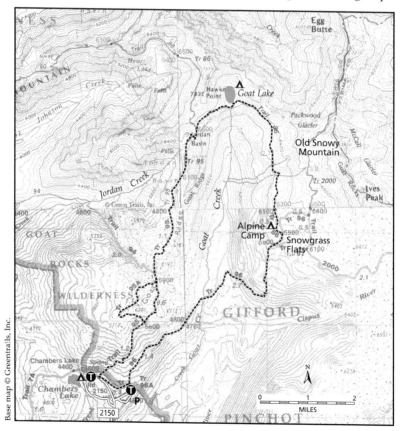

Wildflowers abound in Snowgrass Flats.

time to warm up and swing into a smooth trail pace. Within one hour you cross through a flat area in the valley after crossing Goat Creek on a rustic bridge. Be certain to enjoy the two main ponds and meadows through this area, as they are exploding with mountain-bog orchid and elephant's head wildflowers! Two species of frogs were seen throughout this area as well.

Immediately after these meadows the grind up to Snowgrass Flats begins, gaining 1400 feet over the next 1.5 miles—about one hour of hard work, but the work is soon rewarded. At the first big switchback near the 5200-foot level, listen for the sound of thundering water—you'll have to scramble a few yards off-trail to see the stunning falls responsible for the noise, but side trails lead to good vantage points where you can view the falls and the mossy rocks surrounding them. From this point on, the views get better with each step as you hike north to Goat Lake in about 3 miles.

Be careful along this stretch, as it may prove difficult to watch your feet since your eyes will be drawn to the endless views and wildflowers! Approximately 1 mile from Snowgrass Flats the trail passes a small tarn which, given calm conditions, reflects the side of Old Snowy Mountain with utmost beauty. The last mile to Goat Lake slowly gains elevation and is out of the trees entirely. Looking behind you reveals a view beginning to form over the Goat Creek valley with Mount Adams towering to the south, which is a sight to hold close to your heart. Looking toward the Goat Lake basin as you approach, the view is outstanding of Hawkeye Point, towering above the Goat Creek outlet tumbling more than a thousand feet before leveling off in the valley.

Goat Lake makes the perfect halfway point lunch spot when hiking this in a day and a nice place to camp if backpacking. The basin is void of trees, and icebergs float in the lake throughout most of any typical summer. From here the trail continues on to the 6600-foot pass southwest of the lake. This stretch of trail offers continuing views of Mount Adams along with ever-increasing views of Old Snowy Mountain across the valley. Once at the pass be certain to take in this one last view of the entire valley from one of the most scenic pass crossings in the Cascades!

The beauty of this loop is that the fun doesn't abruptly stop here. From the pass the trail descends quickly 600 feet into beautiful Jordan Basin. It is here where I saw a large variety of wildlife: dozens of pikas, seven deer, and one very large male coyote crossing above the trail, likely hunting the large pika population. Once the trail enters the forest again after 1.5 miles of open terrain hiking through Jordan Basin, it follows a series of up and down portions before the final 1400-foot drop back to the trailheads. Upon reaching the second trailhead area for the Goat Ridge Trail, taking the side trail 0.5 mile will connect you to the Snowgrass Flats Trail.

88 : TUMWATER MOUNTAIN

Round trip ■	**19.5 miles**
Loop direction ■	Clockwise
Hiking time ■	1 to 2 days
Starting elevation ■	2400 feet
High point ■	5200 feet
Elevation gain ■	2800 feet
Best hiking time ■	Late June through November
Map ■	Green Trails Spirit Lake, No. 332
Contact ■	Mount St. Helens National Volcanic Monument

Vanson Peak sat right in the blast zone of the Mount St. Helens eruption of 1980, so there is plenty of lingering effects of that 1980 event to explore and admire. The trail passes a couple of pretty lakes and great views of the gaping maw of Mount St. Helens's crater.

To get there, from Morton drive east on U.S. Highway 12 about 5 miles, passing under a tall concrete viaduct. Turn right just past this structure

Base map © Greentrails, Inc.

onto Kosmos Road, and then left onto the Riffe Lake access road. Continue south past Riffe Lake, cross the Cowlitz River, and turn left onto FS Road 2750. Drive east about 0.7 mile where the road rolls in a big 180-degree curve to the left. Continue south to the end of the road and the trailhead.

Warm up for the loop with a gentle 2-mile trek up the Goat Creek Trail, gaining just 200 feet through lush old-growth forest to reach a fork in the trail. Bear left to stay alongside Goat Creek for another 0.5 mile before climbing modest switchbacks up the west flank of Tumwater Mountain. You'll be strolling the shores of Tumwater Pond at about 5 miles from the trailhead. From the lake, the trail follows the curving summit ridgeline of Tumwater Mountain and then drops southward, staying on the extended

Rutted trail on flank of Tumwater Mountain (Photo by Dan Nelson)

ridgeline for several miles of small elevation gains and losses to reach Deadmans Lake at 11.2 miles.

Turn north at Deadmans Lake and follow Goat Mountain Trail 217 for 2.3 miles to a trail junction on the flank of Vanson Peak. As you walk this ridgeline, you'll notice that the southwest face of the ridge is largely sheared of trees, while the northeast face still boasts a healthy forest—this is how the volcanic blast hit the area. The superheated air from the eruption seared the face of the ridge directly in line with the blast, but the force was moving so fast, it didn't touch the leeward side the ridge.

At the junction near Vanson Peak, a short 0.5 mile hike to the west leads to Vanson Lake—good campsites here—while the loop route leads to the right (east) along the south side of Vanson Peak, then descends to Vanson Creek valley and follows the creek down to Goat Creek, closing the loop at 17.3 miles. Turn left and follow the Goat Creek Trail 2.2 miles back to the trailhead.

89 ┆ COLDWATER LAKE

Round trip	■	11 miles
Loop direction	■	Clockwise
Hiking time	■	7 hours
Starting elevation	■	2400 feet
High point	■	4000 feet
Elevation gain	■	1600 feet
Best hiking time	■	Late June through November
Map	■	Green Trails Spirit Lake, No. 332
Contact	■	Mount St. Helens National Volcanic Monument

Coldwater Lake shows the magnitude of change that this area underwent as a result of the May 1980 eruption of Mount St. Helens. Prior to May 18, 1980, Coldwater Lake didn't exist. Now, it's a vast 3-mile long lake that supports a strong population of healthy trout, not to mention an array of birds—both perching birds along the lush shorelines and waterfowl on the rich waters. Great herds of elk roam the blast-cleared slopes above the lake, and raptors soar on the towering thermals that rise off the ash-covered slopes. These birds hunt small mammals living in the dead trees littering the hills as well as tasty fish swimming in the broad lake.

To get there, from Interstate 5 at Castle Rock, drive east on State Route 504 to the Coldwater Ridge Visitors Center, and continue along the highway 2.2 miles to the Coldwater Lake trailhead and boat launch area.

From the parking area, start up Trail 211 along the north shore of the lake, rolling along the bank of the lake. The trail skirts the base of Coldwater Ridge, weaving through a tangle of trees laid low by the blast.

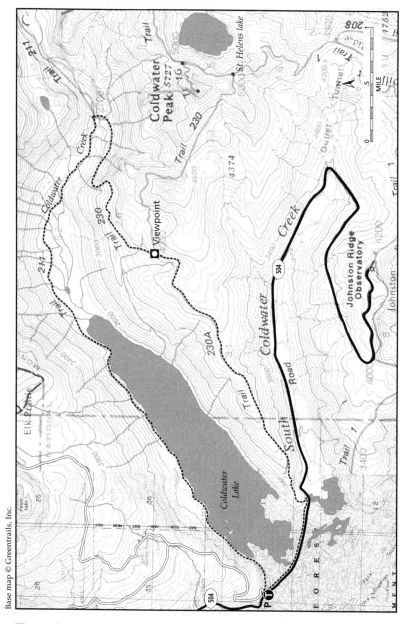

Base map © Greentrails, Inc.

The trail stays clear of the lake itself, as the scientists working with the monument hope to minimize erosion of the fragile, new lakeshore.

Still, while it doesn't dip to the waters' edge, the trail does follow the shoreline the entire 3-mile length of the lake, and then continues up the

Old-growth hemlock and cascading waterfall near the trail around Coldwater Lake

Coldwater Creek valley another 2.2 miles to a trail junction on the right. Leave the Coldwater Trail here and turn right onto Trail 230A. In the first 5.2 miles to the junction, you'll have gained just 300 feet, but now, as you head up Trail 230A, you'll start working harder.

In the next 2.6 miles, you'll gain 1300 feet to a 4000-foot viewpoint overlooking the lake, and Coldwater Ridge to the north. From there, the trail follows the long ridge west, descending gradually over the next 3 miles to South Coldwater Creek Road. Once on the road, turn right and walk the shoulder about a mile back to the parking area at the start of the loop.

90 MOUNT ST. HELENS WEST

Round trip	**11 miles**
Loop direction	Clockwise
Hiking time	7 hours
Starting elevation	3200 feet
High point	4880 feet
Elevation gain	1680 feet
Best hiking time	Late June through October
Map	Green Trails Mount St. Helens, No. 364
Contact	Mount St. Helens National Volcanic Monument

This trail provides an excellent example of the random nature of a volcano. The trail rolls through vast areas devastated by the blast, yet, in the next step, you'll walk into lush old-growth forest that didn't lose a branch to the violent eruption. There's also evidence of the power of recovery in nature.

You'll see trees killed instantly by the intense heat that swept away from the crater, many of them still standing though stripped of bark and limbs, so they look like a forest of telephone poles, yet between these silver snags

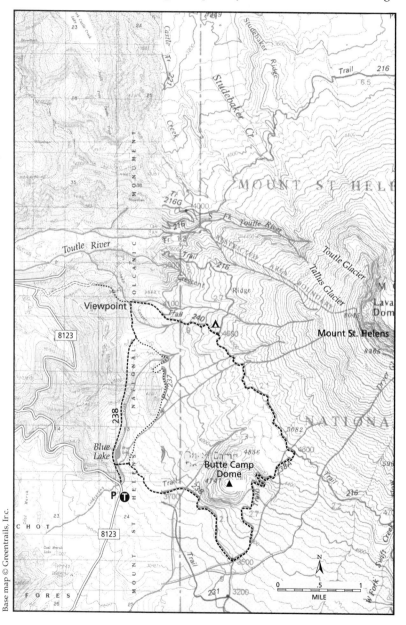

Base map © Greentrails, Irc.

grows a vibrant young forest of new trees, many of which took root less than a year after the blast.

To get there, from Jacks Restaurant and Store in Yale, follow State Route 503 Spur (Lewis River Road) east 4.5 miles to a junction with Merrill Lake Road (FS Road 81). Turn left onto FS Road 81 and drive 11.7 miles to a junction with FS 8123. Turn left onto FS 8123 and drive 2.3 miles to Blue

In spring, patches of snow dot the ash laden slopes of St. Helens, creating a 'watercolor' look. (Photo by Dan Nelson)

Lake trailhead. This single-lane gravel road has one rough spot just before the trailhead where mudflows and floods have crossed the road. It is passable for passenger cars.

We began our hike at the Blue Lake trailhead of Toutle Trail 238. The trail junction just behind the bulletin board is unsigned; the left trail leads to Blue Lake. The Toutle Trail quickly crosses Cold Springs Creek on a bridge and then follows the creek for about 0.3 mile to Blue Lake. This seven-acre lake was created by mudflows from previous eruptions about 600 years ago that blocked Cold Springs Creek. New deposits since 1980 can be seen filling in the lake basin. Silver snags in the lake attest to its recent rebirth. Blue Lake is not blue, but emerald green. It is open for catch-and-release fishing with artificial lures, or flies and barbless hooks.

Beyond Blue Lake, the trail climbs gradually but steadily through rare old-growth noble fir forest to an old clear-cut at Huckleberry Saddle at 2 miles. Meadows provide a good view of the west face of Mount St. Helens. Two small creeks flow through the area, providing water for a nearby campsite at the saddle. Blue Lake Horse Trail 237 intersects the Toutle Trail at the saddle. Stay on the Toutle Trail, reenter old-growth forest, and descend steeply for 0.7 mile to Sheep Canyon.

At the junction with Sheep Canyon Trail 240, continue straight ahead and cross a small stream on a bridge. No horses are allowed beyond this point in other to protect scientific research sites. A small campsite is located on the east side of the creek. The Sheep Canyon Trail climbs steadily, intermittently approaching the edge of Sheep Canyon for views of the 1980 mudflow and the sawed-off mountain.

As we climbed, the forest gradually changed to silver fir and then to a subalpine zone of lodgepole pine and western white pine at the junction with the Loowit Trail. Turn right on Loowit Trail 216 and head south around the slopes of Mount St. Helens.

The trail stays just below timberline, with many views up the mountain. Above the trail, trees killed by the heat of the blast are being replaced by pioneering new forest. Lupine, paintbrush, heather, and other wildflowers are reclaiming the volcanic ash and pumice–covered slopes. We climbed above the trail to a rocky outcrop for a lunch break with a view.

Back on the Loowit Trail, we quickly came to the first of two large glacial canyons. When I last hiked this way in 1994, the trail was washed out in the bottom of the first canyon but it was easily crossed in deep pumice. Seven years later the pumice is entirely gone and the canyon is steep, V-shaped, and deep. The trail has eroded, leaving only the boot tracks of prior hikers. This slope is like the inside of a glacial moraine—all dry, loose rock and sand constantly sliding and eroding.

(Note: The trail managers at Mount St. Helens National Volcanic Monument worked on the eroded trail segment and replaced the trail tread. Before heading out this way yourself, however, call ahead and check the current conditions as this area is prone to erosion and could wash out again.)

The opposite wall of the canyon is a short scramble up rubble and moist sand back to the trail. Once across, the route climbs across high meadows with rocky outcrops and continuous views of the mountain, reaching the highest point on the loop. The second ravine is smaller and easily crossed, and then the trail goes from small ridge to small ridge with shallow draws and open basins in between.

Just past Butte Camp Dome, the trail enters a research area where camping is prohibited and hikers are required to stay on the trail. At the junction with Butte Camp Trail, descend along the path, dropping from the open slopes into thick old-growth forest, to reach Lower Butte Camp—a pleasant level area of small meadows at the base of Butte Camp Dome. A cold spring gushes from the base of the dome and feeds a creek, which meanders through the meadows.

The trail then descends moderately through open stands of lodgepole pine and western hemlock. At the junction with Toutle Trail 238, turn left and hike the final 2 miles back to the Blue Lake trailhead.

91 SHEEP CANYON LOOP

Round trip ■	**7 miles**
Loop direction ■	Counterclockwise
Hiking time ■	4 hours
Starting elevation ■	3420 feet
High point ■	4720 feet
Elevation gain ■	1300 feet
Best hiking time ■	Late June through October
Map ■	Green Trails Mount St. Helens, No. 364
Contact ■	Mount St. Helens National Volcanic Monument

Glorious views of the west face of Mount St. Helens await you on this gentle trail. You'll experience the power of the volcano by exploring the mudflows and blast-leveled forests that cover this area.

To get there, from Jacks Restaurant and Store in Yale, follow State Route 503 Spur (Lewis River Road) east 4.5 miles to a junction with Merrill Lake Road (FS Road 81). Turn left onto FS Road 81 and drive 11.7 miles to a junction with FS Road 8123. Turn left onto FS Road 8123 and drive 6.3 miles to the road's end and trailhead for the Sheep Canyon Trail.

Sheep Canyon Trail 240 climbs gently through old growth forest to Toutle Trail 238. Just before the junction, at 0.6 mile, look for a viewpoint of the canyon and Sheep Canyon Creek Falls. The creek drops over a basalt outcrop for about 75 feet. Just upstream is the trail junction. Continue up the Sheep Canyon Trail, climbing steadily through old-growth noble fir into a subalpine zone of lodgepole pine and western white pine to a junction with the Loowit Trail. It takes about an hour and 15 minutes to reach this junction.

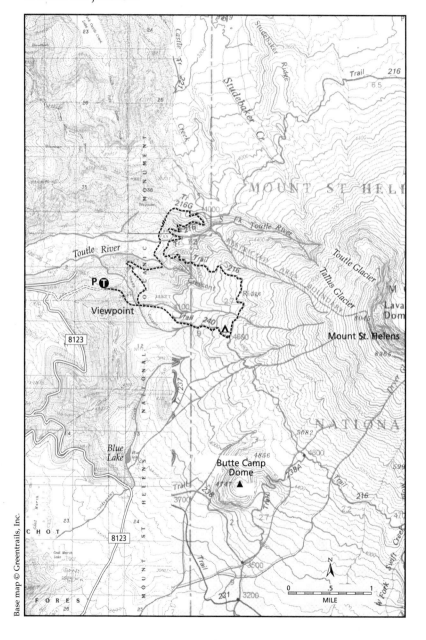

Tall wooden posts mark the sometimes obscure Loowit Trail. (Photo by Dan Nelson)

On the Loowit Trail, hike north toward the canyon of the South Fork Toutle River, crossing the head of Sheep Canyon on the way. You'll walk through dramatic edge effects of the 1980 blast where one tree is dead but its neighbor lives, and then into the blast zone proper where the forest overstory was killed, but the heat released the understory of young trees that were buried under a protective cover of snow at the time of the eruption.

The trail reaches the rim of the South Fork Toutle at a large rock outcrop on Crescent Ridge where the view of the opposite canyon wall shows the composition of the interior of Mount St. Helens. There are views across the canyon of the blast zone, the Spirit Lake Memorial Highway, and Hoffstadt

Bridge, Coldwater Lake and visitors center, Johnston Ridge Observatory, and the Mount Margaret Backcountry Ridge on the northeast skyline, including Coldwater Peak, The Dome, and Mount Margaret. Above you looms the headless mountain.

The Loowit Trail switchbacks downhill steeply, with an elevation loss of about 1400 feet, along the canyon rim to a junction with the Toutle Trail, where you turn south and climb back over the ridge to Sheep Canyon and close the loop, once again walking in old-growth forest. Spectacular fall colors on Crescent Ridge, highlighted by white snags and the bulk of Mount St. Helens in the background, enticed us to stop frequently for photos. Each view seems better than the one before.

92 MOUNT WHITTIER

Round trip ▪	**14.9 miles**
Loop direction ▪	Counterclockwise
Hiking time ▪	9 hours
Starting elevation ▪	4200 feet
High point ▪	5883 feet
Elevation gain ▪	1680 feet
Best hiking time ▪	Late June through October
Map ▪	Green Trails Spirit Lake, No. 332
Contact ▪	Mount St. Helens National Volcanic Monument

The summit of Mount Whittier extends out as a long ridge rather than projecting as a single knob. This makes for a great place to stroll along and gaze in awe at the tremendous devastation wrought by the eruption of Mount St. Helens more than two decades ago. This loop route carries you through the heart of the blast zone, rolling through the scorched Earth and leveled forests of the Mount Margaret Backcountry Area.

To get there, from Randle drive south on FS Road 25 to its junction with FS Road 99 (found just past Iron Creek Falls). Turn right (west) onto FS Road 99 and drive 9.2 miles before turning right (north) onto FS Road 26. Continue about 1 mile on FS Road 26 to the Norway Pass trailhead.

From the trailhead hike west along the Norway Pass Trail, climbing steadily through blown-down forests as the trail angles southwest to a ridge crest. The way then turns northward, following the ridgeline to reach Norway Pass at 2.1 miles. From the pass, enjoy great views down the ash-laden valley to Spirit Lake. Note the huge cluster of logs that cover the lake surface—the remains of the once great forest that surrounded the beautiful lake.

Continue north 1 mile from Norway to Bear Pass and the start of the loop section. For best views, stay right to do the lakes portion of the loop first. The trail rolls north, weaving through acres of timber stacked like toothpicks in a box. In the next 5 miles, you'll pass several small lakes, set in the blast-scoured landscape like fine gems in a tarnished ring. You'll skirt the eastern edge of Grizzly Lake, travel between Obscurity and Boot Lakes, and swing around the southern shore of Panhandle Lake to reach the north side of Shovel Lake.

At 7.9 miles, the trail splits. Stay left to climb the Mount Whittier Trail southeast and in just a mile, you'll be on the summit ridge, oohing and ahhing over the scenery laid before you. To the south resides the still-steaming mass of Mount St. Helens—you can peer directly into the breach of the northeastern face of the once-great mountain to see the building lava dome in the crater. Between you and the crater stands Coldwater Peak and The Dome. To the north are the many pretty lakes you just hiked past, and far to the east stands Mount Adams.

Continue along the summit ridge another mile to a trail junction on the flank of Mount Margaret. Turn left to traverse the 1.8-mile-long ridge back to Bear Pass, 11.8 miles from the start. Turn right and hike the 3.1 miles back to the trailhead.

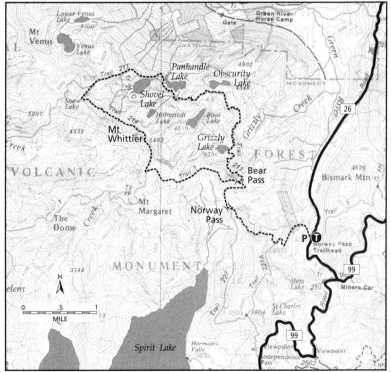

Trail through remnant forest (Photo by Dan Nelson)

93 ¦ SPIRIT LAKE VIEW LOOP

Round trip	■	8 miles
Loop direction	■	Clockwise
Hiking time	■	5 hours
Starting elevation	■	4200 feet
High point	■	4500 feet
Elevation gain	■	300 feet
Best hiking time	■	Late June through October
Map	■	Green Trails Spirit Lake, No. 332
Contact	■	Mount St. Helens National Volcanic Monument

Harry Truman (the old codger, not the president) called Spirit Lake home and refused to leave this Spirit Lake Resort when geologists warned about the impending eruption. He's still there somewhere, as is the great lake he loved. But Spirit Lake looks nothing like it did before the 1980 blast. What once was a blue jewel set in an emerald forest is now a gray pool covered with the dead logs of that former forest. The hills around the lake have been scoured clean of standing trees, and huge amounts of mud and ash flowed into the lake, changing its shape and size.

To get there, from Randle drive south on FS Road 25 to its junction with FS Road 99 (found just past Iron Creek Falls). Turn right (west) onto FS Road 99 and drive 9.2 miles before turning right (north) onto FS Road 26. Continue about 1 mile on FS Road 26 to the Norway Pass trailhead.

Savvy hikers will get to the trailhead early; not to avoid crowds of hikers (well, they will be here as well on a nice summer weekend) but rather to be hiking in the coolness of early morning while having the sunrise hitting the open slopes around you.

Hike west on the Boundary Trail about a mile through the dusty ash-laden landscape to the junction with Independence Ridge Trail 227A. The scenery around the trail is total devastation, with a few strong signs of returning life—flowers and shrubs are coming back to this scorched zone. At the trail junction, turn left (south) onto the Independence Ridge Trail and head toward Independence Pass.

After more of the same starkly beautiful landscape (marked with a few living trees here and there which were protected from the volcanic blast by growing a little bit on the north side of the ridge), the trail turns westward at a junction with the Independence Pass Trail on the left. Stay right and hike out around a low ridge point into a moonscape of blasted forest—a forest that is now trying to reestablish itself—and awesome views of Spirit Lake with the backdrop of Mount St. Helens.

The recovery of this area is evident not only from the flowers, bushes, and trees that are springing up, but also by the plethora of wildlife that has returned. Most impressively, massive Rocky Mountain elk have moved back into the area and the beasts can often be seen along this ridge.

From the knob at the end of the ridge, about 3.3 miles from the trailhead, hike north staying at or near the same elevation for another 2.5 miles to reach Norway Pass. All along this stretch, enjoy great views down to Spirit Lake and across to Mount Margaret.

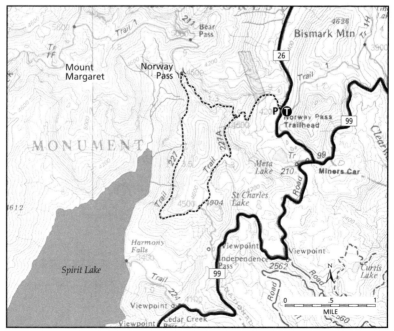

Base map © Greentrails, Inc.

Mount St. Helens and Spirit Lake seen from the Norway Pass area

At Norway Pass, turn right and hike the Norway Pass Trail and then the Boundary Trail 2.2 miles back to the trailhead.

94 NANNIE RIDGE/WALUPT LAKE LOOP

Round trip ■	**12.3 miles**
Loop direction ■	Clockwise
Hiking time ■	8 hours, day hike or backpack
Starting elevation ■	4000 feet
High point ■	5800 feet
Elevation gain ■	1800 feet
Best hiking time ■	Mid- to late summer
Map ■	Green Trails Walupt Lake, No. 335
Contact ■	Gifford Pinchot National Forest, Cowlitz Valley Ranger District or Packwood Information Center

More a triangle than a loop, this route offers breathtaking views from the summit of Nannie Peak—just as you might expect from the site of a former fire lookout tower. You'll see more than views on this hike, though. You'll find wonderful wildflower meadows along the crest of Nannie Ridge, a clear, cold swimming experience in Sheep Lake, a walk along the spine of

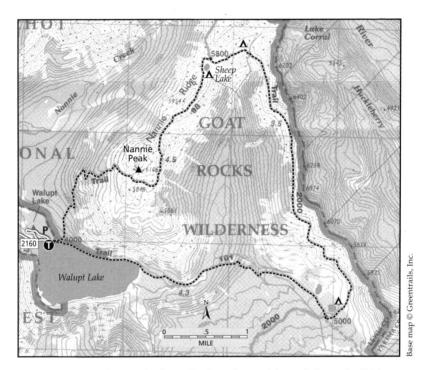

the Cascades on the Pacific Crest Trail, and a cool forest hike in the Walupt Creek valley.

The trail is short and gentle enough to enjoy as a long day hike, but the fine (though few) campsites at Sheep Lake, with their astounding views of Mount Adams (especially at sunset, when the alpenglow has the snowy peak of Adams aflame with orange light), can be tempting, as many backpackers can attest.

To get there, from Packwood drive west on U.S. Highway 12 for 2 miles and turn left (south) onto FS Road 21 (Johnson Creek Road). Continue about 19 miles on the sometimes-rough gravel road before turning left (east) onto FS Road 2160, signed Walupt Lake Campground. The trailhead is about 5 miles farther at the end of this road near the pretty campground on the shores of Walupt Lake.

The loop can be hiked in either direction, but I prefer to do it clockwise—you'll find yourself facing more views this way as you hike. The trail begins near the eastern end of the campground. Nannie Ridge Trail 98 climbs north through dense pine forests for more than a mile, crossing a couple shallow creeks (often dry late in the year), and gradually gaining elevation. As the trail nears the 1.5-mile point, the forests begin to open with spacious clearings scattered throughout. Here's where the fun begins. Hit the trail in late August and you'll find these clearings a deep shade of purple, provided you get there before the other hikers and the bears. Huckleberries the size of marbles and sweeter than honey cover the lower slopes of Nannie Peak (indeed, there are so many here, I don't mind sharing this information).

The trail continually steepens over the next mile, and deep ruts cut many of the switchbacks—be sure to stay on the true trail and don't use the shortcuts or the braided sections of trail (braided trails are sections where hikers and horses have created multiple, parallel trails that weave back and forth together, forming a broad network of trails instead one simple path).

At 3 miles, the trail tops the ridge crest just below the summit of Nannie Peak. A short, 0.5-mile side trail leads to the summit of the peak, and it is well worth the effort to scramble up this boot-beaten path to enjoy the outstanding views and wonderful mountaintop meadows. The views are dominated by the big three volcanoes—Mount Rainier to the north, Mount Adams to the south, and Mount St. Helens to the southwest—but the jagged crests of the Goats Rocks peaks to the northeast are not to be missed.

The trail continues east from Nannie Peak, following just below the crest of Nannie Ridge—the trail drops several hundred feet below the ridge

The side trail to Nannie Peak offers stunning views of Mount Adams.

for a while in order to avoid some towering cliffs. At 4.5 miles, you'll find Sheep Lake at the junction with the PCT. The best campsite is on the knoll to the south of the lake where you'll enjoy evening views of alpenglow on Mount Adams.

To complete the loop, turn south on the PCT and hike along meadows and ponds. Backpackers should note that if Sheep Lake fills up with campers, there are some fine sites along the headwaters of Walupt Creek just 0.5 mile down the PCT from the lake.

As the PCT weaves past a cluster of small ponds 3.5 miles south of Sheep Lake, turn right onto the Walupt Creek Trail. The trail follows the southern fork of the creek 4.3 miles back to the trailhead at Walupt Lake.

95 ▪ COLEMAN WEED PATCH

Round trip ■	**14 miles**
Loop direction ■	Counterclockwise
Hiking time ■	8 hours, day hike or backpack
Starting elevation ■	4000 feet
High point ■	5700 feet
Elevation gain (loss) ■	1700 feet
Best hiking time ■	Mid to late summer
Map ■	Green Trails Walupt Lake, No. 335
Contact ■	Gifford Pinchot National Forest, Cowlitz Valley Ranger District or Packwood Information Center

Don't let the name scare you off—what some folks call weeds, hikers call wildflowers. The meadows this trail visits are home to some of the finest blooming flowers in the country, and the views beyond aren't too bad either.

Look up from the brilliant floral display and you'll see Mount Adams on one side, Mount Rainier on another. The jagged crest of the Goat Rocks peaks stretches to the north, and the deep blue waters of Walupt Lake lie below your feet, straight down the steep ridge wall.

To get there, from Packwood drive west on U.S. Highway 12 for 2 miles and turn left (south) onto FS Road 21 (Johnson Creek Road). Continue about 19 miles on the sometimes-rough gravel road before turning left (east) onto FS Road 2160, signed Walupt Lake Campground. The trailhead is about 3 miles down this road on the right.

Dense forest shelters the trail for the first 1.5 miles as it climbs gradually to the southwest, along the flank of a steep ridge. Views here are limited, but the cool forest is home to a variety of animals, from owls to elk, so pay attention to the surrounding woods and you might catch a glimpse of some of the beasties.

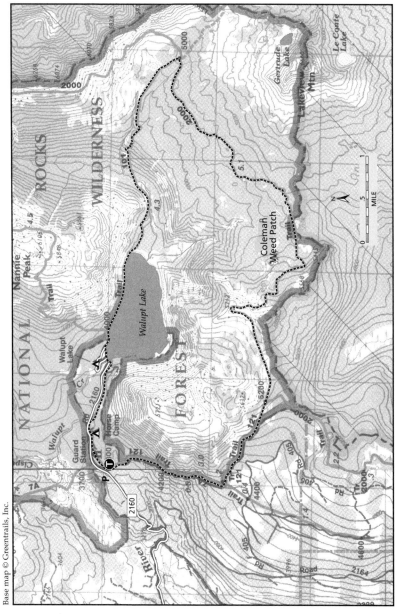

At 1.5 miles, the trail steepens considerably, but the climb is still modest—you'll gain a touch over 1000 feet in the next 1.5 miles. During this stretch, the trees thin and the forest is broken by the occasional forest glade. The Pacific Crest Trail is reached at 3 miles, and here is where the fun really

Magenta Indian paintbrush (Castilleja spp.) *in Coleman Weed Patch meadows*

begins. Turn left onto the PCT and hike into the splendid country before you.

Meadows, speckled with small groves of stunted subalpine evergreens, line the high route. Between the trees, acres of "weeds" sprout colorful blossoms throughout the summer—paintbrush, lupine, phlox, mountain daisies, heather, and columbine are a few of the plentiful flowers that grace these fields. Come autumn, when the blooms have died off, huckleberry bushes color the meadows with their red autumn foliage and deep purple fruit (provided other hikers and bears haven't harvested the delicious berries first!).

From the point where the PCT is reached, hike north to find the best views along the route at 4.5 miles where the PCT crosses the top of a prominent knoll on the ridge crest. The top of this bluff offers an excellent place for lunch as you soak in the panoramic views—all around the slopes of the hill at your feet are wildflower meadows, and beyond are the snowcapped peaks of Mount Adams and the Goat Rocks.

To complete the loop, push on another 3.6 miles as the PCT loops above the meadows of Coleman Weed Patch and under the flank of Lakeview Mountain to reach a junction with the Walupt Creek Trail at 8.1 miles. Turn left and descend the creek trail to Walupt Lake, then find a small connector trail that parallels the road from Walupt Lake about 1.6 miles back to your starting point.

96 MOUNT ADAMS NORTH

Round trip	■	**9.5 miles**
Loop direction	■	Counterclockwise
Hiking time	■	5 hours
Starting elevation	■	4200 feet
High point	■	4500 feet
Elevation gain	■	300 feet
Best hiking time	■	Late June through October
Map	■	Green Trails Mount Adams, No. 367S
Contact	■	Gifford Pinchot National Forest, Mount Adams Ranger District

Broad meadows and fragrant sun-filled forests await you here. The dry pine and fir forests along these trails are carpeted with woodland flowers and fruit-heavy huckleberry bushes. On the high portions of the loop, you'll enjoy outstanding views of Mount Adams and its many personalities. The rocky cliff faces, the crevasse-torn glaciers, the flowing white snowfields, and the noble crown of the summit are all visible most of the way up the trail. On your return, you'll face the older, more scarred cone of Mount Rainier and the gaping maw at the top of Mount St. Helens.

To get there, from Randle drive 1 mile south on FS Road 25 and then turn left (east) onto FS Road 23. Continue 29 miles to a junction with FS Road 2329. Turn left and drive east 2.5 miles to the West Fork trailhead (Trail 112).

From the trailhead, hike southeast along Trail 112 as it climbs moderately up the West Fork Adams Creek valley. Much of the first mile of trail is surrounded by clumps of beargrass with their tall, bulb-topped flower stems. The trail rolls through lush old pine forest, and through glades full of vanilla leaf or others awash in trillium.

At just under 2 miles, a small side trail on the right leads to Divide Camp. Skip this unless you plan to spend the night and continue up the main trail. At 2.8 miles, the trail ends at a junction with the Pacific Crest Trail. Here, you'll find yourself staring straight up at the snowy expanse of Adams Glacier and beyond to the summit of Mount Adams.

Turn left onto the PCT and stroll 1.5 miles north as the trail contours around the flank of Adams, staying mostly in high alpine meadows and low scrub forest. At 4.3 miles, the PCT crosses East Fork Trail 113. You can enjoy a short trip here by turning right and scrambling a mile up rocky slopes to a climbers' camp at 6900 feet. But to complete the loop, turn left at

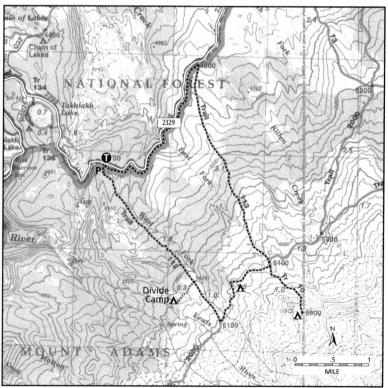

Base map © Greentrails, Inc.

Clumps of beargrass stand tall among wildflowers in Snowgrass Flats.

the junction and descend along the East Fork Trail, cutting through more berry-rich meadows and flower-filled forests to the trail's end at 7.4 miles. Here, you'll be at a trailhead on FS Road 2329. To close the loop, turn left and walk about 2.1 miles along this road back to your starting point.

97 TAKHLAKH LAKE LOOP

Round trip ■	**2.6 miles**
Loop direction ■	Counterclockwise
Hiking time ■	2 hours
Starting elevation ■	4385 feet
High point ■	4460 feet
Elevation gain ■	80 feet
Best hiking time ■	Late June through October
Map ■	Green Trails Mount Adams, No. 367S
Contact ■	Gifford Pinchot National Forest, Mount Adams Ranger District

Here's one for the kids. The trail is short, but it offers a great lesson in the volcanic history of the region. It explores the shoreline of Takhlakh Lake and climbs into a small band of basalt lava that flowed from Mount Adams thousands of years ago.

To get there, from Randle drive 1 mile south on FS Road 25 and then turn left (east) onto FS Road 23. Continue 29 miles to a junction with FS Road 2329. Turn left and drive east about a mile to the Takhlakh Lake Campground.

From the campground on the southwestern side of the lake, head east along the lakeshore trail, enjoying the cool forest and blue waters as you walk. At the southeast corner of the lake, the trail splits. The forest, pierced by the trail, boasts a bounty of huckleberry bushes (the fruit typically ripens here in mid-August), and you'll pass several small glades carpeted with shimmering green leaves of vanilla leaf plants.

At the junction turn right and climb a short 0.5 mile south through the forest before curving eastward and edging up into a band of black basalt lava. This rock is jagged and tends to get quite hot during the sunny days of summer, so make sure the kids are warned to be careful—you might even consider having them wear gloves if they want to handle the volcanic rock and scramble on the mounds of lava. The trail loops through the end of the lava field and curves back down to the trail junction at the lakeshore, about 1.9 miles from the start. You can now either hike the 0.4 mile back to the trailhead on the trail you came in on, or you can turn right and follow the other side of the lake and hike 0.7 mile, looping all the way around the lake to return to your car after a 2.6-mile walk

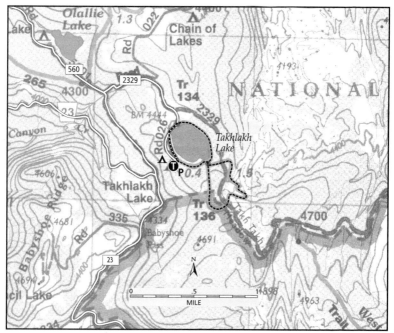

Base map © Greentrails, Inc.

Large masses of vanilla leaf in bloom are regularly seen in spring.

98 QUARTZ CREEK RIDGE

Round trip ■	**17.2 miles**
Loop direction ■	Counterclockwise
Hiking time ■	1 to 2 days
Starting elevation ■	3400 feet
High point ■	5100 feet
Elevation gain ■	1700 feet
Best hiking time ■	Late June through October
Maps ■	Green Trails Lone Butte, No. 365, Mount Adams West, No. 366, Blue Lake, No. 334, and McCoy Peak, No. 333
Contact ■	Gifford Pinchot National Forest, Cowlitz Valley Ranger District

Quartz Creek basin holds some of the finest stands of ancient forest left in the heavily logged Gifford Pinchot National Forest, and this route takes you through some of those mighty cathedral forests. But it also takes you through high ridge-top meadows and across view-rich peaks, providing wonderful panoramic vistas. You can peer across the broad expanse of the

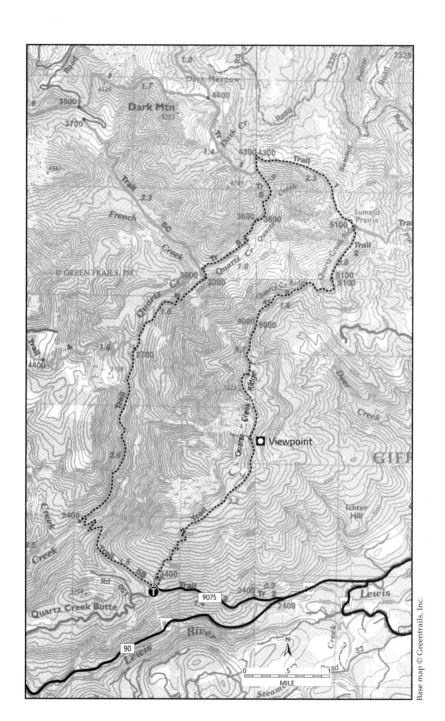

Dark Divide Roadless Area and stare up at Mount Adams and north to Mount Rainier.

To get there, from Cougar drive northeast on FS Road 90 (Lewis River Road), to the Pine Creek Visitor Information Center. Continue past the center about 19 miles and turn left (north) onto FS Road 9075 (Quartz Creek Butte). Drive to the road's end and trailhead.

Hike north along the Quartz Creek Ridge Trail 2 as it climbs steeply in the first mile, gaining 1000 feet, before the pitch lessens and the hiking becomes easier. You'll continue climbing for the next 2 miles, but at a much gentler rate, so you can enjoy the increasingly nice views. The trail follows the spine of Quartz Creek Ridge, and in the periodic meadows and viewpoints, you can look down to the west at the deep green ancient forest in the Quartz Creek valley. To the east, you can often see Mount Adams standing tall and proud on the horizon.

The trail crosses a particularly nice viewpoint at 3.2 miles, and from there, the trail continues north for a ways before bending eastward at about 5 miles out. You'll contour

Picking huckleberries along Quartz Creek Ridge (Photo by Dan Nelson)

around the eastern flank of the ridge now, staying between 5000 and 5100 feet, before the trail turns sharply northward and intercepts the Boundary Trail 1 at 7.3 miles in the upper meadows of Summit Prairie. Turn left (west) on the Boundary Trail and descend through the flowers of the prairie and enter the forest again near the head of Summit Creek. From there, the trail contours west around the Quartz Creek headwater basin. At 9.6 miles, turn left (south) onto Quartz Creek Trail 5 and descend from the ridge above the headwaters to the creekside, following the stream down the valley for the next 6 miles. Along this stretch, many small tributaries feed the creek to create a strong mountain stream. As you descend the valley, the forest, too, grows bigger and stronger. The lower valley boasts great stands of massive Douglas firs and cedars of incredible girth and age.

Leave the river bottom at 15.7 miles by turning left onto a connector trail, Trail 5B, and climbing 1.5 miles east to the trailhead atop Quartz Creek Butte at the southern end of Quartz Creek Ridge.

99 : BIRD MOUNTAIN LOOP

Round trip ■	6.7 miles (or extended loop of 9.6 miles)
Loop direction ■	Clockwise
Hiking time ■	5 hours, day hike or backpack
High point ■	5200 feet
Elevation gain ■	1200 feet
Best hiking time ■	Late summer
Map ■	Green Trails Lone Butte, No. 365
Contact ■	Gifford Pinchot National Forest, Mount Adams Ranger District

Indian Heaven Wilderness is a wonderland of sparkling lakes, jagged peaks, open forests, and, most notably, sprawling meadows filled with flowers and an array of wildlife. A pair of loops around Bird Mountain—the highest peak in the wilderness—allows hikers to experience the best of each of these offerings. The short loop stays close to the flank of Bird Mountain, while the longer loop wanders farther south into bigger meadowlands before turning back to skirt the mountain.

To get there, from Trout Lake head west on State Route 141 for about 8 miles to Peterson Prairie Campground and a junction with FS Road 24. Turn right onto FS Road 24 and drive 5.5 miles to the Cultus Creek Campground on the left. The trailhead is found near the back of the campground loop.

This loop is best done clockwise, so begin on Cultus Creek Trail 33 and start a long, steep climb to the east flank of Bird Mountain. The first 1.5 miles gain nearly 1200 feet in elevation as the trail ruthlessly ascends the Cultus Creek valley. About a mile into the hike, the trail breaks out on a small ridge. Look east from this rocky point and Mount Adams dominates the horizon. Below the viewpoint, the slope drops steeply away and rolls into a long blanket of green between the base of Bird Mountain and the flank of Adams. Face north on clear days and Mount Rainier can be seen. Between the two great volcanoes sprawl the craggy summits of the Goat Rocks Wilderness.

From here the trail turns sharply south as it draws near the cliff faces of Bird Mountain. Pine forests enclose the trail, with occasional meadow breaks and views of the towering cliffs, until the trail passes the crystal-clear waters of Cultus Lake at 2.5 miles. This is a fine lake in which to swim or just enjoy during a leisurely lunch. Beyond the lake, Lemei Rock scrapes the sky. This 5925-foot rock is the remnant plug from the core of a long-gone volcano.

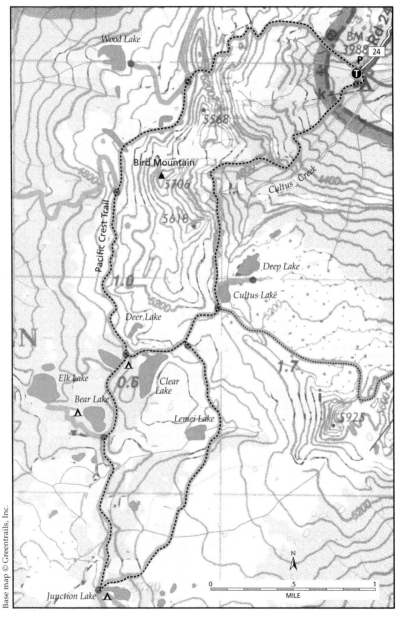

A side trail leaves to the left just a few hundred feet beyond the lake. This path leads to Lemei Rock and beyond. Stay right on the main trail and, in another 0.25 mile, reach a second trail junction. To the left is Lemei Lake Trail 179. This is the split between the long and short loops.

Those planning to do the longer loop should turn left and continue south on this trail. It leads past Lemei Lake—a shallow, somewhat dirty lake—and angles through a series of meadows and wooded sections before reaching Junction Lake at 4.7 miles from the trailhead. Junction Lake, so named because two side trails merge into the Pacific Crest Trail at the lakeshore, is a muddy, frog-filled pond at the base of East Crater. This cinder cone volcano is heavily wooded with spindly pines, and though no trail leads to the top, it is possible to bushwhack to its summit for a view of the crater for which the formation is named.

In the autumn, when the mosquito population and the water levels are both down, there is fine camping in the meadows around the lake. In midsummer, though, this is a boggy, bug-filled basin. Better to hustle through to clearer lakes and breezier (i.e., bug-free) locations.

Turn north at Junction Lake onto the PCT. The trail heads due north along the edge of a wooded ridge. For a bit of variety, hikers can hop off the trail and explore the huge meadows seen to the west, just below the trail. Deer, elk, and a variety of small mammals thrive in these fields of grass and wildflowers. The meadows are crisscrossed with horse and game trails, so knowing the location of the main trail is essential. A map and compass are essential tools for exploring off-trail.

Just a mile north of Junction Lake, the PCT passes a side trail to Elk Lake and Bear Lake on the left. The forest thickens and closes in around the trail for the next 0.5 mile as the route climbs toward Bird Mountain and a junction with Trail 33 (the short loop trail).

Deserved rests in broad meadows like this one are among the rewards of hiking. (Photo by Dan Nelson)

Those hiking the short loop will join the PCT here. From the junction where the long hike splits off, to this junction, Trail 33 rolls less than 0.5 mile through woods and scree slopes at the base of Bird Mountain to reach the PCT. (In comparison, the long loop covered 3.5 miles.)

The PCT heads north from this junction, angling east toward the rocky upper slopes of Bird Mountain. Just beyond the Wood Lake Trail junction, leave the PCT by bearing right onto Trail 108, which leads back to Cultus Creek Campground in another 1.5 miles. Before heading for the trailhead though, stop at the ridge crest just after leaving the PCT and enjoy the views. Or, for markedly better views, climb south along the ridge until the whole of the South Cascades is spread out in all its splendor. Mount St. Helens, Mount Rainier, the Goat Rocks peaks, and Mount Adams can be seen on clear days from this vantage point, less than 0.25 mile off the trail. Don't bother risking the scramble to the summit of Bird as the views are no better from the higher, more dangerous perch.

The trail back to the trailhead is a steep descent through trees, ending at the Cultus Creek Campground entrance.

100 ┊ AIKEN LAVA BED

Round trip ■	**14.7 miles**
Loop direction ■	Counterclockwise
Hiking time ■	9 to 10 hours, day hike or backpack
Starting elevation ■	3700 feet
High point ■	6300 feet
Elevation gain ■	2600 feet
Best hiking time ■	Late June through October
Map ■	Green Trails Mount Adams, No. 367S
Contact ■	Gifford Pinchot National Forest, Mount Adams Ranger District

Mount Adams towers over the South Cascades. The big stratovolcano rises out of a sprawling jumble of lava beds, which make cross-country travel difficult along the flanks of the big mountain. But those same lava flows add a wonderful scenic element to trail hiking. Snowcapped Mount Adams fills the horizon, but at its feet is a world of jagged black rock that slashes at the boots and hands of any adventurer careless enough to scramble off-trail.

To get there, from Trout Lake drive north on FS Road 23 and turn left (east) onto FS Road 82. In about 2.5 miles, turn left onto FS Road 8225 and follow this to its end at a four-way junction. Continue straight ahead, now on FS Road 8225-150 and in about 0.75 mile, park at the trailhead area alongside the road.

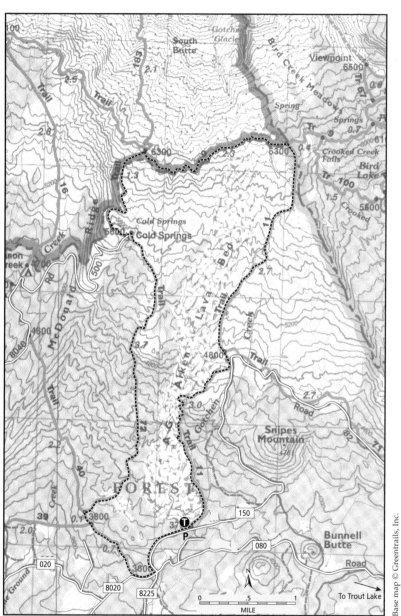

Base map © Greentrails, Inc.

Hike north from the trailhead along Trail 11, hugging the eastern edge of the tall, jagged ridge of black basalt that is the Aiken Lava Bed. The trail stays well under the forest canopy most of the way but during the heat of summer, the black rocks of the lava bed throw a lot of heat back down into the forest; so pack plenty of water, though you'll have access at Gotchen Creek, too.

The trail climbs steadily from the get-go, cutting first through thick, cool forest and then into increasingly open, airy pine forests. Great fields of vanilla leaf bound the trail during the first 3 miles, and beargrass becomes common after that. At 3 miles the trail passes a side trail leading east. From this point on, the forest becomes far more sparse, and meadows and forest clearings become common occurrences. These provide great views up onto the lava bed. At 5.7 miles, you'll intersect the Round the Mountain Trail.

Turn left here and follow the Round the Mountain Trail west, across the upper reaches of the lava bed, and below the sprawling wildflower fields of the western edge of Bird Creek Meadows. You'll traverse the mountain slope for 2.6 miles to reach the popular access trail leading to the south climbing route. Turn left here and descend about 1 mile to the climbers' trailhead parking area at Cold Springs (9.3 miles from the start). Walk through the sprawling

Hikers scramble in the Aiken Lava Bed basalt. (Photo by Dan Nelson)

parking area set amidst the trails and find the Cold Springs Trail on its eastern edge. Head south on this trail (Trail 72) as it rolls down the western edge of the lava bed. The trail drops 3.7 miles to a junction with Trail 40. Turn left and in 0.7 mile, step out onto a small dirt road. Turn left and in about 0.25 mile, you'll come to the four-way junction at the end of FS Road 8225. Turn left to hike the 0.75 mile up FS Road 8225-150 to your waiting car, completing the 14.7-mile loop.

APPENDIX

VOLUNTEER GROUPS

The Mountaineers
300 Third Avenue West
Seattle, WA 98119
(206) 284-6310
www.mountaineers.org

Washington Trails Association
1305 Fourth Avenue, Suite 512
Seattle, WA 98101
(206) 625-1367
www.wta.org
info@wta.org

WASHINGTON STATE PARKS

Park Information and Reservations
7150 Cleanwater Lane, KY-11
Olympia, WA 98504
(360) 902-8844
www.parks.wa.gov

NATIONAL PARK SERVICE
Mount Rainier National Park

Park Headquarters
Tahoma Wood, Star Route
Ashford, WA 98304
(360) 569-2211
www.nps.gov/mora

Olympic National Park

Visitor Center
3002 Mount Angeles Road
Port Angeles, WA 98362
www.nps.gov/olym

Wilderness Information Center
3002 Mount Angeles Road
Port Angeles, WA 98362
(360) 565-3100

North Cascades National Park

Park Headquarters
2105 Highway 20
Sedro-Woolley, WA 98284
(360) 856-5700
www.nps.gov/noca/

U.S. FOREST SERVICE
Gifford Pinchot National Forest

Supervisor's Office
10600 NE 51st Circle
Vancouver, WA 98682
(360) 891-5000
www.fs.fed.us/r6/gpnf

Cowlitz Valley Ranger District
10024 U.S. Highway 12
P.O. Box 670
Randle, WA 98377
(360) 497-1100

Mount Adams Ranger District
2455 Highway 141
Trout Lake, WA 98650
(509) 395-3400

Mount St. Helens National Volcanic Monument

Headquarters
42218 NE Yale Bridge Road
Amboy, WA 98601
(360) 247-3900

Coldwater Ridge Visitor Center
3029 Spirit Lake Highway
Castle Rock, WA 98611
(360) 274-2131

Johnston Ridge Observatory
3029 Spirit Lake Highway
Castle Rock, WA 98611
(360) 274-2140

Mount St. Helens Visitor Center
3029 Spirit Lake Highway
Castle Rock, WA 98611
(360) 274-2100

Packwood Information Center
13068 U.S. Highway 12
Packwood, WA 98361
(360) 494-0600

Wind River Ranger Information
  Center
1262 Hemlock Road
Carson, WA 98610
(509) 427-3200

Mt. Baker–Snoqualmie National Forest

Supervisor's Office
21905 64th Avenue West
Mountlake Terrace, WA 98043
(206) 775-9702
www.fs.fed.us/r6/mbs

Darrington Ranger District
1405 Emmens Street
Darrington, WA 98241
(360) 436-1155

Mount Baker Ranger District
2105 Highway 20
Sedro-Woolley, WA 98284
(360) 856-5700

Outdoor Recreation Center
  (at REI-Seattle)
222 Yale Avenue North
Seattle, WA 98109
(206) 470-4060

Skykomish Ranger District
74920 NE Stevens Pass Highway
Skykomish, WA 98288
(360) 677-2414

Snoqualmie Pass Visitor Center
P.O. Box 17
Snoqualmie Pass, WA 98068
(425) 434-6111

Snoqualmie Ranger District

Enumclaw Office
450 Roosevelt Avenue East
Enumclaw, WA 98022
(360) 825-6585

North Bend Office
42404 SE North Bend Way
North Bend, WA 98045
(425) 888-1421

Okanogan and Wenatchee National Forests

Supervisor's Office
215 Melody Lane
Wenatchee, WA 98801
(509) 662-4335
www.fs.fed.us/r6/oka

Chelan Ranger District
428 West Woodin Avenue
Chelan, WA 98816
(509) 682-2576

Cle Elum Ranger District
803 West 2nd Street
Cle Elum, WA 98922
(509) 674-4411

Entiat Ranger District
2108 Entiat Way
Winthrop, WA 98862
(509) 784-1511

Lake Wenatchee Ranger District
22976 Highway 207
Leavenworth, WA 98826
(509) 763-3103

Leavenworth Ranger District
600 Sherbourne Street
Leavenworth, WA 98826
(509) 548-6977

Methow Valley Ranger District
502 Glover
Twisp, WA 98856
(509) 997-2131

Methow Valley Visitor Center
Building 49 Highway 20
Winthrop, WA 98862
(509) 996-4000

Naches Ranger District
10061 U.S. Highway 12
Naches, WA 98937
(509) 653-2205

Okanogan Valley Office
1240 South Second Avenue
Okanogan, WA 98840
(509) 826-3275

Tonasket Ranger District
1 West Winesap, P.O. Box 466
Tonasket, WA 98855
(509) 486-2186

Olympic National Forest
Supervisor's Office
1835 Black Lake Boulevard SW
Olympia, WA 98512-5623
(360) 956-2402
www.fs.fed.us/r6/olympic

Hood Canal Ranger District
Hoodsport Office
150 N. Lake Cushman Road
Hoodsport, WA 98548
(360) 877-5254

Quilcene Office
295142 U.S. Highway 101 South
Quilcene, WA 98376
(360) 765-2200

Pacific Ranger District
Forks Office
437 Tillicum Lane
Forks, WA 98331
(360) 374-6522

Quinault Office
353 South Shore Road
Quinault, WA 98575
(360) 288-2525

U.S. Fish and Wildlife Service
Nisqually National Wildlife Refuge
100 Brown Farm Road
Olympia, WA 98506
(360) 753-9467
nisqually.fws.gov

INDEX

THE MOUNTAINEERS, founded in 1906, is a nonprofit outdoor activity and conservation club, whose mission is "to explore, study, preserve, and enjoy the natural beauty of the outdoors. . . . " Based in Seattle, Washington, the club is now the third-largest such organization in the United States, with 15,000 members and five branches throughout Washington State.

The Mountaineers sponsors both classes and year-round outdoor activities in the Pacific Northwest, which include hiking, mountain climbing, ski-touring, snowshoeing, bicycling, camping, kayaking and canoeing, nature study, sailing, and adventure travel. The club's conservation division supports environmental causes through educational activities, sponsoring legislation, and presenting informational programs. All club activities are led by skilled, experienced volunteers, who are dedicated to promoting safe and responsible enjoyment and preservation of the outdoors.

If you would like to participate in these organized outdoor activities or the club's programs, consider a membership in The Mountaineers. For information and an application, write or call The Mountaineers, Club Headquarters, 300 Third Avenue West, Seattle, WA 98119; 206-284-6310.

The Mountaineers Books, an active, nonprofit publishing program of the club, produces guidebooks, instructional texts, historical works, natural history guides, and works on environmental conservation. All books produced by The Mountaineers Books fulfill the club's mission.

Send or call for our catalog of more than 500 outdoor titles:

The Mountaineers Books
1001 SW Klickitat Way, Suite 201
Seattle, WA 98134
800-553-4453
mbooks@mountaineersbooks.org
www.mountaineersbooks.org

The Mountaineers Books is proud to be a corporate sponsor of Leave No Trace, whose mission is to promote and inspire responsible outdoor recreation through education, research, and partnerships. The Leave No Trace program is focused specifically on human-powered (nonmotorized) recreation.

Leave No Trace strives to educate visitors about the nature of their recreational impacts, as well as offer techniques to prevent and minimize such impacts. Leave No Trace is best understood as an educational and ethical program, not as a set of rules and regulations.

For more information, visit *www.LNT.org*, or call 800-332-4100.